WOMEN WITHOUT MEN

WOMEN WITHOUT MEN

SINGLE MOTHERS AND FAMILY CHANGE IN THE NEW RUSSIA

JENNIFER UTRATA

CORNELL UNIVERSITY PRESS
Ithaca and London

First published 2015 by Cornell University Press
First printing, Cornell Paperbacks, 2015

Printed in the United States of America

Library of Congress Cataloging-in-Publication Data

Utrata, Jennifer, 1970- author.
    Women without men : single mothers and family
change in the new Russia / Jennifer Utrata. —1st
Edition.
        pages cm
    Includes bibliographical references and index.
    ISBN 978-0-8014-5302-1 (cloth : alk. paper)—ISBN
978-0-8014-7957-1 (pbk. : alk. paper)
    1. Single mothers—Russia (Federation)   2. Families—
Russia (Federation)   3. Sex role—Russia (Federation)
4. Post-communism—Social aspects—Russia (Federation)
I. Title.

    HQ759.915.U87 2015
    306.874'320947—dc23

                                        2014029091

Cornell University Press strives to use environmentally
responsible suppliers and materials to the fullest extent
possible in the publishing of its books. Such materials
include vegetable-based, low-VOC inks and acid-free
papers that are recycled, totally chlorine-free, or partly
composed of nonwood fibers. For further information,
visit our website at www.cornellpress.cornell.edu.

Cloth printing   10   9   8   7   6   5   4   3   2   1
Paperback printing   10   9   8   7   6   5   4   3   2   1

For my family

❧ CONTENTS

✎ ACKNOWLEDGMENTS

The long journey toward a book is oftentimes circuitous; I am very grateful for several sources of encouragement and support at critical junctures along the way. This book would not be possible without the generosity of so many Russians who took the time to share their lives and even their homes with me, including mothers, fathers, and grandmothers from all walks of life. More than anything else, it is the moving stories of ordinary Russians that captivated me and compelled me to write this book. The friendship and kindness shown to me by Russian women, especially Aleftina, Tatyana, Nina, Vika, Yuliya, Svetlana, and Inessa, kept me grounded while dealing with the serendipity of fieldwork, and they offered a wonderful sense of perspective. The warmth, persistence, and stubborn optimism of the Russians I met remain with me as a source of inspiration.

I have also benefited from many sources of institutional and scholarly support. Special thanks are owed to the faculty and graduate students in the sociology department at UC Berkeley, for this project began in conversation with others. Although several faculty members provided excellent feedback and advice, I am especially grateful for my mentors—Victoria Bonnell, Arlie Russell Hochschild, and Claude Fischer—who believed in this project from the beginning and shaped my thinking at key moments along my intellectual trajectory. Each of them has continued to provide support when needed in spite of their multiple commitments. At Berkeley, my passion for sociology was nurtured in myriad ways. Self-doubt seems endemic to the graduate school experience, but I was nevertheless encouraged to be as ambitious as possible in framing Russia as a case study important not only for area studies but for sociology as a whole. The insights of graduate school colleagues and friends such as Jane Zavisca, Tamara Kay, Amy Hanser, Michele Rossi, Allison Pugh, Cinzia Solari, Sarah Gilman, Jennifer Sherman, Jeremy Schulz, Suzanne Wertheim, and many, many more also contributed toward improving the ideas in this book. The supportive friendship of Jill, Jenya, and Becca also made the last years of graduate study more enjoyable.

Several other institutions made this research possible. I was honored to be able to work with Cornell University Press, where John Ackerman, my editor and the former director of the press, provided critical support that spurred me onward. Special thanks are due to two anonymous reviewers whose insightful suggestions helped to improve the manuscript. My research was also assisted by awards from the Fulbright-Hays Doctoral Dissertation Research Abroad program and the Eurasia Program of the Social Sciences Research Council, with funds provided by the State Department under the Program for Research and Training on Eastern Europe and the Independent States of the Former Soviet Union (Title VIII). Funding from UC Berkeley's sociology department and the graduate division was also critical in the earlier stages of research and writing. Finally, a junior sabbatical semester provided by the University of Puget Sound afforded the time necessary for writing and thorough revision, and a research grant paid for the book's index. Several colleagues at the University of Puget Sound have been supportive of my forging ahead with this book project, and special thanks go to Leon Grunberg.

Ideas in this book were sharpened further in conversation with many other colleagues over the years. I am thankful to Sarah Ashwin, Mie Nakachi, Cynthia Buckley, Theodore Gerber, Olga Shevchenko, Jeff Sahadeo, Margaret Nelson, Shannon Davis, and many more scholars who provided wonderful feedback on early portions of the manuscript. Michele Rivkin-Fish offered generous support during the policy symposium "Gender in the 21st Century in Eastern Europe and Eurasia," sponsored by IREX and the Woodrow Wilson International Center for Scholars, and she later read the entire manuscript, providing very valuable feedback. The enthusiastic responses I received after presentations given at the American Sociological Association, Pacific Sociological Association, Association for Slavic, East European, and Eurasian Studies, and Sociologists for Women in Society conferences, as well as at an invited lecture at the University of Wisconsin—Madison's Center for Russia, East Europe, and Central Asia, also helped immensely in making this a better book.

Some portions of two book chapters have been published previously in the form of journal articles, and I am thankful to the publishers for permission to include these materials. Portions of chapter 4 appeared in "Youth Privilege: Doing Age and Gender in Russia's Single-Mother Families," *Gender & Society* 25, no. 5 (2011): 616–641, published by Sage, and portions of chapter 6 appeared in "Keeping the Bar Low: Why Russia's Nonresident Fathers Accept Narrow Fatherhood Ideals," *Journal of Marriage and Family* 70 (December 2008): 1297–1310, reproduced with permission from Wiley-

Blackwell. Although integral to the outcome, some sources of support run deep and wide, spilling beyond the scope of any single project. Mary and Thomas, my parents, nurtured my development in countless ways over the years. The friendship of my sister, Laura, buoys my spirit. From our early days together in the former Soviet Union and Washington, DC, to more recent adventures in Berkeley and Tacoma, my husband, Robert, has long provided steadfast support, encouraging me in my endeavors, both big and small. Finally, I cannot imagine sons more loving than Isaac, Oliver, and most recently, Gabriel, each of whom offers a heady mix of challenge and joy that brightens my days. This book is dedicated to my family, both near and far.

✒ Note on Transliteration and Subjects

I follow the U.S. Library of Congress system of transliteration, with the exception of spelling some proper names and other words in ways that are more familiar to English-speaking readers, such as Katya instead of Katia. In addition, all names are pseudonyms. I occasionally omit or change a few identifying details to protect subjects' anonymity, but my descriptions of people and places are factually accurate and based on field notes and interview transcripts. Finally, all translations from Russian are my own, unless otherwise noted.

WOMEN WITHOUT MEN

Introduction
A Quiet Revolution

"But does anyone really care about single mothers?"

Despite having heard this question repeatedly from Russians during my research, I found it unsettling. After all, the growth of single-parent families is one of the most profound transformations of family life in our time. Because I was immersed in the vast sociological literature on what is typically framed as the "problem" of growing single motherhood around the world, I also knew that many people are concerned about single mothers and their children, at least in terms of their increased poverty risk. Finally, whether people think much about single motherhood or not, perhaps more people should care. Although nonresident fathers inspire little public discourse, single mothers juggle solo breadwinning and caretaking and frequently do so with minimal supports while facing considerable stigma.

When I began studying Russian single mothers, I assumed these mothers would struggle to an even greater extent than other Russians with the burdens of the transition from state socialism to market capitalism. What I learned, however, was more complicated and surprising. Single mothers do not necessarily differ much from other mothers. Furthermore, many single mothers find their lives simpler in comparison with what they endured before a divorce or breakup. I discovered that in Russia single motherhood is normalized rather than problematized as it typically is in other countries, especially the United States. For most Russians, the preoccupation with navigating multiple crises in their daily lives leaves little room to worry about the idea of mothers raising children on their own.

In spite of this apparent lack of curiosity about the lives of single mothers, I chose the normalization of single motherhood in everyday life as the primary puzzle I seek to explain. Most Russians see the prevalence of single motherhood as unremarkable or as a symptom of other more entrenched social problems, such as the lack of reliable men or the weak, unsupportive state. What does it mean to be a single mother when two-parent families remain the cultural ideal even as fewer people are able to attain this ideal? Furthermore, in a society still transitioning from state socialism to market capitalism, what are the implications of the normalization of single motherhood for family life and gender relations?

The Russian case challenges many Western assumptions about single mothers, pushing our collective thinking forward. This is a significant contribution given that, notwithstanding an extensive empirical literature, there is still no scholarly consensus on the meaning of single motherhood or why it has spread so rapidly around the world. Many puzzles remain.[1] Yet the growth of single motherhood certainly shows few signs of abating, and experts anticipate continued growth in most countries.[2] Given this seismic shift shaping the global social, economic, and cultural landscape, the issue of increasing numbers of single parents—the vast majority of whom, in every industrialized country, are single mothers—has attracted the attention of scholars, the media, and the general public, especially in the United States.[3] Most single mothers work for pay, but because of inadequate supports for the dual burdens of breadwinning and caretaking, their families face an increased risk of poverty. Even though the United States trails far behind other countries in supporting parents who are balancing paid work with unpaid caregiving, rates of single parenthood have tripled since 1960 as a share of American households, and at least half of all U.S. children will spend part of their childhood in a single-parent family.[4] Most single mothers are divorced, separated, or widowed, but more than half of first births to women under the age of thirty now occur outside of marriage.[5] Nonmarital birth rates are higher for some racial-ethnic groups than others (68 percent among African Americans, 43 percent among Hispanics, and 29 percent among whites) and are more common among Americans without a college degree, but the trend is toward increasing single motherhood.[6] Overall, even as patterns of single motherhood and family instability steadily increase over time, and even as patterns come to characterize not only the lives of the working class and racial-ethnic minorities but also the lives of middle-class people, many important questions remain.

Further complicating these unanswered questions are the many problematic assumptions surrounding single motherhood in the United States. Scholars and journalists alike have described the rise of single parenthood as mysterious, as alarming, or as "a huge problem without an easy explanation."[7] We hear, too, about a "sad state of affairs" whereby morals have allegedly been abandoned and single parents lack time or energy to devote to their progeny, while liberals are said to fail at being "morally tough" in championing marriage before childbearing.[8] Despite the obvious instability of contemporary marriage, these stories somehow manage to transform marriage into a primary solution to the problem of single motherhood. Whereas some stories sympathize with the "silent crisis" of single motherhood,[9] others smuggle in considerable moral judgment and condescension. Even as single motherhood has lost some of its novelty, single-mother families continue to serve as convenient scapegoats for problems ranging from family breakdown to high prison rates, gun violence, and the even the alleged "decline of men." The high-profile attention of pundits and politicians reinforces the stigma single mothers navigate.[10] Perhaps the very ambiguity and diversity of the category allows single mothers to serve as a kind of Rorschach test, eliciting a range of reactions, from sympathy to scorn. Like the famous inkblot test, people project their own ideas about single mothers (and about families, gender, race, class, and the state) onto the many women who find themselves combining solo breadwinning with solo caregiving on behalf of their children.

Despite the problematic assumptions surrounding single motherhood, it is clear that the facts of family life differ from our fantasies of what families should be. In Russia as in the West, single motherhood is no longer an anomaly: it is part of a broader and ongoing revolution in family life and gender relations. Indeed, it is rapidly becoming a norm. Social institutions are generally lagging behind and failing to support new kinds of families in meaningful ways. The ideological divide surrounding single motherhood prevents us from developing a deeper understanding of the phenomenon. In many societies, single mothers are viewed by both the left and right as a subset of mothers and often as a problem to be fixed.[11] Yet single motherhood, after all, must have some appeal for women in spite of the challenges, even if it is oftentimes an appeal of last resort.

Some readers may think that single motherhood is a narrow analytical lens. In Russia, however, single mothers are the most ordinary of women. Grappling with the meaning of motherhood, especially its shadow side of "single" motherhood, provides important insights into how much families and gender relations are changing during Russia's transition to capitalism. The Russian case also presents an intellectually important problem for the sociology of family and its assumptions about marriage and two-parent households. These assumptions about single mothers' hardships and miseries, the superiority of two-parent families, the primacy of the nuclear family over extended kin, marriage as a panacea for troubled families, and the purported differences dividing the lives of married and single moms are fairly entrenched in scholarship. An in-depth exploration of the normalization of single motherhood in Russia allows us to see single motherhood with fresh eyes.

✒ Russia's Quiet Revolution

When I began fieldwork in Russia, I kept hearing that single mothers were everywhere. Russians initially reacted to my research like Pavel, a cab driver in Moscow who exclaimed: "You're here in Russia to study single mothers?! Well . . . looks like you came to the right country!" Others offered advice on finding mothers to interview. Memorably, one cashier gestured across a busy street and said: "Just walk into any courtyard, sit down on a bench, and look around. Half of the women there will be single mothers!" Russians speak matter-of-factly about single mothers, as if their ubiquity simply goes without saying.

Many people qualify their remarks by noting that single motherhood may not be ideal but is nonetheless part of the way things are in the topsy-turvy world that is the New Russia. Seldom is there much moralizing about it. Russians argue that a weak state no longer supports families as it once did and that weak men all too frequently fear responsibility and seek solace in the bottle. Considering these circumstances, Russians ask, who can really blame normal women for going it alone as mothers? Few consider single motherhood any great tragedy. Instead, and in vivid contrast to the United States, ordinary Russians generally see single motherhood as a nearly inevitable by-product of two intractable problems—a critical mass of weak men and a weak state. Men, Russians of all kinds argue, are too often irresponsible and weak-willed in the face of difficulties, tempted by both the traditional vodka bottle and several newer, capitalist temptations. The state, in turn, makes glowing promises of a brighter day to come but has cut back its supports for families in general and for women and children in particular.[12]

When reflecting on single motherhood, many Russians hark back to the Second World War, another period when men were scarce and single mothers supported their children with the help of their own mothers. Both women and men note that difficult economic circumstances and political instability are hard on families during the transition to capitalism. Stefan, a married father, observed: "So many families have fallen apart, just like after the Great War. He earns little, she wants him to earn more because Misha needs new shoes, so he drinks more to escape the nagging and the stress. Then she realizes she's better off without him. It all starts there." While observing May Day celebrations in Moscow, I chatted with Sasha, a retired military man who mused: "Russia has long been a country of single mothers. It's nothing new."

Western researchers and journalists also describe Russia as a country of single mothers. At a conference, an American scholar remarked dryly: "Single mothers. In Russia. Aren't they all?!" Other conversations provoked similar responses. In reference to the iconic image of the sorrowing mother and child sacralized in Russian Orthodoxy, Barbara Heldt has argued that single motherhood "is almost an inevitability in Russia."[13] In the mid-1990s, the *New York Times* portrayed Russia as "matriarchal," teeming with single mothers:

> The collapse of the Soviet state has changed everything in Russia—except the relationship between the sexes. Expectations are low, but divorce rates remain high and the numbers of single mothers, either divorced or never married, keep growing. . . . In a trend that is as unmistakable to sociologists and social workers as it is distressing, millions of maids, factory workers and university professors alike have grown inured to *raising their families without men*. Instead they have come to rely on mothers, sisters and aunts in the kind of matriarchal society—and downward spiral of poverty and limited horizons—that in the United States has become a hallmark of the poorest urban areas.[14]

These views of Russia as a land of single mothers and a matriarchy are oversimplifications that obscure the complexity and fluidity of family life. Although the view of Russia as a country of single mothers may capture some aspects of its reality, one should not take this view too literally. Some observers quickly invoke matriarchy when confronted with the strength and endurance of Russia's women in the face of adversity, but Russian society remains firmly, objectively, patriarchal.[15] In spite of the significant challenges they face, many single mothers are doing remarkably well, at least relative to other women. They are willing to accept some hardship in pursuit of increased personal independence and a sense of control over their own lives and those of their children. Russia is a country where matrifocal families predominate in daily life, even though the two-parent, nuclear-family cultural ideal remains stronger than ever. In matrifocal families, the mother–child unit is more central culturally than the father–child unit or the mother–father conjugal relationship. Matrifocality does not imply domestic maternal dominance but rather suggests a more elaborated role of the mother in family life as well as the weakness of the conjugal relationship.[16]

Ultimately, the question of whether Russia should be understood as a country of single mothers depends on what it means to be single for the growing number of mothers who experience this scenario. The narratives that follow tell the surprising story of what the transition to market capitalism looks like from the perspective of Russia's many single mothers, women of all kinds keeping their families afloat in spite of feeling disappointed in, and indeed abandoned by, both men and the state.

Even though the spread of market capitalism has irrevocably changed what it means to be a mother on her own, Sasha is right that single mothers are not new to Russia. Most of the roughly twenty-seven million Russians who died in the Second World War were men, leaving many mothers single. Russia has long had a very high divorce rate. It had the highest divorce rate in the world after the United States in the 1970s and continues to have one of the highest rates of divorce today, by some measures the world's highest or second highest.[17] Marriage is less common nowadays, and it is even less stable than before.[18] More recently, since the collapse of the Soviet Union in 1991, nonmarital births have risen steadily to account for nearly one in three births. Some of these births may occur within cohabiting unions, but the increase in cohabitation is also relatively new, its meaning uncertain.[19] Finally, since 1992, working-age men have been dying earlier than ever before, on average at age fifty-nine. Russia has the world's largest gender gap in life expectancy, leaving many mothers on their own. Most Russians still live in two-parent families, but the overall trend is "towards the declining prevalence of dual-parent households and increasing numbers of single-parent households."[20]

⚼ Everywhere . . . and Nowhere

Although I kept hearing that single mothers are everywhere in Russia, I discovered, paradoxically, that single mothers are simultaneously nowhere in particular. Russians agree on the statistical normalcy of single motherhood—everyone knows that single motherhood is all too common to be surprising—but single mothers are nevertheless semantically invisible.[21] The category of

FIGURE 1. A single mother and her daughter wait for a bus in Kaluga's city center. They were expecting a special delivery of produce from their grandmother's garden plot about an hour outside of the city center by way of the bus driver. Photograph by the author.

single motherhood is ambiguous, fluid, and almost up for grabs, with little agreement on who single mothers are. Single mothers do not constitute an underclass but are spread throughout Russian society. As gender and family relations are shifting, what it means to be a mother raising children on her own is fluid and heavily contested.

One rainy spring morning early in my fieldwork, I witnessed these contested meanings surrounding single motherhood rather vividly. I slipped into a coffee shop for a few moments before continuing on to an interview nearby. Hoping for a few leads, I struck up a conversation with the women working the counter. Unwittingly, my queries provoked a heated discussion.

The shop manager turned toward one of her sales clerks, asking a woman in her late thirties whether she wasn't a single mother since her husband had passed away a few years earlier. She replied: "Tatyana Mikhailovna, but how am I really single? My mother helps me with everything! We're a team. Probably single mothers are those who are really on their own." A second sales clerk interrupted to ask me: "Are divorced mothers also in your study? The state used to dock men's pay, but now men get away with avoiding child support if they so choose! Of course, their kids do at least have fathers out there, unlike some other mothers." Before I had a chance to respond, the widowed sales clerk interjected: "As a foreigner you should know that we also have some mothers who are officially single, collecting state support, but they are not really single mothers. Many are living with a guy, and he is helping her out. I don't have any guy helping me out, so I am on my own. Luckily I have my mom around."

As I pondered which of these leads to pursue, Tanya, the shop manager, cautioned me: "Here in Russia you cannot assume that just because a woman is living with a guy that he is necessarily supporting her and her kids. Maybe that's true in America, but not here. Nowadays lots of men simply don't want to get married or be responsible for families. I mean, some may help out occasionally, but there's no guarantee."

All three women began talking at the same time, debating what it was that made mothers qualify as single. There was little agreement, and versions of this conversation recurred during the ensuing months. Of course, single motherhood is an ambiguous category by definition. But in Russia this ambiguity surrounding single motherhood is further amplified. A widowed mother is not exactly single if her mother is helping her out . . . or is she? Given how little most men contribute toward housework and child rearing in Russia's two-parent families, a widowed mother with her own mother's household, child care, and pension support might even be better supported overall than many married or divorced mothers. While it is possible that a divorced mother has a former husband supporting the children financially, this cannot be assumed since most women receive little or no child support and Russian fathers typically become estranged from children after divorce.[22] An unmarried mother might be living with a man, but how much support she receives in these cases is unclear. Even if a single mother remarries (and fewer Russian women than men remarry after divorce), women argue that she is still "practically single" because "most men don't help much, especially if it's not their own kid."

I could not be late for my appointment, so during a lull in the conversation I made my way toward the door, promising to return soon. As I hurried down the shop steps, Tanya stepped outside and called me back: "Wait a minute! I think I have just the woman for you. Olga Petrovna is a *real* single mother—she has no husband, mother, relatives, or anyone else supporting her!"

This coffee shop conversation was one of many incidents demonstrating the lack of cultural consensus as to who counts as a single mother in today's Russia. Following other internationally comparative studies, I define the category of single motherhood as any mother raising at least one child under eighteen without the child's father or another male partner, whether unmarried, divorced, separated, widowed, or married but effectively abandoned.

Yet although I delimit the boundaries of single motherhood in this way, rather than ignoring the slipperiness of the category, I follow Russians' lead in taking the ambiguity and fluidity of single motherhood as a useful and theoretically productive starting point.

Analyzing single motherhood from below forces us to grapple with contradictory, even messy, aspects of the experience we might otherwise miss. More and more women around the world are becoming single mothers, even if this is not what they had hoped for and even if they express strong support for two-parent families and marriage.[23] The reasons why women are doing so are complex, but it hardly makes much sense from a narrow economic perspective for women to go it alone as mothers, especially in countries with minimal supports for families raising children. Rates of single motherhood have gone up even as state support for families has declined over time, both in Russia and in many other Western countries. The idea of single motherhood may often be slippery, given how culturally variable the experience of single motherhood is, but this slipperiness is exacerbated in today's Russia, which manifests a growing fluidity in family life that many people remain reluctant to accept. Mothers and their children are often the bedrock in this story, with men often a more intermittent presence.

The issue of family change in Russia is further complicated by the fact that so many Russians have lacked adequate support during the transition to capitalism. How, in this situation, can one determine whether single mothers have faced greater challenges than so many others? Some still assume that single mothers have it harder than others, yet single mothers themselves question this assumption, arguing that married women bear heavier burdens. The case of Russian single motherhood pushes us to rethink the notion that single mothers necessarily differ all that much from other mothers, depending on the specific context and level of social support in their lives.[24]

Tanya's comments in the coffee shop suggest that it is a lack of support that truly makes a mother single in Russia, regardless of official partnership status. Most Russians define single motherhood, or "real" single motherhood, in terms of this lack of support, whether the lack is due to a missing husband, boyfriend, or—most tragically for Russian women—the absence of one's own mother. I follow Tanya's lead in remaining attuned to the significance of social support in the lives of mothers, refraining from making generalizations about support on the basis of women's official marital status. Single motherhood may seem self-evident; in practice it is seldom so. Instead, single motherhood is a metaphor for how supported, or unsupported, mothers feel in their everyday lives as they juggle paid work with the unpaid work of the home and children.

Illuminating the key paradox of everywhere and nowhere—between the ubiquity and utter normalcy of Russian single motherhood and the lack of agreement as to who counts as a single mother and what it means to be single in the New Russia—is the main task of this book. Single mothers are visible in that no one is surprised that they are everywhere, yet they are simultaneously invisible in that most Russians do not pay attention to the challenges women face in raising children on their own. Single mothers are not distinguished much from other mothers working and raising their children.

✒ Studying Russian Families

Building trust and developing rapport with a wide spectrum of single mothers in Russia took persistence and patience. I was an outsider, an American woman neither single nor a mother at the time. Furthermore, as eager as many single mothers are to talk, they are also extremely pressed for time. I found myself drawing on prior experiences with Russian families, and ultimately I chose to live with local families while conducting research, thus easing my entry into the field. Years before I began this fieldwork, my experiences in the former Soviet Union had begun to shape how I see women's work and family life in the region. In the early 1990s, I had worked as an English teacher in Bukhara, Uzbekistan, for the U.S. Peace Corps, living with two different ethnically Russian families near the old city, and visiting St. Petersburg and Moscow for the first time while staying with relatives of these families. Certainly, life in Uzbekistan differs significantly from life in provincial Russia, but in those early years the influence of Russian and Soviet culture was palpable throughout the region. I spent several more months in the former Soviet Union in 1998 while working as an American company's representative in Tashkent (where my Russian tutor was a single mother), and in the summer of 2000, I studied advanced Russian while living with a divorced mother and her adult daughter in St. Petersburg. Through these varied experiences, I developed a feel for everyday life that served me well during my fieldwork.

When I lived with a Russian widowed mother and her adult daughter in Bukhara, I had been awestruck by all that women managed at work and at home during a period of nearly 300 percent inflation in the early 1990s. Whether women were Tajik, Jewish, Uzbek, or Russian, they bargained for carrots at the local bazaar and made soup from scratch as an "easy" weeknight meal after a full day of paid work and commuting on crowded public transport, before an evening consumed by shopping, dinner preparations, cleanup, caring for children, hand-washing laundry, lesson planning, and grading. They worried about how to improve the morale of their husbands during uncertain economic times, often feeling as if the survival of their families ultimately depended on them. It often did. These mothers, most of them married but often singularly responsible for family survival nonetheless (depending on the amount of support they received in their marriages), in some ways resembled the Russian women described in these chapters. Such women are the unsung heroines of family life in the transition from state socialism to market capitalism, masters of that critical realm of life that Russians tend to dismiss, if not disparage, as *byt* (everyday life).[25]

In Russia, the world of *byt* is one of soul-killing, quotidian struggle—mostly, though seldom acknowledged as such, women's struggle (although women deal with much more than *byt* alone), in stark opposition to the revered spiritual realm of the famous Russian *dusha* (soul). Pesmen describes *byt* as "a belittling term denoting petty concerns of the material kind or the mundane, soul-killing necessities of the grey-hued 'this life.'"[26] It was in the early 1990s when I first became intimately familiar with the intensely gendered nature of Russian *byt*: whether I was proffering my ration card at the state store with fellow teachers, waiting in line for our monthly allocation of sugar or flour as the shopkeeper chatted with friends oblivious to our presence, or watching seventy-year-old *babushki* (grandmothers) hauling several kilos of potatoes and onions onto crowded trolleybuses, many aspects of women's daily lives were both time-consuming and utterly routine. Whether as single mothers or as grandmothers, Soviet women and the Russian women who are their successors are experts at managing the mundane work that holds families together, the work that makes those famously heady flights into the realm of *dusha* possible. My desire to better understand women's work, particularly among women managing a double transition, to single motherhood and to life under capitalism, eventually led me to provincial Russia.

I conducted most of my twelve months of fieldwork in the midsized provincial city of Kaluga, an *oblast'* (roughly equivalent to a state) capital city of 345,000 in northwest Russia, during two separate six-month trips in 2003 and 2004. One of Russia's oldest cities, Kaluga has a population that is slightly older, more educated, and less ethnically diverse than that of other provincial Russian cities, but it has average demographics and rates of unemployment. Even though Kaluga is only 200 kilometers southwest of Moscow, just a few hours by express train, in terms of labor market opportunities and living standards, it is more typical of where most Russians live than the larger, Western-oriented metropolises of Moscow and St. Petersburg. Over half of Russia's urban population lives in small and medium-sized cities. Differences between Moscow and St. Petersburg (where most foreigners spend their time) and the rest of Russia are striking. In Kaluga, I never left home without a small flashlight or two, which were indispensable for navigating poorly lit streets and the dark corridors of the apartment buildings where I traveled to meet with mothers, often late into the evening. In Moscow, those same flashlights looked like curious artifacts to me, to be tucked away until I returned to what Russians call "the provinces."

I prioritized depth over breadth by making Kaluga my primary site, but during my second six-month fieldwork trip, I conducted some interviews in Moscow ($n = 20$) as a check on the generalizability of my findings. Altogether during fieldwork, I conducted 151 formal in-depth interviews with ordinary Russians, each averaging three hours in length.[27] Ninety of these interviews were with single mothers. Through focusing my efforts in Kaluga, I was better able to immerse myself in families and in social networks to develop a broader portrait of family life beginning with single mothers but not ending with them. Apart from single mothers, I interviewed Soviet-era single mothers and contemporary grandmothers ($n = 20$) whose myriad forms of support shape the lives of single mothers so fundamentally, but I also conducted in-depth interviews with married mothers ($n = 20$) and nonresident fathers ($n = 21$).

Interviews were important for building trust and developing rapport, but I primarily sought to engage in what Mitchell Duneier calls "in-depth, context-driven fieldwork";[28] that is, I participated in single mothers' and their family members' lives as fully as possible and took notes over time, avoiding a strict reliance on formal interviews. What our subjects tell us in interviews cannot be taken merely at face value but is also a public fiction that ethnography can further illuminate. Participating in people's lives over time, and considering how institutions such as labor markets, marriage markets, state policies, or institutionalized sexism, racism, or ageism affect people is critical. Admittedly, I was sometimes frustrated that there is no factory, street, school, or precise site from which to study single mothers, so interviews in people's homes became more indispensable than they might have been had I another potential field site to consider.

Among recent studies of single motherhood, my approach is somewhat unusual; in many accounts, the family members who are a salient part of mothers' lives (either rhetorically or in daily practice) are relatively silent or are at most faint voices in the background.[29] Given the importance of social networks in the lives of single mothers, I used these additional interviews and observations to analyze single motherhood from multiple angles, further sharpening this story of Russia's quiet revolution in family life.

Still, I wanted to understand the contours of women's lives beyond the interview context. Though gaining access to Russian families at home without explicitly being treated as a guest was daunting, I managed to do so with several family networks over time. Because single mothers are so busy between home and work, few have much leisure time, and when they do have it, they often relax at home with a few friends rather than assembling in larger groups. Other times I had to be flexible to gain broader access to diverse single mothers, such as when I spent an entire day with a single mother inside a homeopathic *apteka* (pharmacy) kiosk outside a Moscow subway station, squeezing in some questions whenever there was a lull between customers. In interviewing men, especially, I had much less control over the precise time and circumstances of the interviews, which sometimes began at 10 p.m. in a noisy café or dark local bar, with one occurring in a taxi after a father's evening shift.

Becoming enmeshed in several networks of single mothers and generally avoiding official channels, I used in-depth interviews extensively to build trust and gain access to all kinds of single mothers. Through everyday conversation and field notes, I was able to check on and advance what I learned through interviews, triangulating among participant observation, formal interviews, and informal conversation. Relying on snowball sampling, I conducted all interviews by myself in Russian, without an interpreter. Because of the Soviet-era legacy of people using friends and networks of acquaintances to get things done, snowball sampling helped to extend my networks beyond an initial set of contacts in Kaluga.[30] This method was also critical for building trust, given the sensitivity of my subject matter, which included discussions of marital breakup, out-of-wedlock childbirth, abortion, intimate partner violence, material hardship, and unofficial sources of income. I hired several local typists to transcribe recorded interviews in the original Russian, which I coded and analyzed using a grounded theory approach. Interview topics, in no specific order, included the advantages and disadvantages of single motherhood; routes to single motherhood and reasons for divorce or breakup; work histories; challenges of balancing work and family responsibilities; the value of children and problems in raising them; material hardships; sources of kin and social support; views on how life had changed since the breakup of the Soviet Union; feelings about remarriage, cohabitation, and finding a man; other problems women faced as mothers, as women, or as single mothers; and future plans and expectations for themselves and their children. Given the lack of scholarly and public attention paid to the growth of single motherhood in Russia, an inductive, open-ended approach was imperative. Although I discussed a range of topics with mothers, I was sensitive to what mothers wanted to discuss most urgently and frequently followed their lead.

I saw nearly half of the mothers interviewed at least a second or third time for a follow-up interview, a local outing, or as a guest in their homes, which enabled me to probe further regarding interview topics and deepened my knowledge of mothers' lives over time. I learned the most, however, from those dozen or so mothers from both working- and middle-class backgrounds who become key informants; with these mothers, I watched their kids, joined them for evenings around the kitchen table, and spent time with them celebrating birthdays at home or visiting parks or cafés. I did not explicitly provide monetary compensation for interviews, as doing so is considered cold and off-putting in Russia; most people see granting an interview as a favor rather than a transaction requiring payment. Nevertheless, I wanted to show my appreciation and reach out to poorer women or those with few social networks. I always brought along fresh fruit, boxed chocolates, or a cake to interviews, and after the interviews I offered various small souvenirs from California (such as books of picture postcards or small toys for kids) as a token of my gratitude.

Though my samples are not random, they are purposefully diverse. I included representatives across the spectrum of single mothers in the general population, stratifying by income, education, age, marital status, employment, and living arrangement. Respondents ranged from twenty-three to fifty-four years of age, and slightly over half had higher education. Reflecting national trends, most single mothers were divorced and had one (63%) or two (24%) children,[31] though one in four had never been married.[32]

Even though Russian women at first wondered what could be interesting about their lives as single mothers, in time most were flattered that I wanted to learn from them and spoke very candidly with me. As an American researcher who was neither single nor a mother, I was always aware of negotiating my triple-outsider status. I participated in shaping, in an ethical manner, how others saw me in order to gain richer data, negotiating varied socially constructed scripts depending on whether I was interviewing Soviet-era mothers, divorced fathers, or married or single mothers.[33]

When pressed about motherhood, I explained that I hoped to become a mother at some point in the future, and most Russians refrained from asking further questions (perhaps suspecting infertility). I consciously downplayed my marital status, but I need not have been so concerned. Most women projected their own ideas onto my marital and motherhood status. Divorced and widowed mothers felt I could better empathize with their perspectives

FIGURE 2.   Three mothers who had all been part of the same school dance troupe growing up reunite with about fifteen to twenty others at a picnic in a park outside of Kaluga. (The author is on the left.) Children were mostly left at home with relatives, typically grandmothers, for the day's outing. Photographer unknown.

as a married woman, with several stating so explicitly, whereas most unmarried mothers seemed to consider me as single as they were. Because I had no visitors while in the field, some women did not really consider me married at all. Several women informed me that most Russian women could not, or would not, leave a "good man" behind for months at a time, and conversations with Russian men confirmed this belief. Finally, being perceived as a somewhat naive American seemed to encourage many Russians to articulate taken-for-granted aspects of gender relations and family life. Many enjoyed telling me how things *really* are in Russia.

☙ Russian Families through the Lens of Single Motherhood

The chapters that follow explore what it means to be a single mother in the New Russia from a variety of perspectives, gradually untangling the paradox of how and why single mothers are both "everywhere" yet "nowhere in particular." The narratives focus on the experiences and worldviews of single mothers raising children under eighteen, but through the lens of single motherhood the book also interrogates the broader meaning of the quiet revolution occurring in Russian families. While the growth in the population of single mothers does not comprise the entire quiet revolution in family life, the belief that women can make it on their own—without a man, without the state, and even without the conventions of official marriage—is central to these wider changes.

Chapter 1 provides a window into the lives of Soviet-era single mothers, most of whom felt protected as workers and as mothers even as they faced considerable social stigma as women on their own. Russian women have long coped with male absence, infidelity, and irresponsibility for children, and these patterns intensified during the post–World War II period when the state introduced the category of "single mother" (*odinokaia mat'*) and legislated women's responsibility for children, in effect marginalizing fatherhood and institutionalizing male irresponsibility. Today's single mothers face the reverse scenario: little stigma but little social protection. While the landscape of single motherhood has changed, several of the problems that plagued marriages in the late Soviet era, such as male drinking and domestic violence, have only worsened in postsocialism.

In chapter 2, I explore how and why women minimize the import of the material hardships they face on the path to single motherhood and indeed are adamant that these difficulties are not the main story of their lives. At the same time, they generally reject feminism and fantasize about meeting a "real man" who would take some responsibilities off their own shoulders. The contradictions revealed in this chapter, where strong women relish their freedom but long for a responsible, sober man at their side, illuminate the paradoxes of gender relations in the New Russia.

Even though the route to single motherhood is important for understanding how single mothers interpret the experience, chapter 3 examines how the dominant cultural code of single motherhood, what I call *practical realism*, constrains single mothers in their daily lives. In the vacuum left by the absence of adequate support from men or the state, mothers embrace a neoliberal ideology of self-reliance, encouraging one another to work on transforming themselves and their way of being in the world. In contrast to Soviet times, today's single mothers are expected to demonstrate their competence without complaint, proving their dignity and worth to others. In order to meet these expectations, single mothers often turn to other women, mainly their own mothers. As chapter 4 shows, most grandmothers are pressured to help single-mother daughters, serving as the reserve army of feminine self-sacrifice. Still, the negotiations for support and the power relations between single mothers and their mothers are complex. Single mothers talk about wanting a man, but what most really need turns out to be a babushka.

Single mothers, their children, and their own mothers constitute the core of Russian family life, but married mothers and nonresident fathers figure in the lives of single mothers and their families as key points of comparison. Given Russia's matrifocal families, there are what I call "blurred boundaries" between single and married mothers, with many similarities in women's daily lives. Most Russian single mothers become single through divorce, and married motherhood is always haunted, to varying degrees in a divorce culture, by the specter of single motherhood.[34] Many married mothers also rely heavily on their mothers and other women for practical and moral support, have considered divorce, and contribute to the general discourse on the unreliability of men and the state. Chapter 5 investigates a subsample of married mothers through the prism of single mothers' experiences. Importantly, and contrary to assumptions in the sociological literature that married mothers have it easier than single mothers, many Russian married mothers are more burdened in their daily lives and have far less control over their income and their bodies than do single mothers.

In chapter 6, we learn that many fathers, too, often end up accepting Russia's dominant negative discourse on men, a discourse that keeps the bar for fatherhood low. Rather than directly refuting women's claims as some might expect nonresident fathers to do, Russian men agree that most men are "by nature" irresponsible and less capable of adaptation than women. Men ultimately reinforce a status quo whereby women bear primary responsibility for children and family and not much can really be expected of men in the near future. Broader patterns of men's detachment from family life are historically shaped and based on cultural assumptions of women's strength and men's relative weakness. Finally, the concluding chapter reflects on the implications of Russian single motherhood and this case of normalized gender crisis and fluidity of family formation in the transition to capitalism.

Through the lens of single motherhood, whether at the core or the periphery, the contours of Russia's quiet revolution in family life become clearer. This focus on the increase in single motherhood also challenges our own entrenched assumptions about women without men. Perhaps the revolution is quiet, after all, because the gender crisis Russia is experiencing is hardly considered a crisis at all by most. Instead, normalized gender crisis is simply the way things are in Russia. Although many single mothers want to be able to count on the state and on men in their efforts to raise their children well, most women end up making a virtue out of the necessity of becoming stronger, adapting as best they can to neoliberal market capitalism. As much as they might like to count on men and the state, most single mothers find themselves counting on motherhood instead—on themselves and their own efforts and on their own mothers. This fatalism about the gender status quo, where men are often weak and the state is unsupportive and women ultimately have only themselves to rely on, has profound consequences for Russian family life and for society.

✒ CHAPTER 1

From State Protections to
Post-Socialist "Freedoms"

The Changed Context of Single Motherhood

> Materially I lived like most people did. So I didn't
> really suffer. And back then [in the late Soviet period]
> money wasn't all that necessary. . . . I suffered more
> morally, because my children didn't have a father. . . .
> But things have changed. My daughter doesn't even
> want to get married! She's quite modern in this way
> for it's a different generation now. They've all
> watched *Santa Barbara*.
>
> —Natalya, divorced, 65-year-old retired
>   schoolteacher

Paradoxes abounded in the lives of Soviet-era single mothers. Natalya, unlike her daughter, did not come of age watching *Santa Barbara*.[1] Understanding the cultural contradictions of contemporary single motherhood requires grappling with what single motherhood meant before the collapse of state socialism. Natalya knew little about the kinds of freedoms and choices considered by the younger generation of mothers today. She knew she had to get married in order to become a mother and be considered a respectable woman. Even though she ultimately divorced, she had considered divorce mostly as a last resort. Divorce had become quite common by the late Soviet period, but cohabitation and nonmarital births were still relatively rare back in the 1970s.

When Natalya was raising her daughter, narrower social mores prevailed. In spite of the more radical ideas that had been considered in the early days of Bolshevik rule, the Soviet state was rather traditional about gender, doing little to challenge the status quo apart from its strong commitment to women's full employment. Natalya received regular child support and her job was secure, so she felt "protected" by the state in this regard. But at the same time, Natalya felt judged by society. She cared deeply about her children's lack of a father in the home and the moral judgments surrounding her divorced status. Soviet single mothers, especially the unmarried but to a lesser extent also divorced mothers, were officially supported, but they faced considerably more social stigma than do single mothers today.

Single mothers in the New Russia, in contrast, cannot count on either child support or a lifelong job. The vast majority work, but few feel protected as mothers in the workplace. Instead, most face discrimination as mothers, at least if they aspire beyond the lowest-paying jobs. They speak of "relying on themselves alone" and are unfazed by a variety of family arrangements, with couples perhaps living together, having a child before marriage, and even getting divorced more than once if need be, all without significant social repercussions. Premarital sex, cohabitation, nonmarital childbearing, and multiple divorces are both more common today and more socially acceptable.

Of course, even beyond Russia, single mothers navigate varying amounts of contradiction and stigma. A mother may relish the increased freedom and control she has in raising her kids, yet at the same time struggle with managing on a single income. She may be proud of her efforts to make it on her own, yet at the same time wish there were more social supports for the formidable challenges of juggling solo breadwinning and caregiving. Or she may appreciate raising her kids without having to negotiate child rearing details with a partner, yet still long for some assistance when dealing single-handedly with a child's defiance.

But beyond the contradictions one might expect to find in the lives of single mothers, Soviet mothers had to navigate mixed messages: they felt protected by the state, yet judged by society. Indeed, Soviet single mothers experienced almost the reverse of what Russian single mothers experience today. Soviet single mothers of all kinds were at least tolerated and mostly supported officially by the state as worker-mothers, but in everyday life they were made keenly aware of the stigma of their second-class single status. This was especially so for unmarried mothers, but divorced mothers faced stigma as well.

To paraphrase Natalya, Soviet single mothers materially had a standard of living similar to that of other mothers. Single mothers were not set apart from other citizens. Those who could not rely on the support of their own mothers or relatives struggled more than others to ensure that their children did not lack anything that they perceived children in two-parent families enjoyed. But when they took a four-hour train ride to Moscow every couple of weeks to locate proper-fitting shoes for their kids or sausage for the family dinner table, they did so alongside many other ordinary Russians riding that same train. Russians joke sarcastically about this "equality in poverty" they once experienced: "We were all equal back then . . . we were equally poor!"

Kalugans of all kinds relished telling me an anecdote based on a common Soviet ritual in the town: "What's long and green and smells like sausage? An *elektrichka* [suburban electric train] arriving from Moscow!" Everyone knows the joke, and many Kalugans have either been on that train or had a close relative riding it for them. Of course, for some women, traveling by train to buy good shoes or sausages had been humiliating and far from a laughing matter. Many report being treated with disdain, if not scorn, by native Muscovites. Yet most ordinary people, especially women expected to be masters of mundane matters of *byt*, had spent time waiting in those lines and riding that same green train.[2] The sense of solidarity with others struggling and facing similar problems is much weaker today, mainly because of the onset of neoliberal market capitalism and accompanying ideologies of self-reliance (see chapter 3). Soviet citizens recall feeling solidarity with others facing similar kinds of struggles in acquiring deficit goods. Fewer citizens faced the extremes of hunger or deprivation that exist today.

At the same time, Soviet citizens, including single mothers, did face inconveniences and material challenges. Sometimes this involved dealing with frustrating deficits of various consumer goods or limited choices regarding child care arrangements. But most still had a great deal that they could reliably count on. Unlike women today, most Soviet single mothers could count on getting regular child support, basic medical care, child care, on having enough provisions to get by and feed their families, and on feeling secure in their jobs even when they had to stay home with a sick child. Many enjoyed being able to travel to Eastern Europe or elsewhere in the Soviet bloc on vacation or qualifying for a voucher for a stay at a sanatorium as a single mother with a child. Today many single mothers cannot indulge in a cappuccino at a street corner café.

The context of single motherhood has changed dramatically. This is not merely an issue of Soviet single mothers looking at their years of raising children through rose-colored glasses or even one of perceptions of single motherhood changing. Although nostalgia may sometimes affect women's recollections, and single motherhood is certainly more normalized and more common (and thus perceived differently) today than it was in the Soviet era, many of the problems single mothers face have either objectively changed or worsened. For instance, Soviet mothers did not worry much about finding a decent job because jobs were guaranteed, nor did they worry as much about children's fathers paying child support because such support was deducted from the salaries of fathers, all of whom worked for state enterprises. In the new Russia, the state no longer guarantees anyone a job, and the enforcement of child support payments has declined precipitously even as more

men are working unofficially (frequently earning more than their official salaries indicate) in the private sector. And even Soviet-era problems that are
not brand-new, such as men's heavy drinking, have only worsened in the
post-Soviet period.

Moreover, during the postwar and late Soviet periods, when cracks in the
system did surface, mothers felt entitled to complain to the authorities and
to have their concerns addressed by the state. After all, they were workers
and mothers serving the state in a respected dual role. Doing their jobs well
contributed not only to their own families but to society as a whole. Women
such as Irina, a Soviet single mother, observe: "It was a different time back
then. All that mothers do at home is important of course, but these days it's
no longer really valued. At least not as it was before. Women are no longer
protected as mothers."

Besides the retrenchment of state support for women and families, women's
feelings of entitlement to a set of social protections have changed or are at
least much more muted among the newer generation of single mothers.
The ground has shifted, and most mothers feel there is little chance of going
back. Few have much faith anymore in society placing considerable value
on a mother's unpaid caregiving. Women's work used to be lauded, and however symbolic the state's praise sometimes was, it meant something to some
women. But most of this appears to be in the past. Much of the work that
women once did for society is now considered a private issue and a choice,
no longer a public duty deserving of tangible support, much less symbolic
honor. Its problems notwithstanding, late Soviet state socialism provided some
guarantees and stability. These guarantees and the accompanying sense of stability are now gone.

❦ The Soviet Gender Order: A Façade of Liberation

Women were more protected by the state as workers and as mothers in the
Soviet period, but this does not mean that they were liberated or equal to
men in practice. Far from it. In spite of more equality in poverty in Soviet
times than exists in today's vastly unequal Russia, to be a Soviet single mother
always raised eyebrows as to a woman's morality or to her skill in being able
to keep a man around. Marriage in Soviet society gave a woman much more
than a stamp in her passport and an official status; marriage gave her a stamp
of respectability. Women could turn to the state for support in what was considered women's natural double burden in juggling paid work and motherhood, and they could turn to the Communist Party to try to keep philandering,

heavy-drinking husbands in check. But a good woman was expected to quietly juggle her many responsibilities, including her man.

Having a man brought significant social status to women in everyday life. Regardless of the extent to which he was faithful, sober, or helpful, just having a man at home conferred status. Without a man, a woman was considered less respectable in society, and she might be seen as personally at fault for failing to hold onto her man. As one Soviet mother reflected: "People saw a husband as only raw material. A good woman should be able to not only keep him but to make a man out of him." A woman on her own, Soviet mothers explained, had somehow failed as a woman. And as another Soviet mother observed, "Most of us knew that probably another woman would look at that same troubled guy and take on the challenge. Men in Russia don't stay single for long . . . unless of course they are completely a lost cause!"

This was a peculiar kind of "liberation" indeed. In the Soviet gender order, the state mandated women's participation in the labor force while letting gender traditionalism flourish at home and in everyday life, creating a mere façade of liberation. Soviet women had been liberated in the sense that they had no choice but to labor alongside men in factories and enterprises while occupying lower-paid, second-tier jobs relative to men. In all kinds of workplaces, women were considered second-class workers because of their many responsibilities at home. At the same time, women were expected by the state and society to do all of the "women's work" at home, with little or no help expected from men, turning to the state as ultimate father and patriarch if and when troubles at home proved to be too much. Motherhood was politicized, and women were supported as worker-mothers by the state, whereas fatherhood was marginalized, with the state downplaying men's patriarchal authority at home but doing little to transform gender relations. The Soviet state paid lip service to gender equality, relying on women's paid labor while at the same time underpaying women for their work.[3]

Relative to what has been written about women's "second shift" of housework and child care in the West, where inequalities at home persist in spite of women's integration into the workplace, Russia is a more extreme case. The inequalities between women and men at home in Russia, even though women have long worked full time, are rather stark. The state did not encourage men's participation in housework and child rearing, since men were to instead focus their efforts on working, managing, and leading state enterprises. Male dominance was left unchallenged as a norm in the Soviet period, even though the state tried to shift the basis for masculine identity to work rather than private patriarchal power. Furthermore, women's notorious double burden was especially onerous since apart from child care the state's social services were, according to Ashwin and other scholars, "woefully inadequate."[4] Given consumer shortages and the lack of modern conveniences in the Soviet period, many women describe going to work as a respite from all of their responsibilities and burdens at home. In spite of women's increased participation in paid work, they were always expected to manage the home and children, all while coping with shortages of consumer goods and lacking many conveniences and shortcuts available in other parts of the world.

This chapter analyzes how and why, despite official tolerance and considerable social protections relative to today, the social status of Soviet single mothers was always so problematic. Using original data gathered in interviews with Soviet single mothers and historical accounts, it also highlights the main contours of the changed context of single motherhood, which subsequent chapters will flesh out further. Generalizing about the Soviet era is difficult given significant policy shifts over time. Nevertheless, understanding contemporary single motherhood demands that we look back to the period after the Second World War, when the number of single mothers skyrocketed and state policies had the effect of legislating male infidelity.

Women certainly raised their children on their own prior to the Second World War. Yet it was the state's postwar policies that reinforced patterns of family life—such as male absence, infidelity, and lack of responsibility for children alongside female perseverance, intergenerational support systems, and responsibility for children—which continue to influence Russian families today. The post-Socialist state is no longer tying men to families as it did in the past, nor is it supporting women as worker-mothers as it did in the late Soviet period. With the state's retrenchment, and men's varying commitments to family life alongside continued heavy drinking, nowadays single mothers feel at times heroic and free, yet, at the same time, unprotected and often truly on their own.

✎ Legislating Soviet Single Motherhood

Russians today do not always agree on who precisely counts as a "single mother," but this very ambiguity surrounding gradations of single motherhood has historical precedent. Whether or not any state or society frets over the growth of single motherhood or instead accommodates family changes by supporting parents of all kinds while minimizing differences among mothers, some women have long raised their children with little or no support from men. This may be due either to men's literal absence or to men's more figurative absence in the form of a lack of practical support at home. The Soviet Union was no exception in this regard. Since the early days of the Soviet Union, mothers raised their kids alone, even though this situation, throughout Soviet history, has seldom been considered a serious social problem.[5] Single parenthood (which in the vast majority of cases is single *motherhood*) was not seen as a problem by the state, but the category of single motherhood itself is also relatively recent. Single mothers were created as a legal category, establishing single motherhood as an official status conferring state benefits, only in the aftermath of what Russians call the Great Patriotic War.

✒ The Postwar Period (1944–1967)

The Soviet Union lost approximately twenty-seven million soldiers and civilians during the war, about half of all Second World War casualties.[6] In a four-year period, nearly 15 percent of the Soviet population had perished.[7] The war's losses left an indelible imprint on Soviet society as nearly everyone had been personally affected by them. Even today the losses of the war are a palpable reference point for the Russian people.

What remains less recognized is how much Russia's normalized gender crisis has been shaped by the far-reaching effects of the Second World War. The gender crisis has complex, multiple origins, but the war's aftereffects, including the state's ensuing legislation, shaped the contemporary gender order. Russia lost a staggering number of men during the war, intensifying the sex ratio imbalance and producing an unusually large number of single mothers. Women's responsibility for children and family life became institutionalized during this period, as did men's marginalization in families.

Officially, there were no single mothers in the USSR until 1944, when the term "single mother" (*odinokaia mat'*) appeared in a July 8th decree.[8] The 1944 Family Law focused on "increasing government support for pregnant women, mothers with many children, single mothers, and strengthening preservation of motherhood and childhood" and on establishing "the honorary title 'Mother Heroine,' the foundation of the order 'Motherhood Glory,' and the 'Motherhood Medal.'"[9] The law collapsed the distinction between war widows, who were respected by their communities and entitled to government support, and unmarried mothers, who were much more stigmatized. Because the term "single mother" in popular usage also included war widows, the state probably hoped to defuse controversy by using the term for unmarried mothers. In hopes of encouraging women to help replenish the population, the state sought to diminish distinctions between war widows and divorced or unwed mothers, if not eliminate those distinctions altogether.[10]

The law caused a vast increase in the number of illegitimate births. The pronatalist government encouraged all women to bear children; in the absence of a father, the state would support single mothers. The state wanted men to marry, form families, and raise children, but at the same time it encouraged men to impregnate unmarried women, or at least it encouraged men to sire more children than they could afford to support. The 1944 law "inculcated a specific set of postwar gender relations," and by sanctioning adultery, Mie Nakachi demonstrates persuasively that it "undermined its simultaneous desire for stable families."[11]

Resurrecting a double standard of sexual morality that had been abolished after the Bolshevik Revolution, a single mother's sexual partner now had no legal responsibility for children created. Single mothers could no longer register their children under fathers' names. Fatherhood became defined as merely a legal obligation related to official marriages. Men had long been marginalized in family life, but this period intensified their marginalization.[12] Motherhood, however, produced immediate social repercussions, and women carried full responsibility for children born outside of marriage.[13] Unable to file for child support, unmarried women could either receive government aid for child rearing or send their children away to be cared for in state-run orphanages. The law also strengthened the ban on abortion, prevented common-law couples from obtaining legal recognition, and established measures to discourage divorce.[14]

During the postwar period, the state offered support to single mothers while encouraging men to impregnate women without assuming any familial responsibilities. But even before the passage of the 1944 Family Law, the war had begun to wreak havoc on families. In addition to millions of men dying at the front, evacuations made it difficult for families to maintain contact, and new sexual liaisons produced new families. But prior to 1944, mothers at least could name the fathers of their children and make a claim on them for support. The 1944 Family Law changed this by adding, according to Nakachi, "the category of de jure 'single mothers' to the preexistent de facto ones."[15] After the Second World War and the passage of the 1944 Family Law, approximately one-third of all births were outside of marriage.[16]

The 1944 Family Law had far-reaching, inequitable repercussions, especially for women. Yet although women certainly experienced stigma as single mothers, the amount they experienced is unclear. Many accounts suggest that the state discouraged any moral condemnation of single, unmarried mothers because it needed women, regardless of their specific circumstances, to give birth. Besides, because so many men were lost in the Second World War, some Russians may have viewed unwed single mothers and women who had lost potential husbands with considerable sympathy, at least for a time, compared with how they were viewed at the same time in the West or would be later on in Russia.[17] On the one hand, the Soviet cult of motherhood meant, according to Kanji, that "Soviet lone mothers were held to be deserving because they had fulfilled their maternal duties to the state, which perceived that higher population numbers meant more prestige, and, at a practical level, more workers and soldiers."[18] On the other hand, single mothers were still stigmatized in relation to women who had legal husbands. Even though single mothers were officially supported by the state because of its concerns about replenishing the population, single mothers were probably less supported by society.

In any case, scholars such as Carlbäck note that there were "relatively few people expressing a negative view on the situation of lone mothers and fatherless children."[19] However, considering the repression of the postwar Stalin years, it is difficult to gauge any kind of public opinion on single motherhood until the mid-1950s. We know that many women were not pleased with the law's gender status quo. Women wrote to newspapers such as *Literaturnaia gazeta* to protest the inhumanity of the law and the difficulties it created for women and children who had no way to bring philandering fathers to justice. A 1948 study by a party functionary was never brought to light officially but revealed systemic patterns whereby male partners would abandon women as soon as they discovered a pregnancy. Other letters from single mothers argued that as long as fathers were permitted to be irresponsible, women would not have more children. The state, however, responded slowly to people's dissatisfaction with the law.

In 1955 the abortion ban was repealed. Even though the state relied less on force and more on normalizing techniques of power after this ban was lifted, it still sought to regulate gender and sexuality through education and the medicalization of abortion.[20] In December 1965 the state simplified divorce procedures. A new Family Code was introduced only in 1968.

☛ The Late Soviet Period (1968–1991): Tactical Shifts

During the late Soviet period, a different set of mixed messages prevailed. Soviet family policy had long been marked by a tension between the two conflicting priorities of female independence and equality, as stressed in legislation, and the state's efforts to strengthen the family as a key social in-stitution. But during this period the state began relying on moral suasion rather than legal prohibition for both divorce and abortion.

The 1968 Family Code ushered in a new era in reproductive politics. In addition to honoring motherhood symbolically and encouraging women to replenish the population, the 1968 laws attempted to reduce the private costs of rearing children by investing further in maternity leave and child care fa-cilities. Although many of these policies failed to achieve their objectives, especially considering the significant gender wage inequalities in the Soviet Union and the notorious double burden that Soviet working women bore on the home front with little or no help from men, the state's tactics had undeniably shifted from the postwar years.[21]

After 1968, even though the size of monthly child allowances did not in-crease,[22] there were other significant changes. Mothers were permitted to register any male name of their choosing on a child's birth certificate, break-ing down the division between legitimate and illegitimate children.[23] The law allowed voluntary acknowledgment or firm evidence of paternity, thus eliminating the stigma, for children and their mothers, of a blank space on a child's birth certificate. Paternity was no longer tied to legal marriage alone, and women could make claims on their children's fathers for support. Al-though tactics had shifted, the years of encouraging state-sanctioned adul-tery for men likely had longer-term effects.

During this period, the state upheld the two-parent family ideal, but at the same time it encouraged men to "alter their behavior and become more conscientious husbands and fathers." Unmarried single "spinsters" and their solitary lives were pitied during an antiabortion public health campaign (in spite of the legality of abortion after 1955), and the state increasingly, ac-cording to Randall, "urged men to perform their masculinity by serving as more explicit heads and masters of their families."[24] Although the party still framed fatherhood in terms of the many negative behaviors men should avoid, it did more in this period to control men's behavior, disciplining men who neglected children, beat wives, or broke up another person's marriage.[25]

Although Western scholars have retrospectively conceptualized this over-all period as the *zastoi*, or stagnation, in reference to the USSR's declining social and economic development, many Russians did not experience life in this way. In contrast to the postwar period, and in spite of continuing family problems, these years meant relative stability and prosperity for many.[26] Though instability in family life may have continued, it was of a different kind. There were far fewer nonmarital births during this period, dropping to just 10.6 percent from the high of 33 percent of all births after the war.[27]

The state gave special rights and responsibilities to motherhood, and it was motherhood, rather than marriage, that conferred these rights and responsibilities. For example, in divorce no alimony was paid to wives unless they were disabled, but child support was legally mandated and enforced. Neither a pregnant woman nor the mother of an infant under one year of age could be divorced without the woman's consent.

But although nonmarital births became less common, the 1968 legislation caused the divorce rate to increase sharply, from 179 to 309 per thousand marriages in the mid-1960s.[28]

By 1979, the Soviet Union had the world's second-highest divorce rate, even though unofficial divorces and separations were also common.[29] Because the Soviet state concentrated on protecting the rights of women as both mothers and workers, there were relatively few separate benefits for single mothers during this period. Benefits generally accrued to women as mothers, regardless of the type of motherhood.

Nevertheless, whenever the state did distinguish between single and married mothers, it sought to provide additional support to the former. According to Russian labor legislation, single mothers with children under the age of fourteen could not be dismissed from their jobs. If a single mother lost her job, she could challenge the decision and have it quickly overturned. In addition, state enterprises maintained quotas in terms of the number of single mothers on their rosters and on waiting lists for housing. In this way, some single mothers were able to obtain housing more quickly than couples might. Considering the financial position of single-mother families, trade union organizations often gave vouchers for single mothers to send their children to pioneer camps and sanatoriums. Besides providing for children's day care and schooling, including children's meals, mothers received an allowance when they were unable to work because of their children's illnesses (for children under the age of fourteen).[30]

Yet in spite of these provisions for single mothers, given the stigma surrounding unmarried motherhood, women still considered single motherhood only as a last resort. Although studies of the experience of Soviet womanhood are somewhat limited, with many focusing on the postwar rather than late Soviet periods,[31] most Soviet women were made to feel incomplete if they had not experienced motherhood. After all, many of women's rights and responsibilities became tied to their special status as mothers, rather than to their status as women or as workers. Childlessness was stigmatized and pitied even though divorce not only became common throughout this period but has continued to increase well into the present.[32] The state regulated the terms and conditions of women's employment, putting restrictions on the range of occupations in which they could be hired; gave some financial benefits to women; subsidized child care; and regularly issued official statements acknowledging the contribution that the development of the services sector could eventually make toward alleviating the burdens of housework. There were fluctuations over time, with maternity leave becoming more generous during the 1980s, but the amount of support women were given still left women on maternity leave coping with a reduced income.[33]

In contrast to the postwar period, late Soviet single mothers raised their children during a time when everyday life seemed stable in spite of the increasing frequency of divorce, the dominance of traditional gender ideologies, and the stigmatization of women forgoing marriage or childbearing. Women were encouraged to look to the state and their work for support as mothers instead of to individual men.

✌ The Experience of Late Soviet Single Motherhood

Although there is a gap between ideology and lived experience,[34] most research has focused on official Soviet family policy and ideology. Though the research on what single motherhood meant to women in Soviet times is limited, clues can be found in both the films and cultural artifacts of this period, as well as from listening to Soviet single mothers reflect on their experiences. Late Soviet single mothers are the immediate predecessors of today's single mothers. Even though today's high rates of nonmarital births mirror postwar rates, there are many aspects of the late Soviet single motherhood experience that provide invaluable context for understanding Russia's quiet revolution occurring in family life. The sexual revolution, for instance, began toward the latter part of the late Soviet period but reverberates throughout the post-Soviet era. Divorce and abortion became widespread, too, and rates of both remain high today.

To better understand the experience of unmarried and divorced single motherhood in the late Soviet period, I draw on films and historical accounts as well as on retrospective interviews with twenty Soviet single mothers. In-depth retrospective interviews offer a unique perspective on what it was really like raising children alone after the passage of the Family Law of 1968. In retrospective interviews, late Soviet single mothers become oral historians, sharing stories about raising children between 1968 and 1991.

Most women argue that although they faced some challenges as single mothers in the late Soviet period, today's single mothers face many more difficulties, even in spite of some increased freedoms. While some challenges are particular to the post-Soviet era, other more familiar problems have worsened in size and scope. I interviewed a broad range of late Soviet single mothers. Just over half of the mothers had higher education, and most had one (65 percent) or two (30 percent) children.[35] By the late Soviet period, marriage was nearly universal, and it was very rare for women to bear a child outside of wedlock. My sample reflected the general pattern of mothers marrying relatively early, divorcing after a few years, and either remaining single, remarrying, or, in the post-Soviet period (as cohabitation became more widespread), living together with a boyfriend. Only four of the twenty Soviet single mothers I interviewed had given birth out of wedlock, and of these only one was never married.

⚓ Compulsory Marriage and Motherhood

During the late Soviet period, the state and society reinforced the idea that marriage and children are compulsory for women. Ideas of pitiable single women living lonely lives without a husband or children were predominant, and single women were pitied, dismissed, or "laughed at mercilessly."[36] With the possible exception of the progressive intelligentsia, the Soviet system considered the unmarried sector of womanhood morally unstable, and the word for "old maid" (*starukha* or *staraia deva*) is very pejorative.[37]

A whole subgenre of late Soviet films touches on the plight of the pitiable single woman. Perhaps the most famous film about a single woman is the 1987 tragicomedy *Lonely Woman Seeks Life Companion* (*Odinokaia zhenshchina zhelaet poznakomit'sia*), in which a forty-three-year-old woman so desperately wants to get married that she posts notices around town seeking male companionship. In the 1983 film *Rooms for Singles* (*Odinokim predostavliaetsia obshchezhitie*), the story centers on a female textile worker living in a dormitory who dreams of marrying but spends her free time matchmaking on behalf of other women in her building. Even the hit 1979 film *Moscow Does Not Believe in Tears* (*Moskva slezam ne verit*), a commercially successful film seen by eighty-five million people across the Soviet Union, alludes to the sex ratio imbalance and stereotypes about single women.[38] In one scene, Katya, the single-mother protagonist and factory director, visits a city singles club, where single women are turned away as members but men are accommodated since, according to the club's director, there are "five single women for every forty-year-old bachelor" in Moscow. When Katya meets her future beau, he remarks that she has an "unmarried," searching look about her.

The state's official support for both working motherhood and gender traditionalism is also reflected in *Moscow Does Not Believe in Tears*. Katya rises to the pinnacle of Soviet success as a factory director, but she is portrayed as unhappily single, making do with a passionless affair with a married man. When she meets and falls in love with Gosha, a metal worker taken with Katya but troubled by her superior work status, she, too, seems concerned that her success is rather unfeminine. This was one of many late Soviet films reflecting a mixed message about single motherhood and a traditional message about the place of women in society: single mothers who work hard can rise to the top of their chosen professions, and Soviet society cares enough about them to provide them with some benefits, but in the end, according to Gillespie, "a woman's place is with her man, and she should not earn more than he does."[39]

Marriage was considered an essential stage in a woman's life course. Traditional mores and gender ideals held sway over mothers during the late Soviet period. From the late 1960s, the state was in the business of reinforcing ideals of natural gender difference, with Soviet egalitarianism giving way to what Gray considers "an obsession with gender roles."[40] Too many women living outside of marriage, or avoiding marriage altogether, implied that women were not conforming to traditional family ideals. Marriage was the gold standard, and state policy was based on women's so-called natural responsibility toward the family. Women were pressured from all sides, from families, friends, coworkers, and state policies, to not only get married but to do so sooner rather than later. Besides respectability, marriage was a prerequisite for career advancement. Love in the heterosexual romantic sense was not considered as essential for marriage or happiness. A few Soviet single mothers I interviewed spoke of marrying for love, but they felt somehow lucky or even naive. A larger number of women, including those who married for love, explained that they married mostly because they felt it was time or because they wanted to have a family, with marriage considered the necessary precursor.

Ludmila, a divorced factory worker who had moved to Kaluga from Siberia, described why she married: "Marriage here is just conventional. First of all, I was already twenty-one years old. . . . By then it's time! If one waits too long to get married then they start to talk about you. At least back then, now it's much freer of course." When I asked her what marriage had meant to her, she replied: "When I came to Kaluga I was pretty much alone. He was a local resident and I moved into his home." Ludmila explained that she soon realized that she could not live long with his entire large family, so she switched careers. Just as some women got married to qualify for better housing, others changed jobs to places that allocated apartments more quickly or provided better day care arrangements. In Ludmila's case, she took a low-paying job at the local housing agency (*domoupravlenie*), mainly because along with her job she was given a room in a communal apartment: "The salary was small, but I went to work there to get an apartment. The salary was much worse than at the factories but because my husband earned good money at a factory job I could go to work there for less money, since I knew I would get an apartment." Particularly in a society with more women than men, which was especially the case in the postwar era but persisted subsequently, an asymmetrical marriage market makes marriage very attractive to men by giving them more choices in terms of partners and in setting the terms of a marriage.[41] Meanwhile, a married woman could tell herself, and others, that someone wanted her.

Irrespective of social class or educational background, Soviet women perceived that it was harder to get married after age twenty-five. Aleftina, a divorced cleaner and former librarian, said that because someone she liked asked for her hand in marriage, she agreed; she had not thought much about the specifics of what married life would entail. In her case, she felt ill prepared for the demands of living with difficult in-laws (where her mother-in-law was beaten in front of the children when her father-in-law drank too much), dealing with her sick child at the day care center, and balancing her librarian job and never-ending household and shopping responsibilities: "I simply thought that a woman must have a child before she turned twenty-five. The notion that this was the way things ought to be done was spread throughout popular culture, films, and books about love. It was just a part of our psychology . . . that a woman had to be married by this age, with at least one or two children." Aleftina explained that she, her husband, and child ended up moving back in with her own mother for some peace and quiet, though then all four of them had to live in just one room.

Soviet women saw a narrow window of opportunity in which to marry. Zoya, a retired teacher, admitted that she married because she was afraid of ending up alone. Her mother did not care for the family, but Zoya felt that marriage was just a game and it was high time she, like her friends, got married. There was a stereotype, Zoya added, that you needed to marry, start a family, and then get on with your life and that without marriage, getting ahead was just not possible.

In stark contrast to the contemporary period, in the late Soviet era a lack of money was no obstacle to marriage. Early marriage and childbearing often signify a lack of opportunity in the West, but demographers note that in Soviet Russia it indicated a lack of risks. Shotgun weddings were probably very common in Russia, and regional studies found that a high proportion of births conceived nonmaritally led to marriage, representing 30–40 percent of all first births and 50–60 percent of adolescent births.[42] The state supported women's anxieties in rushing into wedlock, and women over twenty-five were referred to as "aging first-time mothers." Even in 1989, when the changes of perestroika were under way, only 6 percent of Russian women were single at age thirty.[43]

Since families had to demonstrate need for housing by proving either that they resided in inferior, unsafe conditions or occupied space smaller than nine square meters per capita, the housing shortage also encouraged marriage and parenthood. If couples wanted to live together, they had little choice but to marry. "I lived in a dormitory," Lada explained. "That also probably influenced me in terms of wanting to get married. I had always lived in a house and I was sick of dormitory life." Even though single mothers might "jump the queue at the notoriously crowded day care centers," get a small cash benefit, or, after 1981, obtain first priority on housing waiting lists, nearly everyone preferred to marry instead.[44] Any guarantees provided to single mothers (and there were not many given that Soviet mothers in general were supported much more than single mothers in particular) paled in comparison to how difficult it was to live respectably outside of marriage.

In light of the housing shortage, young adults often lived with their parents or in subsidized dormitories until they received an apartment from the state. Employment after graduation was guaranteed, education was free, and most young people could count on parental help. Parents helped adult children with money and with household tasks such as shopping for deficit items, growing food on *dacha* (garden) plots, cooking, cleaning, and raising the grandchildren. Other families relied on state-run day care centers. Young people could either live poorly on their own incomes or accept help from families. Soviet women, too, emphasize their generation's lack of mercenary motives for marriage by contrasting it with current practice. Irina, a divorced teacher, argued: "Today people are more practical. . . . They plan. They consider whether or not they have money. Or when they need a baby, and when they don't. Back then there was a different psychology. . . . I didn't understand that one needs money to live!"

Pregnancy was regarded as a first step in family formation, and marriage symbolized adult status and independence from the parental family. Although abortion rates were extremely high in the late Soviet period (in part because access to contraceptives was limited),[45] abortions were feared during the early childbearing years. Because many people thought that women should not have an abortion before bearing their first child, believing it could make them sterile, the rate of abortions was lower among childless women.[46] Vera, a divorced teacher currently living with her boyfriend, explained that she married at the very early age of sixteen (special permission was needed to marry at this age) because abortion was believed to have life-altering consequences: "The question of abortion arose but right away everyone said no. Abortion was widespread, definitely, but everyone probably understood what the consequences would be: I might never be able to have children. . . . Even now, people still say that you shouldn't have an abortion if it's your first pregnancy. One of my classmates got pregnant during her last year of school and had an abortion before graduation. Unfortunately, she still doesn't have children."

Lada also mentioned that she had long wanted a baby. Once she found out that she was pregnant, getting married was the next step. She reflected, "Back then it was not acceptable to just live together. If there had been the option of living together, I wouldn't have registered the marriage. But living together was considered shameful." Although living together, or *grazhdanskii brak*,[47] is widespread in the post-Soviet period, the practice was rarer previously. Several women, grimacing, noted that the words used in Soviet times to refer to men and women who lived together without being married, *sozhitel'* or *sozhitel'nitsa* (roommates) and *sozhitel'stvo* (cohabitation), had an ugly ring to them. Few wanted to announce that they were living in such circumstances.

Because marriage garnered respect, status, housing, and career options in Soviet society, it was ubiquitous. But motherhood, too, was considered compulsory for women; it was a civic duty and the natural destiny of every woman. When push came to shove, becoming a mother was one of the main reasons to marry. If marriage was not possible, becoming a mother could still enable a woman to fulfill her so-called feminine destiny, even if others could then judge her for her lack of morals. However much the state officially supported unmarried mothers with its pronatalist policies, bearing a child outside of marriage conferred a lower status on a woman, notwithstanding her other professional or personal accomplishments.

Of the four women in my sample who gave birth outside of marriage, only one had never been married. Galya gave birth to her daughter in 1983, when she was thirty years old. In her words, she had been too naive and trusted her boyfriend, who was divorcing his wife at the time and had promised to marry Galya after the paperwork was finalized. He left her when she was eight months pregnant, while she was still living in a dormitory room. Galya received some privileges from the state, but like other women, she viewed these benefits as minor in light of the social stigma she endured. Still, her workplace put her at the top of the waiting list for housing, and she received her own apartment in 1984.

Despite her polished, feminine appearance, friendly manner, and professional accomplishments, Galya admitted that she always felt badly about her
lack of social status as an unmarried woman.[48] Sometimes her coworkers had
teased her about her unmarried status, always in a jocular way, but it felt "like
getting a slap in the face": "Probably it was hardest to endure the social status. What can I say, our city is provincial and at that time, to be a single mother
[*mat'-odinochka*] . . . well, I wouldn't say they'd throw stones at you, no, that's
an outrage. But many people of my generation felt that, well, they had husbands and an official status, but you're without a husband and it's just a different social status. This really oppressed me. Maybe not that strongly, maybe
the situation just weighed me down somewhat, but all the same it was unpleasant." In terms of the unpleasantness, Galya remembered it getting back
to her that one of her girlfriends advised the others that one could completely befriend only married women; it was too risky letting unmarried
women into one's home. With infidelity, along with heavy drinking, a major cause of marital breakups in the Soviet Union, some married women
felt they had to protect their husbands from being led into temptation. People celebrated many Soviet holidays at home, drinking and eating together
with family and friends, so single mothers may have felt especially isolated
during major holidays.

Some Soviet single mothers argued that whether it was stigmatizing to
give birth outside of marriage depended on a woman's particular circumstances and even social class. Natalya, a retired teacher, remembered her girlfriend who worked at a technical college, still unmarried at age twenty-nine.
All of her colleagues told the woman, "Time is flying. If you want to have
a baby, now is the time . . . you can always meet someone later on." Eventually her friend followed their advice, and though still unmarried, she is grateful for her child.

The terminology surrounding single motherhood provides some insight
into how much single mothers were tolerated rather than being fully accepted.
The word for single (or lone) mother, *odinokaya mat'*, is relatively neutral
and in popular usage frequently refers to all kinds of single mothers, including unmarried, widowed, or divorced mothers. Russian social scientists refer to these various kinds of single-mother families as maternal or "incomplete
families" (*nepolnye sem'i*).[49] Unfortunately, for many Russians the word for
"incomplete" (*nepolnye*) families is closely associated with the word used to
describe inferior or defective (*nepolnotsennye*) families, in contrast to complete (*polnye*) or full-fledged (*polnotsennye*) families. Besides these general terms,
the pejorative version of the word for single mother, *mat'-odinochka*, refers
specifically to unmarried mothers who give birth out of wedlock. A related

slang expression, "single-night-mother," reflects stereotypes about single, un-wed mothers. The phrase *mat'-odnanochka* plays on the word for single mother to indicate that the child was conceived after a one-night stand, casting as-persion on the morals of the unwed mother. Some Soviet mothers described neighbors gossiping about the very idea of a woman who *naguliala rebenka*, a slang expression that suggests that a woman got pregnant because she slept around.

Notably, Soviet mothers believe women are freer in the post-Soviet pe-riod to have children regardless of their marital status—as long as they can provide adequately for them. While providing adequately under market cap-italism has its own pressures and ambiguities, of a different kind than those that Soviet mothers experienced in providing for their families in a society with less inequality, most women greet the liberalizing of narrower Soviet social mores as a breath of fresh air.

But rather than simple freedom, today single mothers face a different set of constraints. Irina, like most Soviet mothers, feels that women today do not face stigma in raising their children alone, even if they have never been married. In the New Russia, however, a woman's material situation shapes many aspects of her life, including how much others judge her as a single mother. Irina observed: "Now people look instead at a person's whole situ-ation. If she is rich, if she has a good business, if she makes good money, well so what if she's a single mother? . . . But if she is poor, and if she also has a child, then people will think, 'why in the world did she go and have a baby?' "

✐ Divorce: An Accessible Last Resort

Along with compulsory marriage and motherhood, divorce became extremely widespread in the late Soviet period, especially in urban areas. Divorce was not welcomed on an official level, but it was not nearly as stigmatized as un-married motherhood. Some slang words for divorced women pronounced judgment on their morals—the term *razvedenka* (slang term for a divorced woman) was a pejorative—but these words were used much less than the similarly derogatory phrase for a single, unwed mother, *mat'-odinochka*. As the number of divorces escalated, so did the acceptability of divorce increase as well. In a culture that encouraged the idea that women could "make some-thing" out of a man, in some ways divorce was still seen as a form of failure for women. But as long as women were married for a time, which in itself brought her some status, divorce became an accessible last resort. Although there were some status differences between officially married and divorced women, the more profound status difference was between married and never-married women. In an insightful study of Soviet autobiographies, Rotkirch argues that "In contrast to the single woman, the *divorced single mother* was a possible role in Soviet everyday morality."[50] Gray observes that among the intelligentsia in the late Soviet period, it was "just splendid, and utterly normal" to be a single mother.[51]

Yet even as divorce became a normal occurrence, being single in such a pro-marriage society automatically took a woman's status down a notch or two. Many divorced women felt uncomfortable socially. Olga explained: "I endured such humiliation, such disappointment from my marriage. . . . But people treated you differently when you were not married. If a woman was not married then she had the attention of everyone, she was watched vigilantly. 'And where is she going? And who is she going there with?'"

Mothers particularly felt the judgment of others if they dared to divorce for a second time. After a heartbreaking first marriage in which she caught her husband cheating on her, Marina felt pressured by her family to accept the marriage proposal of a coworker at her factory, to give her daughter a "normal family." Although she did not love him, he courted her and helped her father repair cars for extra money. Her father insisted that he was a good man and that Marina's daughter needed a father. However, he turned out to be worse than her first husband, drinking heavily and beating her. But Marina, a factory worker, still did not rush to divorce him: "Six years. I put up with him for six years. And this second time I didn't divorce because I felt uncomfortable in front of others. I mean it was my second marriage and I was once more getting divorced? I had these kinds of thoughts."

Marina also described feeling that as a woman she needed to have a man at home. Not having a man at home affected not only her own social status but the status of her parents. She argued that "everyone wants a complete family" (*Vsem khochetsia polnuiu sem'iu*) in order to feel protected (although in her own case she could hardly be considered protected at home). Living in a closed society, in which social networks and ties with others mattered a great deal for accessing scarce goods and services in daily life, led Soviet women like Marina to behave cautiously because of what others thought of their actions.

Although Marina is unusual for divorcing more than once in the late Soviet period, the reasons why she initiated divorce are not unusual. The Soviet women I interviewed did not divorce because they no longer loved their husbands or because their husbands failed to help much on the domestic front, even though these situations were described. In some ways, traditional

FIGURE 3. Three generations of Russian women. The youngest daughter on the right, a single mother, had just returned from a trip to Moscow to look for freelance work. Her son, far right, had stayed behind in the care of his grandmother and great-grandmother. Photograph by the author.

gender ideologies, in which fathers were encouraged to concentrate their efforts on working and bringing home their paychecks rather than helping their working wives on the home front, probably exacerbated the divorce rate. But most women divorced their husbands because the men drank too much, were abusive verbally and physically, or were chronically unfaithful. Soviet analysts, too, cited alcoholism as the main cause of divorce, with infidelity a second major reason.[52]

⤴ The Context of Late Soviet Marriage and Family

In addition to societal attitudes toward single mothers, whether unmarried or divorced, understanding late Soviet family life requires grappling with three important aspects of the context: women's reliance on the state for keeping husbands in line and enabling their workplace participation; the frailty of heterosexual relations and women's dependence on kin relations and especially on their children's maternal grandmothers for practical support; and the normalization of men's heavy drinking and domestic violence. In contrast to the late Soviet period, the contemporary Russian state has a mostly toothless set of protections for mothers as workers. While still critically important, the intergenerational support system under market capitalism faces new pressures. And finally, several key causes of marital breakdown, especially male drinking, have only worsened in the post-Soviet period.

☛ Protected by the State

Soviet single mothers lived modestly, but most were confident about being able to at least make ends meet. Soviet women feel it was much easier for Soviet single mothers to provide basic necessities for their families than it is today. There is much more social inequality in the post-Soviet era, including high levels of inequality among single mothers. Furthermore, mothers, regardless of marital status, were supported as worker-mothers by the state. Women could not rely on the state alone and needed to be employed in order to live, and to live well most also needed the support of their own mothers. But the Soviet state provided some protections and guarantees for mothers of all kinds; these protections are much fewer today. In the late Soviet period, women worked for pay, the state supported mothers in caring for children, and the party was "a sympathetic ear to which errant husbands could be denounced."[53]

If there was a problem in receiving child support, for instance, women felt entitled to go through official channels. In most cases, women did not go through official channels to complain about a husband's drunken behavior or failure to pay child support, preferring to circumvent the state. But some appreciated having legal recourse available. Ludmila, who married a second time mainly because of "the status that unmarried women had in society," explained that it took her awhile to completely get rid of her first husband, even after the official divorce (he was still officially registered in Ludmila's apartment): "After he struck our daughter, Evgenia, after there was too much fighting, I went to the police. I had them check up on him because he was living with another woman but coming here to rattle our nerves. I mean we were officially divorced! The other woman had a four-room flat, so he had someplace to live. Back then there were communist laws in place where you could go to complain to the 'profkom' or 'mestkom' about a husband's bad behavior. It provided some justice." Most late Soviet mothers discussed having had rights, guarantees, protections, and a strong belief in the future while raising their children. Of course, what may seem rudimentary to some may feel to other mothers like security about being able to provide the basics of life—food, shelter, clothing, education, work—for oneself and one's family. Women's assessments of the Soviet period depend a great deal on their assessments of their current standard of living as well as the opportunities and challenges faced by their own adult children. But Soviet single mothers agree that there were more protections for mothers and workers in the Soviet period, along with fewer opportunities and choices.

There was little support for single-parent households as such; state support was based on the fact that the family contained children, and that the household was poor, rather than on the absence of a parent. Poverty was never officially recognized in the Soviet Union; instead, the authorities referred to *maloobespechenost'*, or possessing few resources. But single mothers, like war veterans, comprised one of the groups the state targeted for assistance. In the Soviet Union, the dual breadwinner model dominated, and both spouses generally had to work to feed the family. With few exceptions, the earnings of just one parent were insufficient to support the family; therefore, bringing up a child alone, even with child support payments and state subsidies, posed a challenge. The state provided some payments to unmarried single mothers, but such payments did not cover the earnings of absent fathers.[54]

Soviet women routinely limited family size, privileged motherhood over career advancement, and faced shortages of consumer items and services. Yet while state payments and child support never replaced an absent spouse, most scholars concur that "a comprehensive array of universal and specialized social welfare programs provided a relatively adequate and secure safety net for single and unmarried mothers and their children."[55] Overall, Soviet single mothers offer relatively positive assessments of their experiences: "It's impossible to raise a child alone now. Before it was possible." The state's official support for women combining paid work and motherhood, whether it was guaranteed day care, free afterschool activities, reliable work, or child support enforcement provisions, was critical to women's sense of overall well-being.

Because everyone was employed by the state, child support laws were enforced vigilantly. Today single mothers cannot count on regular child support as their own mothers did. Lusya, a fifty-five-year-old divorced lathe operator, felt supported by the state in her efforts to obtain child support from her daughter's recalcitrant father: "Before it was better because although some husbands tried to pay less they still had to pay child support. And then . . . well, I found out where he [her former husband] worked, right? And I said, he works over there, check on his job and on how much he earns. And then people would check. I got child support every month." Some men paid on their own, without having child support deducted from their paychecks, because it was embarrassing for some to have child support withheld at work. As Lada put it, "He didn't want to feel ashamed at work, so

I didn't file for support. He paid me on his own instead." Most women responded like Olga when asked about child support, calmly stating: "I filed for child support and received it without any problem. . . . I could count on getting it if he was working."

Women emphasized that the amount of child support they received was not large but paid for some essentials every month. Nonresident fathers paid 25 percent of their monthly salaries to support one child, 33 percent for two children, and 50 percent for three or more children. For instance, Aleftina's former husband earned good money as a welder. Because her daughter was ill as a child, she left her librarian job and went to work as a cleaner in a factory. Had she not been able to rely on regular child support, she explained, it would have been very difficult to support her daughter as a cleaner working limited hours: "Back then child support was strict. It's only now that someone can get a guard's job for a hundred rubles and then go to work somewhere else for six thousand with his wife knowing nothing about it. In Soviet times, this was impossible because one had a labor-book and one could only work at the place where one's labor-book was registered. Therefore things were easier for divorced women. Women were socially protected on all sides. They tracked down husbands for not paying child support and could condemn them." Aleftina pointed out that even the accounting departments at enterprises were interested in making certain that everything was clean so that nothing could be said against them. Accountants, she added, could also be fined for enabling working men to shirk their child support obligations.

Nevertheless, there were some cracks in the system and exceptions to the general rule of reliable child support. In large part because Soviet society relied heavily on *blat*, or personal networks and connections, some men evaded paying child support, or at least paid less child support than they owed. Although certain practices were prohibited, they were still possible with the help of the right personal connection, as suggested in the Russian phrase *nel'zia, no mozhno* ("one should not, but it's possible").[56] Marina, one of the most ardent defenders of the Soviet period, explained that although most of her friends received child support, in her own case her husband was able to get away without paying much because he avoided regular work: "I didn't get any child support because he tried to avoid working. He didn't want to work. He'd quit job after job, running from place to place. . . . I'd get ten rubles and then maybe another ten rubles after six months had gone by. He simply tried to get out of paying." Irina also mentioned that she "got a huge stack of paper, but little or no money." The papers said that the authorities were searching for her husband but were still in the process of tracking down his whereabouts. Still, most women had faith in the overall system.

Soviet fathers, however, had little connection to their families after divorce, often withdrawing from relationships with children.[57] Child support was the main contribution fathers were expected to give to children. After several months in the field, I was no longer surprised when I heard that fathers, who generally lived in the same city as their children (especially in Soviet times), saw their children once or twice per year, if at all. Soviet mothers worried about their children not having contact with their fathers, but they did not seem to imagine how it could be otherwise.

Although there were fewer inequalities between people, and thus between mothers, in the Soviet era, late Soviet single mothers describe just how pervasive the system of *blat* was in everyday life. Personal connections and networks helped women with getting their child a day care slot just as they may have helped others to buy meat without having to make the long train trip to Moscow. For example, many Soviet mothers described the challenge of ensuring places for their children in day care centers (even though day care was guaranteed), but there were various ways around the problem. Some mothers changed jobs to places that had available openings in affiliated day care centers, while others worked in day care centers for a year or two to obtain a spot for their child. Some women, like Irina, were able to rely on influential acquaintances, in this case her mother, to get her child a place in a day care center. Irina recalled: "It was hard to get a place. But my mother . . . well, we have an expression called *po-blatu*. That was how things were back then. Everything was done *po-blatu* . . . connections. My mama was a director at the milk factory. Not the head director, but she still had influence."

While many women spoke of access to day care as an important right of the late Soviet period, others noted that in spite of these so-called rights, women had very few choices with respect to the conditions or terms of the care provided to their children. So if a woman did not like the day care center affiliated with her workplace, she was generally out of luck unless she changed jobs. Women felt positive about the entitlements and guarantees mothers had access to in the Soviet period, but at the same time, they argue that single mothers today are much less constrained by traditional mores and benefit from expanded choices and opportunities. Aleftina, for instance, changed careers entirely, accepting clear downward mobility, because she was dissatisfied with the day care arrangements at her job and saw no other way out. She was unwilling to put her child in the day care center, so eventually she became a factory worker instead of a librarian: "The library gave me a place at a day care center, but it was a twenty-four-hour center and I would have had to leave my child there all week. . . . I visited the center, looked at the conditions there, and I didn't like it. It was cramped, they didn't go out for walks much, and I was supposed to just leave my daughter there every Monday while I worked at my job all week and then pick her up on Friday. . . . So I quit my job and went to work at a factory."

While *blat* may have helped some mothers obtain a day care slot or find a new job with a shorter waiting list for housing, it was also helpful for the arduous daily task of shopping. Given the shortage economy under state socialism, people often engaged in time-consuming activities in order to procure (*dostat'*) necessary items. Shoppers could spend hours going between specialized stores and waiting in various lines, and people who arrived at the stores too late were often out of luck. *Blat* connections and shopping cooperatively with friends helped women save some time, and these connections were frequently more important than money. In Russian households, women typically were responsible for shopping (in addition to working outside the home, cleaning, cooking, child rearing, and managing the family budget), and single mothers were probably more involved with *blat* practices in order to maintain their family's well-being.[58]

Although procuring necessary products and services for one's household was time-consuming, single mothers had varying perspectives on it. For women like Marina, a divorced factory worker barely making ends meet in the post-Soviet era, the time spent procuring items had been a tolerable nuisance: "While I was raising Lena on my own, we always had a full fridge. We could eat eggs to our heart's content. Now there's no way we can do that . . . the price has gotten really high. . . . To get things back then we traveled to Moscow. Moscow is close, so this was no trouble. We traveled there, bought things, and, well, this was the only shortcoming. But I'd bring those products home and I would have shoes and clothes for myself and for my child and a full fridge. And now I can't get clothing and shoes for myself." For Marina, being "protected on all sides" meant not having to worry about being robbed, getting thrown out of one's apartment, going hungry, lacking child support, or going without medical care. Single mothers today worry routinely about all of these kinds of issues.

Unlike Marina, most Soviet single mothers appreciate not having to wait in long lines any longer or travel to Moscow for consumer goods. Although Ludmila was as appreciative as Marina of the social protections and rights that workers and mothers had in the Soviet era, she has few fond memories of the constant scramble involved in juggling work, child rearing, and all of the waiting in line and traveling necessary to get decent clothing and food: "Things were hard materially. I mean now we at least have products available, but before the shelves were often empty. And when there's nothing and you have a baby . . . well, it was a question of where to obtain things. We traveled to Moscow, and those of us with children organized with one another collectively at work. I would take three kids and then go to get in line for things. Can you imagine? And in order to avoid being snitched on, we'd put the bags in an extra stroller. . . . We took turns with one another." Although Ludmila admitted that life could be challenging in the Soviet era, she still emphasized that many things were better before: they received paid sick days and work was stable. They believed in the future. There were shortages of some products, but no one was dying of hunger. Although she had never had a dacha, those who did could provide themselves with their own cabbages and potatoes. Some women even managed to avoid train trips to Moscow altogether. Alana, a retired English teacher who claimed she "had no material difficulties in Soviet times," led groups on organized trips to Moscow by bus. She was able to get in line to buy various products during the day and still go to the theater at night. Whereas she felt secure about getting by, she explained, mothers today have to think constantly about overcoming material difficulties. The new shortage item is money.

✦ Supported by Mom

In late Soviet Russia, there were few shortages or difficulties in life that one's own mother could not help overcome. The bonds between mothers and their children were in many ways stronger than those between husbands and wives. The frailty of heterosexual relations and importance of intergenerational kin bonds between adult daughters and their own mothers has a long legacy, and these two phenomena are interrelated. This legacy endures into the present,[59] even though today these intergenerational bonds face unprecedented pressures (see chapter 4). Describing the frailty of heterosexual relationships, some scholars note that mothers often complain about husbands as "second children" in their autobiographies, with children, rather than husbands, being the source of much more stable, rewarding sources of love. Indeed, Soviet women describe husbands "getting in the way" of the close bonds that develop between mother and child. Others admit that they had wanted to get married in order to have a baby and cared less about the husband part of the package.

While men's absence in the aftermath of the Second World War is a big part of this legacy of grandmother support in families, Kukhterin also notes that the party supported the "definition of the home as a female-policed realm."[60] Women typically received most of the tangible support for carrying out domestic duties from their own mothers. Most Soviet mothers routinely described moving back with their own mothers either before giving birth or shortly after having a new baby, in order to receive extra help not provided by husbands. Some either chose to stay with their mother or insisted that their husband move in with his mother-in-law. When Irina's mother, for example, visited her in Ukraine, she "saw my unhappiness and told my in-laws we would be going home for a while so she could help me out with the baby, then barely four months old. Everyone understood that we would not be coming back."

Many mothers depended on their own mothers for help with child care, buying gifts, finishing their education, finding a better job, doing housework, and shopping. Considering the amount of help Soviet single mothers report receiving from their mothers, it is somewhat surprising that many claim that in Soviet times, unlike the present era, it was still possible to raise one's child alone. Few actually did so. The support a single mother receives from her own mother, then as now, is most frequently taken for granted. But the comments of Soviet single mothers make sense considering that they could also count on some state supports, guarantees, and protections.

Galya, an unmarried late Soviet single mother, distinguished between providing for her child's needs and ensuring that her child never felt deprived compared with other children in two-parent families. She could only do the latter, she explained, thanks to the help of her mother: "I could not buy a car, that was rather expensive for me, but I could create a cozy home, go on vacation, and dress my child. Of course, we weren't showing off. If one of my relatives offered me some of their children's second-hand things, I took them. . . . At the same time I tried to make sure my child's pride was never wounded. I tried to make sure that she had everything that others had. I was only able to do this with the help of my mom. And later on with the help of our relatives, my aunt and my three cousins in Moscow." When I asked Galya how she would have managed without her mother's help, she explained: "I would have survived, but I would not have been able to ensure that my daughter didn't feel deprived. With my mom's help, we could make my child equal with those children who lived in complete families."

Soviet grandmothers stepped in to compensate for the state's inadequacies and the frequent absence of men. Even those single mothers who did not receive help with child care or housework from their own mothers usually pointed to several key contributions that their mothers had made to their lives. Aleftina, for instance, had a hard time working and caring for her sick daughter. She could not have imagined how she would have coped without her mother's help in shopping for deficit goods: "My mom took the first train to Moscow, at 4:30 in the morning, and she got home at 11 at night.

She'd get to Moscow at 9 a.m. and she stood in different lines all day, until 6 p.m. This was just for food because if we needed clothing we would all go so we could try things on. Shopping for clothes required a separate trip." Although Aleftina was never close to her mother, her mother's support was invaluable and allowed Aleftina to focus more on spending time with her daughter. Similarly, Zoya, an active party member, found time for party committee work and pursued a second higher-education degree in Moscow, mainly thanks to the assistance she had from her own mother in raising her children after her divorce.

Women expected their mothers to support them and typically received at least some support even if the relationship itself had its conflicts. Because money was not the main critical factor for household well-being in the late Soviet era, several scholars, such as McKinney, have observed that "an unmarried mother living with her mother or grandmother might in fact be better off in many ways (though not financially) than her married counterpart, since the older woman would have been more likely to provide assistance with childcare and housework than the average Soviet father."[61] Irina, like Aleftina, was not close to her mother, yet she credits her mother for giving her the opportunity to pursue higher education and helping her out of an awful marriage. Because her mother had been a party activist and had *blat* connections through her job that allowed them to eat relatively well, Irina's entire life changed after her mother committed suicide. With a five-year-old son to raise without her mother's help, from then on Irina always felt like a *real* single mother. Unlike most other mothers interviewed, she struggled materially, living paycheck to paycheck. Her father paid her apartment rent (minimal in Soviet times) and contributed toward her son's clothing, but she bought herself nothing and felt very alone.

☙ Coping with Male Drinking and Domestic Violence

Problems of drinking, along with domestic violence, have long plagued families, and in Russia these problems were in full force during the late Soviet period. Women divorced husbands mainly for these often interconnected reasons (along with chronic infidelity), and as the next chapter will show, these problems still break up many marriages. However, not only are these problems long-standing issues in Russia, but according to most indicators they have actually worsened in the post-Soviet period, alongside fewer state supports and increased economic pressures on families.

Drinking, primarily vodka, is a widespread cultural ritual. Russia is the world's hardest-drinking nation, with a primarily male drinking culture and high rates of binge drinking and other risky drinking practices. The tradition of binge drinking is several centuries old.[62] Male drinking, whether among former husbands, sons, fathers, or other relatives, was voluntarily brought up in nearly every interview, whether with late Soviet or contemporary single mothers, married mothers, or nonresident fathers. Survey data affirm that about one-third of Russian males binge drink at least once per month. High levels of consumption are not new but have deep historical and cultural roots, with consumption quadrupling from the 1940s to 1980s and increasing still further today. Furthermore, just as important as the high levels of consumption is what Russians drink (mainly vodka, but frequently also alcohol substitutes and *samogon,* or illegally home-distilled spirits) and how (episodic binge drinking).[63]

Russians consume approximately 4.75 gallons of pure alcohol per person annually, more than double the amount considered a health threat.[64] With an average consumption of one bottle of vodka for every adult male every two days, heavy drinking has serious consequences for the stability of family life, frequently causing divorce.[65] In virtually every study, alcohol is identified as the most important cause of marital breakdown in Russia, with alcohol frequently linked to other problems, including domestic violence, infidelity, and a lack of material support. The Soviet state led various campaigns against alcohol. Some women raising children in the late Soviet period appreciated that the state supported women's efforts to keep male drinking in check. Marina explained, "There were sobering-up stations [*vytrezviteli*] and generally if a man was drunk you could call them and they'd pick him up and take him there. Even though you had to pay a fine from the general budget, at least there was something you could do about the rowdiness. Now it's useless . . . there is nothing like this!"

Indeed, today men's drinking has become further normalized and entrenched. There are some class differences in how alcohol is consumed, with some business elites increasingly managing their drinking carefully or abstaining entirely, but this is a minority phenomenon. Since the post-Soviet collapse, opportunities for drinking are more extensive. There are more drinks available around the clock in Russian cities and more places to drink compared with the Soviet era, where most people drank in private homes. Today there is also less state intervention in condemning and regulating drinking practices. With less state regulation, cheap, fake, and even lethal vodka has flooded the market, compounding the deleterious effects of drinking.

Russia also has the world's largest gender gap in drinking. Women do drink in Russia, and the numbers of women drinking have actually increased during the post-Soviet period. But drinking is primarily a ritual of masculinity. Apart from special occasions, women are much more likely to gather around a table drinking tea.[66] For example, a study in Novosibirsk found that 30 percent of Russian men compared with 1 percent of women reported binge drinking at least once a month.[67] A 2011 World Health Organization (WHO) report stated that "By far the highest proportion of alcohol-attributable mortality is in the Russian Federation and neighbouring countries, where every fifth death among men and 6 percent of deaths among women are attributable to the harmful use of alcohol."[68]

Men's drinking has been more central to their identities as workers, where practices of drinking distinguish men from both women and nonworkers. For men, there is a great deal of social pressure to drink given that drinking copious amounts of alcohol remains a defining ritual of masculinity.[69] In Russia, it is through drinking wherein men become "real men."[70] Russian culture condones heavy drinking as an essential part of masculinity, and drinking in groups is a firmly rooted and socially expected aspect of male friendships and work. It may also be viewed as a normal masculine response to life's stresses and failures. In other words, "drinking has been seen both as a drug for failed masculinity and as compensation for it."[71]

Men's limited domestic responsibilities create more opportunities for leisure drinking, and drinking may also allow men to escape from their responsibilities. Drinking creates a vicious circle since it appears to then reduce fathers' emotional and financial contributions to their families.

Whereas women are expected to prioritize family responsibilities, deriving a sense of being needed in the family, men's place at home, and in their families, is heavily dependent on their ability to bring home money.[72] Drinking, a compensatory form of masculinity, is a culturally accepted way for men to experience a sense of being needed in the world, especially if men cannot find much respect at work or at home. Some scholars emphasize how much drinking helps in establishing and tightening social bonds among men or how much drinking is necessary for men getting work done. Recent research also suggests that the lack of constraints in the post-Soviet period limited Russians' freedoms, with men's drinking defined in opposition to authority and responsibility, providing some space from the state, from work, and from the family.[73]

Although the causes are multifaceted, heavy binge drinking is associated with the crisis in male mortality that intensified in the 1990s. Today the gender gap in life expectancy remains high at twelve years, with men's life expectancy now at sixty-two years and women's at seventy-four.[74] Heavy drinking among men as well as a high incidence of accidents, violent deaths, and stress-related illnesses are some of the problems contributing to men's lower life expectancy.

Whatever the more positive aspects of ritual drinking, the effects on family life are rather grim. Women (and children) are often left to cope with the effects of men's drinking, in a similar manner to how women have long been expected to compensate for the inefficiencies of the Soviet state by bearing a triple burden of paid work, domestic work, and service to the state—patiently and tirelessly. My research reveals close connections between men's drinking and men's estrangement from family life and even domestic violence.

Although to a lesser extent than drinking, violence emerged quietly but consistently in one-quarter of my interviews with mothers, frequently overlapping with discussions of men's drinking, as the following encounter described in my field notes makes clear. Sitting in the living room looking at family photos, Ludmila, a forty-two-year-old grandmother, paused at one photo, a formal, black-and-white portrait of a couple dressed up in their finest for a friend's wedding. The woman in the photo smiled demurely, next to a stoic man with his arms around her, protectively. "He struck me that same night," Ludmila said almost inaudibly, her eyes fixed on the photograph of her younger self with her second husband. Ludmila's daughter Lena, who had joined us for part of the evening, seemed startled and glared at her mother, muttering: "Mama. You needn't say such things in front of her." I instinctively put my hand on Ludmila's shoulder. Ludmila replied, "I didn't hide anything from Zhenochka. . . . She knows things about our family."[75]

That first night, Ludmila explained, led to many more years of violence. "He drank. He drank and drank and who knows why he did it." Had we been alone, we might have talked more, but Lena, herself a single mother, was eager to shift the focus away from the violence that her mother had endured for several years before divorcing a second time. Lena nonchalantly told me of an old Russian proverb, one that I had heard a disturbing number of times: "You've heard the Russian saying, right? If he beats [you], he loves [you] [*byote, snachit lubit*]!"

I wondered whether the women perceived differences between how willing women were to tolerate this kind of abuse in the Soviet period and how much they did so now. Ludmila, after all, was a Soviet-era single mother who genuinely had felt really protected by the state in some ways while raising her child, at least in her factory job and in her work as a mother. But certainly she had not felt protected at home. Lena blurted her answer out, declaring that "Fewer women put up with this today." Ludmila seemed much less convinced. "Fewer," she agreed. "But it still happens a lot."

My own research as well as the literature on domestic violence in Russia leads me to agree with Ludmila. The problem of domestic violence, thanks to global feminist social movement organizing, is much more openly acknowledged today. The Soviet response to violence against women had been "haphazard" at best, characterized by what Johnson (2009) calls gender skepticism. Domestic violence was sometimes regulated under "hooliganism" ordinances, sometimes treated as a "family scandal" with reconciliation as the goal of police intervention, and (especially in high-profile rape cases) "sometimes regulated as a by-product of other concerns."[76] The residential permit system meant that women often had to live with violent men with whom they no longer had a relationship. Most problematically, domestic violence was not seen as a gendered issue that affected women collectively in systematic ways. Statistics were not collected on gender violence, and the prevailing Soviet ideology focused on class violence, remaining skeptical about gender violence.

Recent studies emphasize that the intensity of domestic violence in Russia is greater than in many other countries, such as the United States, with current estimates suggesting that Russian wives are more than twice as likely as U.S. wives to be murdered by their husbands. Cubbins and Vannoy (2005), however, found that "over a quarter of urban Russian married and cohabiting couples have experienced wife abuse at some point in their relationship, a level of abuse similar to that found in U.S. studies.[77] Many Russian women suffer abuse for years before leaving husbands simply because they have nowhere to go.

Overall, given the state's retreat from regulating most aspects of family life, and the collapse of the system of state supports which had provided women with a basic safety net, domestic violence has probably increased in the contemporary period. The post-Soviet state does not provide credible data on the deaths of women at the hands of their spouses, but according to Johnson, "violent mortality rates in Russia are three times the world average,"[78] and increases in drinking, male-perpetrated interpersonal violence, and divorce rates suggest a similar increase in domestic violence.

Collectively, the data on drinking, domestic violence, and the male mortality crisis in Russia hardly allow for an optimistic impression of family life. Most people prefer not to dwell on the intractable problems that are sadly just as much a part of family life as feelings of closeness, solidarity, or even tight intergenerational support systems. But as the subsequent chapters will flesh out from varying perspectives, the darker side of family life is not a mere footnote in this story of single mothers, gender crisis, and social change in the New Russia. Instead, it is a major leitmotif, one which women, especially but not exclusively, have managed—silently and for far too long—and one which has indelibly shaped the very meaning of today's single motherhood. The fact that so many single mothers summon a positive outlook and strive to improve their family's material circumstances, as subsequent chapters describe, has a great deal to do with the context of family life outlined in this chapter as well as with what they perceive around them as normal family life.

The context of single motherhood has shifted irrevocably, from the postwar period, which created the category of single mothers, to the dissolution of the Soviet Union in the early 1990s. Although there are some new freedoms for women, and for mothers, in that they do not feel judged in society, for many women these freedoms in reality mean a lack of protections as well as new pressures. During the late Soviet period, state support, however incomplete, nevertheless made a huge difference in the lives of single mothers. But equally important, if not more so, was the support of women's own mothers. State protections have withered away for the most part, and even when laws are still on the books, they are no longer upheld in society. The state has retreated from its former policing of family life. But the privatization of drinking and domestic violence hardly helps women who must manage these problems on top of new economic challenges posed by neoliberal market capitalism. State policies no longer discourage divorce, and marriage is no longer a necessity in order to get a good job or even to be considered a respectable person. Yet apart from its relentless focus on replenishing the population, the Russian state does little to actually support mothers as workers in the way it once did.

Just as problems of men's drinking and even domestic violence have gotten worse, women face a world of fewer state protections and increased challenges in employment, finding child care, keeping their children safe after school, and so on. There is a longing for the order of the past among the older generation, in part because although these women see their daughters as having some new kinds of opportunities, the younger generation also has to deal with a more complex set of issues in juggling work and family, all while having fewer resources to rely on. To be sure, Russian women have long juggled multiple responsibilities. But a qualitatively new kind of juggling act is now being asked of them as single mothers under market capitalism.

Notwithstanding the material challenges Soviet single mothers endured, Vera was one of many who pointed out the silver lining people shared in their hardships: "Everyone had confidence in the future. That was a good thing about Soviet times, and it was simpler too probably. Now not everyone has this confidence in the future." With a great deal of equality and security, as well as help from their own mothers and confidence in the future, most Soviet single mothers did not feel that their lives were especially difficult. But as single mothers, they felt somewhat stigmatized. In a closed society, others judged them, or they believed others judged them, for failing to find a man or failing to reform the man they had found. State protections and guarantees did little to change their lowered social status.

How single women felt, and whether they even identified as single mothers at all, was shaped by how supported they felt as mothers. State support is only part of the story. Women usually felt supported most by their own mothers, or they struggled to find a mother substitute. There were limits on their aspirations and conventions to follow. Although it remains to be seen whether single mothers in the New Russia are as burdened materially and, paradoxically, as free in their personal lives as Soviet single mothers make them out to be, in some ways their lives are the polar opposite of the lives of late Soviet single mothers. While today's single mothers have limited state supports, they experience little or no stigma as single mothers. And they enjoy some opportunities that late Soviet single mothers could not yet imagine.

⤞ CHAPTER 2

Diminishing Material Difficulties
Single Motherhood beyond Survival Strategies

> For some reason everyone thinks, "oh, she's raising a child alone, how hard things must be for her!" But really, for me it's much simpler raising my son on my own! Because fathers don't take on any responsibilities and you end up running around and looking after your husband too, so your child gets much less time with you than when you are raising a child alone. When you're married with one child, it's often more like having two. As we say, "I have two children, one is five years old and the other is thirty"!
>
> —Nastya, twenty-nine-year-old widowed mother, accountant

Single mothers of all kinds routinely challenge stereotypes of Russia's single mothers as poor and unfortunate (*bednye i neschastnye*). Some mothers may be poor and unfortunate, women argue, but there is nothing about a mother's marital status that means she necessarily has it harder relative to mothers in so-called intact, two-parent families. Everything depends on the circumstances. Oftentimes, women insisted—either triumphantly like Nastya or, more frequently, as if it were a dirty little secret they were letting me in on—single mothers' lives are actually simpler than the lives of many women in two-parent families.

Nastya greeted me warmly at the door of her fourth-floor walk-up apartment, wearing white slacks and a frilly blouse, painted toenails peeking out of house slippers. She exuded confidence and was eager to share her experiences, including her late husband's drinking problems and her newfound independence. She divorced for the first time at age twenty ("it was puppy love . . . we were just fooling around and should never have married"), remarried at twenty-one, and was widowed at twenty-seven when her second husband and father of her eight-year-old son, Misha, died in an alcohol-related car accident. She described several challenges in raising her son alone. She was saving up for a computer Misha wanted, trying to be both mother and father at once, and worrying somewhat about his lack of male role models. Nevertheless, she emphasized that married mothers in Russia often face these same difficulties, with the added burden of caring for needy husbands who too often do little to help: "Married mothers often have more work. One needs to look after men more, as a wife, and things worked out so that I was paying more attention to my husband than to my son." She hopes to meet a good man someday who could be a father to Misha, but in the meantime she is not waiting for her prince to come. Instead, she has more concrete goals: finishing her higher education, buying a car, adopting a dog.

Although a single mother, Nastya seldom feels different from, and certainly not more unfortunate than, many other mothers she knows. She faces material difficulties, but so do many cohabiting and married mothers. Her best friend, Faina, who joined us after the interview, lives just upstairs and has two kids to support as well as a husband who does not earn much. Nastya depends on her older sister's moral and material support at times, especially since her parents are far away in Ukraine, but other mothers regularly turn to kin for support. She believes that mothers did have some benefits during the Soviet period, in terms of guarantees ranging from job security to child care and free afterschool activities for children, but at the same time she is glad there is no longer stigma surrounding single motherhood. Besides, she feels there are more interesting opportunities for women to get ahead in life today, even though it can take a while to figure out how to seize these opportunities.

The transition to single motherhood was hard at first, but Nastya argues that being a single mother is much easier than putting up with a burdensome husband or indifferent father. Sure, she acknowledges, it may not be as ideal as raising a child with a good husband and father. But these days, women of all kinds observe, these good men are harder to find. Becoming a single mother is an ordinary, even if unforeseen and temporarily traumatic, event in the lives of many Russian women.

☛ Going against the Grain

I was initially puzzled as to why most single mothers tended to downplay many of the significant material difficulties they had experienced. While hardships, such as skipping lunch to save for bus fare or forgoing small treats for one's child, can be unpleasant to acknowledge or embarrassing to share, all the more so with an American perhaps, there was clearly much more going on with this avoidance. After all, women shared other intimate details of their lives with me, from unplanned pregnancies and abortions to marital unfaithfulness and intimate partner violence.

Besides challenging my own assumptions by diminishing, rather than elaborating on, their hardships, Russia's single mothers are going against the grain of most social science research. People may debate the pros and cons of single motherhood in terms of "family values" and "lifestyle choices," but a major unifying concern for most scholars, policymakers, and citizens alike is how single-mother families fare in terms of their economic well-being and especially how the children of single mothers fare compared with children from two-parent families. When single mothers are doing well economically for their children, most people are less concerned about single motherhood as any kind of problem. The persistent association with heightened poverty risk dominates scholarship on single motherhood, and the general mood is one of gloom, doom, and the tribulations of family breakdown.

In exploring the meaning of single motherhood, I knew that families subsisting on one income rather than two are generally poorer, on average, than two-parent families. References to single mothers in the broader social science literature, especially in the United States, are often followed by discussions of poverty or welfare. Despite growing numbers of more affluent single women worldwide who choose to become mothers, the dominant idea of single mothers as women who are poor and unfortunate continues to shape public perception.[1] Single motherhood has long been associated with a "feminization of poverty," at least in those Western countries where meager state support systems are coupled with a gender pay gap where women still, on average, earn less than men.

Russian women, however, repeatedly assert that their lives have improved since becoming single mothers, contradicting many scholarly assumptions. On top of a rather dismal single motherhood scenario emphasized in many studies, the post-Socialist literature since the 1990s has analyzed the many hardships faced by ordinary Russians during the transition to capitalism, focusing on survival strategies. Given that providing for one's kids with scant supports is a challenge for most single mothers, at least at first, one might assume that the struggle to provide is even harder for Russian single mothers given the insecurities of the transition to capitalism.

Yet many Russian women began interviews by declaring, "My *only* difficulties are material," often impatiently waving their hand as if to brush aside any pesky material concerns of survival and to instead change the subject to something more interesting, significant, and worthy of conversation. But I could not exactly brush these concerns for economic well-being aside, for Russian mothers have experienced all kinds of material hardships. When asked, women described incredible material challenges that they had once faced or that they routinely still endure. Women shared stories of hitting rock bottom in the past or of having to plan incessantly to avoid hitting rock bottom, whether in terms of running out of food or having to borrow money from a friend. But at the same time single mothers diminished the import of material challenges as routine and banal. They were typically eager to move on to other topics, such as their work, children, problems with former husbands, and the difficulties of finding a good man with whom to share their lives.

Back when Ries (1997) conducted her study of Russian talk in the last days of the Soviet era, she reflected, "my first clue about the value of hardship was simply that the people I met were always talking about it."[2] Yet in post-Soviet Putin-era Russia, there is much less talk of hardship, even though people clearly still experience it. Instead, single mothers are intent on not talking much about material hardship unless probed, or alternatively, they talk about it in a way that diminishes its overall importance in their lives. I listened to single mothers and grappled with where they were coming from without simply taking their words or that dismissive wave of the hand at face value. Why do so many women shrug their shoulders over something as critical as material difficulties? How are struggles to provide food, shelter, clothing, and other basic necessities of life for themselves and their children considered relatively immaterial, or at least minor, in the larger scheme of things? Most important, is life truly simpler as a single mother for many women in the New Russia and, if so, how and why? What might this tell us about what ordinary women expect from normal family life and what they perceive around them?

Using different angles, the next three chapters untangle this puzzle of why women diminish the import of material difficulties in their lives. In probing these questions, we gain clues for understanding the rise of single motherhood in many other contexts where two-parent families are idealized and it makes little economic sense for women to go it alone. Mothers' insistence that material difficulties are only part—and not necessarily even the main theme—of their stories runs deep and wide.

The first part of this chapter describes who single mothers are in the New Russia and outlines the major routes to single motherhood. Although there are surely some differences between widows and divorced mothers or between those who get pregnant unexpectedly in their early twenties versus those who seek to have a baby at all costs in their thirties, in the Russian case the similarities among women's accounts are frequently more compelling than subtler differences in how women become mothers. Indeed, this chapter suggests that women's experiences with former partners and husbands indelibly shape how women assess their current situation as single mothers, for many truly appreciate the heightened sense of control and stability single motherhood affords—in spite of the real material challenges many still face. The second part of the chapter details some of the specific material challenges that women have experienced, challenges that many mothers tend to frame as experiences very common among other women, including their own mothers, or experiences which, however unsavory, pale in comparison to the joy of raising one's own child. Furthermore, material difficulties, if navigated well, generally help to make women stronger. Such strength hardly feels optional to single mothers under today's market capitalist system.

↜ Ordinary Single Mothers

Given the Soviet-era legacy of matrifocal families and a widespread negative discourse on men,[3] accompanied by a fluidity of family life circumstances, there is a great deal of diversity among Russian single mothers. Single mothers do not typically feel set apart from other mothers and do not exist as a social group with a shared identity in any meaningful way. Rather than conceptualizing "single mothers" as a social group, it makes more sense to consider single motherhood in Russia as a probable, and possibly temporary, stage in the life course of many ordinary women.

In other countries with high rates of single motherhood, scholars have similarly noted that the risk of single motherhood is shared not by a small subset of the population but by the majority.[4] Most scholarship needs to catch up with this reality by treating single mothers as normal, ordinary women rather than implying that they are somehow aberrational. The falsely homogenizing category of single mother is especially unhelpful in Russia, with its fluid living arrangements, early age of first marriage, and high divorce rates.[5]

Of course, Russian single mothers do differ somewhat from other mothers, particularly in terms of how the experience of divorce or nonmarital birth changes them. But the differences (as chapter 5 explores further) are not as pronounced as much scholarship implies. In Russia, where the vast majority of women eventually become mothers, nearly 60 percent of marriages end in divorce, one-third of all births are nonmarital, and adult male mortality rates are among the highest in the world, single motherhood is not exceptional. Darya, a twenty-three-year-old unmarried mother and lawyer who broke up with her child's father before the birth, reflected on the ordinariness of single motherhood: "Typically a couple meets, the girl gets pregnant, and they marry. After a year or two they divorce. Or as a woman nears thirty she realizes that her personal life hasn't worked out, so she makes up her mind to have a baby on her own. This is also typical nowadays." Women like Darya, who may live together with a man for a while but do not marry him when they become pregnant, represent a newer path toward single motherhood that has increased since the collapse of the Soviet Union.

Even though the average Russian woman is fairly likely to spend some time as a single mother, in everyday life there is very little discussion of single motherhood. Single mothers are ubiquitous to the point of near invisibility. Nastya, like many mothers, alluded to this invisibility, noting, "no one even thinks about single mothers anymore." Though it may seem puzzling to outsiders that single motherhood is rarely discussed as a "social problem" in Russia, in spite of the growing numbers, there are several reasons behind this invisibility of single mothers in public discourse.

First, there is even greater ambiguity in the post-Soviet period concerning exactly who is, or should be considered, a single mother. To some extent, ambiguity is inherent in the constructed category of single motherhood and has long been a part of its construction in Russia. As chapter 1 detailed, since 1944 the legal term "single mother" (odinokaia mat') has referred to an unmarried mother raising a child without a partner, excluding divorced and separated mothers. But in more popular usage "single mother" often applies more broadly to any mother raising a child without a husband or partner, regardless of the specific reason.[6]

However, with increased rates of cohabitation in the post-Soviet era—which Russians refer to as living together in a grazhdanskii brak—confusion is mounting. I excluded mothers living with a male partner at the time of interview from my sample of single mothers, but I frequently met women and men living together while unmarried, and some single mothers I interviewed had also lived with men for a time. Some unmarried mothers live with partners in marriage-like relationships, with partners who help to raise women's children, regardless of whether they are registered as the children's fathers. But even more frequently, unmarried, cohabiting mothers are effectively single, living on a temporary basis with new boyfriends who may do little, if anything, to support resident children. While some cohabiting Russians refer to their respective partners as husbands and wives, arguing that legal distinctions do not matter, others never use these terms. Furthermore, in some cases women refer to a cohabiting couple as married, whereas men in that same cohabiting relationship later clarified for me directly that they were single.[7] Russian scholars have noted that although the increase in non-marital births indicates a major change in the organization of family life, decisions to bear a child outside of marriage are not generally demonstrations of female independence. In sum, no one agrees on precisely who single mothers are, and a mother's status as single or not frequently shifts over time. Rather than forming a distinct group, single mothers tend to blend in with the many other mothers raising their children with the help of female kin.

Second, besides no one agreeing on who single mothers are, few really seem to care. Most official and academic discourse in Russia and abroad also ignores the rise in Russian single motherhood, instead focusing on other demographic shifts that have taken place since the breakup of the Soviet Union. For instance, plummeting fertility rates and alarmingly premature male mortality rates have attracted most of the attention. On the basis of President Vladimir Putin's speeches in recent years, the state is mostly concerned with reversing its population decline and wants to encourage women to bear more than one child for the sake of the Russian nation. But whether women are single, divorced, married, or cohabiting is clearly considered less important.[8] Echoing the Russian state's indifference toward single motherhood, today Russians of all kinds agree that marital status is much less important than it used to be, and marriage rates declined somewhat in the post-Soviet period.[9] As long as a mother is able to provide for her children, most people do not care much about the specifics of her situation.

Finally, single mothers are rather invisible in part due to the very achievements of the Soviet era. Even when single motherhood was more stigmatized, official policies ensured that single mothers were integrated into the mainstream of society. The state generally assisted families with children rather than single-parent families as such and supported the employment of all mothers regardless of marital status. The legacy of these policies is palpable in the post-Soviet period. As a result of this successful integration, single mothers do not differ systematically from other mothers in terms of age, education, living conditions, or employment.[10]

Regardless, the increase in single-mother families in post-Soviet Russia is beyond doubt. Just as the share of children living in single-parent families almost doubled in the United States in the 1970s (from 12.8 to 21.5 percent), a period characterized by economic recession, increasing inequality, and a sharp decline in fertility, so Russia has been experiencing demographic shifts in a similar context of economic and social change since the 1990s. Klugman and Motivans concluded that "The net result of increased divorce, non-marital childbearing and premature mortality during the 1990s has been a greater number of children living in single-parent families."[11] Of course, in terms of the prevalence of single-mother families, the snapshot or static picture of single motherhood based on cross-sectional data always grossly underestimates the number of children who have spent or will spend time in a single-mother family. The more dynamic picture that focuses on lifetime prevalence is a much better indicator of how common single motherhood is becoming as a stage in women's lives.[12]

↝ Abandoned by the State

Single mothers describe feeling unprotected (*bezzashchitnye*) as mothers, lacking both male support and, especially, the support of the state. They explain that they are well aware that no one seems to need their children. Children are for mothers alone, with no one else in society caring much about their fate. In contrast, Soviet single mothers felt supported by the state as mothers and workers.

In the post-Soviet period, motherhood has become a private choice and responsibility rather than a public duty and a social good.[13] Since the early 1990s, state support has decreased steadily for all mothers. Although there is still some state support for working mothers, it pales in comparison to what was available in the late Soviet period. Some of the benefits and allowances introduced in the late Soviet period remain on the books, but very high inflation has made them mostly irrelevant. Single mothers do not generally receive special treatment, with the exception of a miniscule child allowance, which since 1998 is available only to families (whether single- or two-parent) whose average per capita income does not exceed twice the minimum subsistence level. Women typically consider the subject of the "child allowance" or state benefits for mothers unworthy of discussion, calling the allowance laughable at best or insulting and humiliating. As Kiblitskaya notes: "women feel deserted by the state, which no longer guarantees them employment, no longer glorifies and supports their role as mothers, and no longer provides them with a safety net. . . . They have begun to turn inwards, to concentrate on their families."[14] For many, the extensive assistance of female kin (and sometimes friends and neighbors) compensates somewhat for a lack of state support.

Contemporary Russia is similar to the United States in its lack of a coherent framework for social protection. Since the breakup of the Soviet Union, there has been no coherent framework for the social support of vulnerable groups; instead, there is a hodgepodge of provisions administered by local government departments and workplaces. Local or regional authorities are responsible for specific programs, so some benefits to the poorest single-mother families vary somewhat by region, though most of these benefits make little difference to standards of living for Russian families with children.

Scholars agree that there is much less support for mothers than there was previously, and fathers, more than ever before, are often evading their responsibilities with impunity.[15]

Mothers have the right to take maternity leave for up to three years, but levels of this benefit have dramatically declined, and very few can afford to do so. Child care has been cut, so while employers provided and subsidized three out of every four child care places during the Soviet period, the employer share of places is currently less than one in five.[16] The vast majority of single mothers return to work well before the three-year period, out of both necessity and desire. Because of a lack of other options, many rely on the child care assistance of female kin, so women without family assistance have an extremely difficult time finding child care for their children. Some women try to work from home doing odd jobs like tutoring or making handicrafts for sale at local markets, while others use social connections to try to secure a coveted child care slot.

Furthermore, though most women with young children have to work to make ends meet, nearly every mother describes widespread discrimination in looking for work. Repeatedly I heard that "no one wants to hire a woman with a small child." Even having one's child in day care does not help much in navigating this kind of open, systematic discrimination. Private employers assume that women will take frequent sick leave to care for their children. Those with female kin, typically a grandmother, available for on-call child care have fewer problems, especially in securing higher-paid private-sector employment.

The system of collecting and enforcing the payment of child support probably contributes most to women's feelings of being abandoned by the state and subject to the whims of former husbands. Although women are entitled to receive child support from former husbands or from men registered as the legal fathers of children, these laws are seldom enforced. The 1996 Family Code stipulates that child support should be calculated on the basis of all income (including entrepreneurship, private plots, and informal sector activity), rather than official income alone, but this seldom occurs.[17] In the mid-1990s, wage arrears were common and now unofficial employment and uncontrolled incomes have exacerbated nonpayment problems. Many private employers keep official salaries artificially low to evade higher taxes (even though significantly more money is paid to employees), but the amount of child support, in practice, is based almost exclusively on artificially low official salaries; the existence of unofficial income is difficult to prove. Women are forced to negotiate informally with former spouses and to try to feel grateful for what they can get. Most mothers cannot count on getting much. Few believe that turning to official state channels will help them in any way. Instead, doing so may harm relations with children's fathers irrevocably, so that mothers will then get nothing for their children.

✎ Ignored by Society

Single mothers feel unprotected by the state, but they are unanimous in their conviction that much has changed for the better concerning the status of single motherhood in everyday life. Women report little or no stigma, irrespective of their route to single motherhood. Divorce is accepted by most as a fact of life, and though it is still somewhat more prestigious to have been married for a time (regardless of eventual divorce) than to have never been married, women do not feel judged by others for being a single mother as long as they manage to provide well for their children.[18] Relative to the late Soviet period, when women felt pressured on all sides to find husbands by the age of twenty-five, the deadline for finding a decent husband, too, has extended to about the age of thirty. But even those who have never married feel admired, at least by some other women, for their strength and independence. Many, too, feel substantial support for raising their children alone from their own mothers, or from older women who regret having putting up with burdensome or abusive husbands for fear of what others thought, or from those who gave up having children altogether because they never met the right man.

While the lack of stigma surrounding single motherhood relative to the late Soviet period is an important change, society does not necessarily embrace single mothers. Mostly, society ignores them. Several women who had divorced more than once emphasized that nowadays being divorced multiple times is no longer a big deal. Faina, a thirty-two-year-old twice-divorced taxi driver, explained, "I think it was morally bad somehow to be a single mother back then. Before, if you said that you had been married twice then people would think you were a bad woman. And now I can simply say that I've been married twice without feeling embarrassed at all."

But because people still agree that two-parent families are best, even single mothers are influenced by the dominant view that however "normal" (in the sense of statistical normalcy) single motherhood is in the New Russia, it is still far from ideal. It is even referred to by some single mothers as "unnatural." Yet, even this unnaturalness is the fault not of mothers themselves but, rather, of gender relations gone awry in the New Russia. Lena, a thirty-four-year-old divorced single mother, described this contradiction between single mothers' normalcy alongside the unnaturalness of the entire situation, explaining, "I don't feel that anyone is judging me because all around me there are women raising children alone. Today it's an absolutely normal situation, but it's unfortunate because it's not right, it's unnatural really. But now there are a lot of mothers on their own, including my girlfriends. People have started to think in a more modern way about it. In Soviet times it was a bad thing, it was shameful. Because of that people put up with drunken, brutish husbands. Now it's no longer shameful to be a single mom. Frankly, I feel like a fine woman just because I am able to raise my daughter alone!" As Lena's reflections reveal, rather than society fully embracing single mothers, most people in society either ignore them or have gradually come to accept single mothers, as they are so numerous. Women's observations generally support scholars' assertions that attitudes toward single motherhood tend to follow rather than lead changes in family behavior.[19]

While single motherhood is "normal" in Russia, this is mainly because the gender crisis itself is normalized in Russia, not because most Russians see large numbers of women raising children alone as exemplary in any way. But rather than blaming single mothers for their situation, Russians argue that the large number of single mothers is an unfortunate symptom of other problems. For example, the idea that a critical mass of Russian men have problems with drinking, commitment, fatherhood, and responsibility is extremely widespread. Many mothers assert, for example, that no one judges single mothers anymore mainly because everyone realizes how unreliable men have become. Lada, a thirty-year-old factory worker with a four-year-old daughter, argues that she had no choice but to become a single mother: "I don't feel there are many advantages to raising a child alone. But I also don't feel shame. Single mothers used to feel rotten. But now we have so many mothers on their own. It's just so widespread. And everyone knows that women simply cannot rely on men."

Women's own parents, especially their mothers, often support their daughter's decisions to become single mothers, especially now that the stigma is gone. Girlfriends, coworkers, and other older women also offer encouragement and support. Sometimes the support comes gradually. Lada explained that her mother was alarmed at first by her determination to bear a child on her own but eventually came around to her way of thinking: "When I turned twenty-five, I said that I would have a baby. . . . At first my mom was shocked because she didn't know how to tell my father, but I said, 'no matter what you say I'm going to have a baby.' I said, 'You had two children when you were twenty-six and I'm almost twenty-six with no child. Who will be at my side as I get older?'" Most Russian women feel entitled to have one child regardless of the obstacles.

As there are still some lingering status differences surrounding having been married, women who never married make more of an attempt to justify their single status. Life circumstances, they argue, forced them to take the drastic step of having children alone, mainly because they feared missing mother-hood altogether. Women are convinced that although being a single mother is less ideal than having a "complete" family, it is far better than growing old without a child. Tamara, a thirty-three-year-old social worker and govern-ment official who was divorced before giving birth as an unmarried woman, explained:

> A woman raising her children alone . . . I mean, to some extent it's not normal, is it? Because a child should be raised with both parents. But I can't say that I'm seriously suffering or that I feel ashamed or in any way to blame in society. Actually, when I went to work pregnant and my colleagues found out that I was pregnant, they supported me. An older woman who had helped me out a lot when I first started, she's around fifty years old, said that in Communist times things hadn't worked out for her with men and she had been afraid to have a baby alone. She had an abortion because then it was considered awful to give birth without a man. Society wouldn't have accepted her. She would have lost her well-paid job because in Communist times the family was the all-important building block of society: a husband, wife, and child. Even if you were divorced with a child you might not be promoted for your service at work. . . . The state needed to propagandize healthy families. . . . So this woman didn't give birth and now she's fifty years old and without children, without a husband, without anything. And she was always telling me, "Tamara, have the baby, definitely give birth and we will all support you." When I gave birth society had become perfectly comfortable with women having babies alone. . . . Nobody cares anymore! Whether you're alone, with a husband, divorced, or whatever. It's your choice, your business.

Although Tamara is thankful that she felt supported by other women, her comments also reveal that society ignores single mothers more than it ac-tively supports them. Indeed, "nobody cares anymore," which might not be an issue for mothers like Tamara, who have the extensive supports of ex-tended family members. But other single mothers find themselves with fewer supports.

Less-supported women tend to argue that in spite of the lack of shame surrounding single motherhood, they nevertheless would feel more protected and less vulnerable if they had a man at their side—at least if he were a good man. But because of the perceived "problem with men" in Russia, these same mothers frequently go on to argue that their everyday lives are much better than those of the married mothers they know who must manage burdensome husbands. Depending on the particular point of comparison, women shift back and forth in their assessments of their lives. While the general account that single mothers give of their lives suggests that life is simpler as a single mother, given the realities of Russian life, it is not always as triumphant an account as Nastya's, the vignette which opened this chapter. When single mothers compare their lives with those of single mothers in Soviet times, they feel that things are morally better for all single mothers now. Compared with the Soviet era, mothers feel that they have more opportunities, mainly because they are aware of a highly influential minority of mothers achieving material successes unheard of during state socialism. When they compare their lives with those of many of their married friends and acquaintances, single mothers often feel lucky to be living without husbands. But when measuring their lives against an abstract notion of an ideal family with a supportive husband, some single mothers still feel as if their lives are second-rate.

Being a single mother in any society where two-parent families are considered optimal means learning to live with these ambiguities and contradictions. Women learn to do so, with varying degrees of success. Even though women appreciate the lack of stigma surrounding their situation, many cast some doubt on the idea that they are that much freer compared with their own mothers. Instead, the environment in which single mothers must live, work, and support their children has changed. The lack of stigma gives some options to the unhappily married and those yearning to have a child at all costs, but at the same time the rise of single motherhood is symptomatic of a new form of patriarchy. Hochschild (1989) has argued that:

> Formerly, many men dominated women within marriage. Now . . . men dominate women anonymously outside of marriage. Patriarchy has not disappeared; it has changed form. In the old form, women were forced to obey an overbearing husband in the privacy of an unjust marriage. In the new form, the working single mother is economically abandoned by her former husband and ignored by a patriarchal society at large. . . . The more men and women live outside marriage, the more they divide into separate classes. Three factors—the belief that childcare is female work, the failure of former husbands to support their children, and higher male wages at work—have taken the economic rug from under the half of married women who divorce.[20]

The discourses and practices of single mothers in Russia reflect the contradictions of private versus public patriarchy. In the late Soviet period, the state provided some protections for all mothers, including single mothers, yet mothers felt more societal pressure to remain in unhappy, unhealthy marriages. Today, women feel freer to leave such marriages or to have children outside of marriage, and there is much less stigma surrounding these kinds of decisions. Yet while they might be supported by other women, they are mostly ignored by a broader patriarchal society and by male-dominated labor markets. Single mothers may feel free, and many more are opting for freedom in lieu of private domination, but equality is elusive as long as so many women are nearly single-handedly raising the next generation with little support from workplaces, men, or the state.

Routes to Single Motherhood

Becoming a single mother is an event in a woman's life. This event is momentous whether she was previously partnered or officially married. Yet in many cases, contrary to some assumptions in scholarship, the most difficult period of a woman's life was endured well before becoming single. So it is not that the transition to single motherhood is not also challenging to endure, but in many cases it is less harrowing than what came before. These gendered aspects of the transition to capitalism in Russia require further attention, from scholars, the media, and policymakers. For instance, scholars have written insightfully about how Russians have generally experienced the period of *perestroika*[21] as a turning point dividing time into a "before" of security and predictability and an "after" of chaos, crisis, and disorder,[22] but the event of becoming a single mother, and whether life as a single mother gives women an increased sense of control over their lives or makes their lives even more insecure, is equally important to understand. In addition to the before and after of perestroika, many women divide their lives into before and after their divorce or breakup.

Driven to Divorce

As in the late Soviet period, most Russian women become single mothers through divorce. Of the ninety women interviewed, nearly 60 percent were divorced at the time of interview. When including women with mixed marital statuses (who became widows or later gave birth outside of marriage after divorce), nearly three-quarters of all women sampled had gone through a divorce at some point during their lives. Though most had divorced just once, 10 percent had divorced two or three times, and 11 percent have had mixed marital statuses over time.[23]

Russians are the quickest to marry, as well as the quickest to divorce, out of all citizens of the countries in Central and Eastern Europe and the former Soviet Union.[24] Yet while Russian women decide to marry for a variety of reasons, women generally resort to divorce only when the situation is quite grave. Perceptions of gravity, of course, are always subjective; but in only a handful of cases did women mention reasons like no longer loving a man, not getting along, or a man's failure to earn enough money or help with housework as the main reasons for considering divorce. When women did mention these reasons as motivations for divorce, they were typically describing early first marriages that were entered into quickly and ended swiftly, before the couple had children.[25]

In Russia, as in the United States, women generally initiate divorce.[26] In my sample, too, women filed to divorce their husbands in three-quarters of the cases. According to women's reports, men initiate divorce proceedings only if they have decided to actually move in with another woman. Much research still assumes that women "choose" to divorce their husbands, whereas unmarried mothers have less choice about going it alone. But in Russia, unmarried women, as well as many married women, frequently consider abortion as an alternative to carrying a pregnancy to term. The Soviet Union had one of the highest rates of abortion in the world because contraceptives were hard to come by, and Russia still has a very high abortion rate. Few treat abortion as a moral issue, though some fear abortion may carry a risk of future infertility. Although women do ultimately choose to file for divorce, understanding the conditions under which women make this choice is critical.

Most women still consider divorce a choice of last resort. Women want to keep their families together but increasingly refuse to put up with drunken, violent, philandering, or otherwise burdensome husbands. Many struggle for years to preserve their families, in hopes of reforming drunken or abusive husbands, before deciding to divorce. Overwhelmingly, in nearly three-quarters of all cases, women describe some combination of a husband's alcoholism or drug abuse (the former much more frequently), chronic infidelity, or violence as the primary reasons for divorce.[27] Of these often overlapping reasons, Russian mothers describe male alcoholism and chronic infidelity most frequently. It is no coincidence that women tend to sigh and launch into these explanations for divorce as if it were all a familiar story, as they also refer in passing to their own fathers and other men who have had drinking problems or who were unfaithful to their wives.

When women dismiss material difficulties faced as single mothers as routine and not the main story of their lives, this has everything to do with what women experienced prior to becoming single mothers. Many mothers describe feeling as if they were already single mothers before divorcing their husbands and making the dissolution of the marriage official. Some observers might wonder whether women's reasons for divorce are really serious enough—did women really try to hold their families together and, if so, for how long? Statistics are important but can also render invisible the distressing realities that many single mothers experienced prior to their divorces. The contours of women's narratives tell a rather dark story about Russian family life, and it is not the only story to be told. But among contemporary single mothers, these troubled narratives are disturbingly common.

Polina, a forty-six-year-old divorced physical education teacher and mother of two, found working and mothering difficult while married, primarily because she was doing everything alone, without any assistance from faraway kin or from her alcoholic, workaholic husband. She explained, "It was hard physically. I was running here and there, and with little kids, well, they act up even though I was already tired and carrying everything. So I'd come running home and would have to cook dinner—no one would ever cook for me or do the dishes for me—and then I'd have to check my son's lessons, put the little one to bed, and then when everyone fell asleep I'd have things to do. I'd have to do the washing and ironing and cook for the next day."

Although Polina emphasized the physical stresses of running the household and caring for everyone, in addition to her own paying job, all without any help, she did not really divorce for these reasons. For years prior to her divorce, her husband's only contribution to the family was his coach's salary. In exchange for some financial assistance, some of which went right back into supporting his vodka addiction, she put up with fluctuating levels of drunken and aggressive behavior for years. She sighed and said,

He drank. That's why we divorced. I can endure almost anything, and I can learn to accommodate myself to another person. But I can't stand all that drinking. . . . It's just that I really loved him so I kept forgiving him all the time. I felt I couldn't live without him. I tried to leave him several times for a short while before I finally divorced him ten years ago. . . . He wasn't the kind of guy who had long bouts of heavy drinking where he couldn't work. No, no, he always worked. But he would simply come home from work drunk every day. He drank a lot, every day after work. . . . Later he started to drink at work but he was a very

good coach so they put up with it. . . . He got aggressive when he drank.
I was afraid of him.

Polina's husband, returning from work inebriated on a daily basis, did little
to help her and instead caused extra work and fear for her and the children.
So even though Polina has faced significant material difficulties since her divorce, she felt that nothing is worse than what she endured while living as a
married mother. Her story is hardly unique.

Moreover, Polina argued that although her financial resources are meager, at least as a single mother she has more control over them: "Life is better, even materially, since I can better plan where my money will go. We eat
differently now and I buy more dairy products, which are cheaper. But there
are other pluses: I'm free again. I don't always have to cook, or report to
anyone, and I no longer have an extra child." For single mothers, being "free
again" often means being liberated from rituals of gender deference, which
married mothers frequently are expected to perform for husbands.

Natasha, like Polina, lived with an alcoholic husband for six years and spoke
of how much she valued marriage and how much she had wanted a family
at almost any cost. During those years living in Ukraine, she felt like a single
mother, as her husband did not contribute much. She explained, "When we
moved there my husband simply started to drink a lot, feeling like he somehow wasn't realizing himself. But he didn't exert any effort in terms of trying
to make things better. Basically I was always finding him jobs and he would
constantly dislike something about them. He never felt fulfilled and turned to
the bottle. Our last six years together he really drank a lot, and he wasn't working at all. . . . During those six years it was just awful, I mean he let himself
become completely degraded. And when I felt that it truly was over, that there
was no use fighting it any more, I took the children and left." Women are
expected to attempt to reform husbands. Indeed, most women do try to
change husbands' behaviors, cutting their losses and divorcing only when they
see no other way.

Housing problems, as in the Soviet period, also circumscribe women's
choices. It is very expensive for many Russians to rent apartments, and few
can buy them without saving for years because the mortgage and banking
systems are not yet developed enough to allow people with average salaries
to buy property with modest down payments.[28] Most single mothers live in
apartments inherited from deceased relatives or parents, or they live in an
apartment they received during the last few years of the late Soviet period
when state enterprises still allocated housing to employees. Others struggle
with finding an affordable place to live. Given the considerable housing prob-

lems most Russian women face—if not so much a shortage of housing as in the Soviet era, then a shortage of the money necessary to buy or rent housing in an underdeveloped market—it is even more surprising that the divorce rate is so high. When kin can provide a place to live or watch over grandchildren while mothers focus their efforts on higher-paying work in the private sector, women are more likely to consider divorce feasible. A lack of kin support and housing options makes it difficult for women to consider divorce, even in the most excruciating of circumstances. Yet so many women, still, find a way to divorce.

Evgenia, a forty-two-year-old mother of two teenage boys who repairs meters for the local electric company, taught me about the housing crisis in a distinctive way. Evgenia lives in a tiny two-room apartment about forty minutes outside of the city center. She is a survivor, having endured a violent, abusive marriage for years. Although divorced for more than three years at the time of interview, she has been unable to sever all ties with her former husband, a man who abused her physically and emotionally, coming home drunk late at night, insulting her, and ordering her about. Evgenia was also one of the most isolated of the single mothers I interviewed, with no relatives to assist her in Kaluga and parents who long ago passed away in Siberia. Her in-laws and the police never wanted to get involved:

> If a husband has serious problems, then of course there are many advantages to raising your children alone. Because in my situation, well, I wasn't just worried about keeping my kids off the street, or away from bad influences, but I had to protect them at home, from their own father. He would come home drunk, creating an uproar. He hurt me physically and humiliated me in front of the children. The kind of horrors they saw as children, well, I don't know how to treat them for it. . . . I couldn't have any visitors, and if he saw me talking to someone on the street, I would have to pay for it later. At night he'd come home, yelling, "Make me some grub!" Even when I had a broken leg, he came home, pulled the covers off of me and shouted, using foul language: "You can crawl, but you will make me something to eat." . . . This man was ready to kill me if there was no meat in the frying pan. I lived through hell. [long pause] How stupid of me! Now I regret losing those years. But I was intimidated and felt so alone.

Evgenia blamed herself for not divorcing earlier, even though she had grown up witnessing similar abuse and had no kin support in Kaluga. Evgenia was relieved that she finally divorced her husband, explaining to me that she realized she could not die (as her own mother did at the age of forty-five) since she still had two children to raise. However, toward the end of our four-and-a-half-hour interview, Evgenia showed me a foldout bed tucked into the back of the hallway. Because her former husband is registered as an official occupant of the apartment (divorce does not change residency rights automatically), the police told her that she has no right to kick him out completely. He has not laid a hand on her since the divorce, but he sleeps in the hallway when he is not staying with his own parents in the country.

Although Evgenia's case is especially tragic, incidents of violence are far too common. I did not ask single mothers about domestic violence directly unless they offered the information themselves or described the drunken behavior of former spouses (because I learned that the latter so often included acts of aggression and violence). Still, nearly one-quarter of single mothers sampled described violent behavior on the part of former husbands.

Apart from the frequent link between male drinking and violence, the level of kin support in women's lives shaped decisions concerning divorce. Unlike Evgenia, who endured abuse for years in part because of minimal social networks, twenty-six-year-old Yelena, with "amazing" parents and an older brother who would do anything for her, made a much quicker decision to divorce. Although theirs was already a high-conflict marriage, she left her husband immediately after he threatened their newborn baby with a knife:

> He started drinking a lot more after Nastya was born. I don't even remember how the fight started exactly, but when he came home I asked if he wanted to eat. He said "no" and fell asleep in the armchair. Ten minutes passed, he woke up and yelled, "why the hell haven't you fed me?" I tried to explain that I had just offered him dinner, but he started swearing at me, and when I put his plate of food on the table, he threw it back at me, saying: "What are you giving me? It's like you're throwing bones to a dog!" . . . I said "what are you doing?!" and because the little one was sleeping on the sofa I said "you'll wake the baby!" He said, "oh, will I wake the baby?!" then he grabbed a knife, walked over to the baby and pointed it at her, saying: "we'll just see what else could happen!" And that was it. . . . I left that night, went to my neighbor's place, and my father came to pick me up. I stayed with my parents and filed for divorce and child support.

Though Yelena never wavered once she decided to divorce her husband, the steadfast support of her mother, father, and brother clearly buttressed her decisiveness. She now lives in her own apartment, inherited from her deceased grandmother, though she visits her parents frequently and relies on them for emergency child care should her daughter get too sick to attend day care.

Unlike Yelena, who left a dangerous situation before it got worse, Aleftina felt completely unsupported in her decision to leave her husband. She literally had nowhere to go and was fearful for her safety. Her mother passed away when she was twelve years old, and although her sister and father shared a house in Kaluga, she and her two daughters were not welcome back home. Her father, who had abused her mother while Aleftina was growing up, insisted that her situation was normal. She explained, "My father said that as long as he was alive I could not come back here to live. 'Live,' he said, 'with your husband.' . . . He didn't want to see the destruction of the family. He basically said, 'be patient, everyone drinks.' . . . I explained that my husband beat me, but he repeated, 'everyone does this.' Finally my sister said, 'Come here, somehow we'll find a way to live together. Anything so you can get away from there.' And I left. . . . Papa had been sick, and he passed away two months after I arrived with my daughters."

The experiences that many married women endure silently, doing what they can to hold their families together in circumstances no one could envy, certainly shape the wave of the hand with which women often dismiss any material difficulties they face later on as single mothers.

Considering that drinking is referred to so casually by ordinary women and men as "the scourge of Russia," high divorce rates resulting from drinking and violence are perhaps not surprising. But almost as frequently as women describe dealing with male drinking, they describe philandering husbands. Though seldom the sole reason, infidelity is a major contributor toward divorce. Of course, infidelity, and related issues of marital conflict are considered private issues, but there is a public, gendered discourse about these issues, in terms of what one can expect culturally from a married man or woman. Certainly, there are gendered effects of infidelity, and patterns of infidelity shape what single motherhood means to women and how women assess their chances of finding a trustworthy man after divorce.

Russian popular discourse assumes that male rather than female infidelity breaks up marriages. In her study of contemporary Russian men, Kay argues that "the question of extra-marital affairs remains, at best, a matter for speculation and, at worst, an area where conclusions are drawn on the basis of gut prejudice."[29] But infidelity can, and should, be examined as a social phenomenon, at least in terms of what women and men consider acceptable standards for marital behavior in various cultural contexts. For example, in her study of Soviet autobiographies, Rotkirch concludes that "extramarital affairs were both relatively common and relatively tolerated in urban

Soviet culture."[30] There are even fewer moral sanctions on people's behavior in post-Soviet society and even more opportunities for men, especially, to travel for short- or longer-term work opportunities. Therefore, infidelity, too, has likely increased, at least according to both women's and men's (see chapter 6) accounts.

However common, a gendered double standard surrounds marital infidelity. Few women admit to cheating on husbands, though many women describe having affairs with married men while single, seldom feeling guilty about the latter as long as the liaison does not lead a man to abandon his family. Women often feel betrayed by unfaithful husbands, but they seldom file for divorce because of isolated incidents of unfaithfulness. In about half of the cases where infidelity was mentioned, women described husbands who began cheating on them and ultimately left them for another woman when the affair became known. But in the other half of the cases, women described husbands who cheated on them but who still preferred to remain married in spite of "having other women." Some men tried to conceal their behavior or even reform, but men with more economic power sometimes also tried to convince their wives that having romantic liaisons, particularly for businessmen, is no longer a big deal under market capitalism. Single mothers generally leave their husbands for good only after they have been living with chronic infidelity for months or years at a time or when they are enduring infidelity made more intolerable by a husband's drinking, detachment from the family, or failure to support the family financially.

Darya, a forty-year-old mother of three who repairs slot machines, demanded that her husband choose between her and his lover. When he made his choice and was ready to leave her and their three children, she begged him to reconsider. Although angry and hurt, Darya would have forgiven her husband had he chosen to end his entanglement with the other woman, explaining: "I really wanted to save the family. I was in a state of shock, without work, in a strange city, with three small children. . . . It was hard to endure it all." Darya wavered between feeling betrayed, which guided her decision to make her husband choose between her and the other woman, and admitting that had he atoned for what he had done she probably would have taken him back: "Maybe I look at life differently now, knowing more men and seeing what they are, for there are very few decent men these days. . . . Most of them cheat on their wives, probably around 90 percent anyway, but some of them can't manage to do it right and they get caught. . . . I mean there are some who cheat, but who still don't forget about their families—some earn money, bring home money, and still help out with things. But my husband couldn't care less. . . . It was hard morally and materially, but at that time I couldn't forgive him for being able to leave me. I had three kids, and he was just trading me in for another, betraying me. I'm raising his children and he's out there, somewhere."

Like so many Russian mothers, Darya felt resigned to the gender inequities in the marriage market, knowing that former husbands have a much easier time finding new wives than women have trying to find new husbands. Infidelity is hurtful, but for most women the pain could be lessened through a husband willing to nonetheless retain some level of commitment by spending time with his children or by contributing to the family's well-being.

The extensiveness of drunken, abusive, and chronically unfaithful behavior on the part of husbands according to single mothers may strike some readers as extreme. Yet similar narratives are found in other contexts of instability and poverty. In this way, there are parallels between Russian single motherhood and U.S. low-income single motherhood. Among U.S. unmarried mothers, rather than the financial troubles so often assumed to break up families, "It is usually the young father's criminal behavior, the spells of incarceration that so often follow, a pattern of intimate violence, his chronic infidelity, and an inability to leave drugs and alcohol alone that cause relationships to falter and die."[31] Although the quality of men's jobs or lack of sufficient jobs has often been highlighted as a cause of rising single motherhood, there is surprisingly limited evidence for this cause. Russian single mothers, too, instead describe husbands who do not work even when some jobs are available or who fail to contribute, especially financially but also practically, to the family's well-being.

In Darya's case, she felt particularly betrayed because she was doing so much to feed and care for her family, without asking much of her husband in return: "I was such a homemaker then! . . . When he got home, everything would be hot since I was always keeping everything warm so he could eat a hot meal as soon as he got home. I really tried hard . . . so I could not handle that he had betrayed me." Although there is no evidence that a "superwoman strategy" on the part of women helps marriages last, the character and organization of what DeVault terms "feeding work" gives women an almost limitless responsibility for a family's well-being. This could not be more true in terms of what is expected of Russian women. Furthermore, DeVault observes: "The fact that 'what to do' is always up for grabs produces an open-ended sense of the possibilities for improving family life through more work."[32] Indeed, Russian women are expected to be experts at doing a job that is never done.

Yet despite their heavy household burdens, Russian single mothers do not generally divorce because of husbands' failure to help out sufficiently at home.

Although many women long for a partner to help out at home, they do not consider it realistic, given the local context, to even allow themselves to expect much domestic support. Still, single mothers routinely describe glaring inequities in household labor, in which husbands do little or nothing around the house or with children, as a major contributing factor to divorce. As one mother put it, citing the revolutionary Soviet poet Vladimir Mayakovsky, "The love boat was wrecked by daily life" (*Lodka liubvi razbilas' o byt*).

Numerous studies have described Russian women's double burden of paid work and household and child care responsibilities.[33] Most conclude that the division of household labor is starkly inequitable, with women doing the bulk of household labor and child care in addition to paid work. According to Russian Longitudinal Monitoring Survey data, the average Russian woman works—in terms of the time it takes to do paid work, housework, and child care—one extra month per year more than her husband.[34] The inequities Russian women face in bearing most of the second shift represent an intensified but understudied case of what we know about women's continuing second shift burdens in the United States and many other Western countries.[35] A recent study on the division of household labor in Russia describes the patriarchal nature of gender relations at home, noting that "Women are often grateful simply to have husbands who can help provide for the family and who do not abuse alcohol, let alone help with domestic chores."[36] At the same time, the more dissatisfied wives are about the division of labor, the greater the association with perceptions of conflict and thoughts of divorce.

Inequalities on the domestic front exacerbate other marital problems, pushing women toward divorce. Resentment about what was an inequitable division of labor resurfaces when women reflect on the possible advantages of single motherhood. Irina, a thirty-one-year-old divorced accountant, confessed: "This is probably feminism, but I like that I don't have to do the laundry, iron, indulge someone, and defer to someone's moods. I also like that no one is attached to me, yelling at me because somewhere, something ruined his mood." As Hochschild (1989) observed in her landmark study of the unequal division of labor at home among working parents, couples seldom struggle simply over who does what; instead, they struggle over the giving and receiving of gratitude. Irina had been unhappy not only with the inequitable division of labor but with the emotion work that she, as a wife, was expected to perform, including deferring to a husband's bad moods. This kind of household work, emotion work, and gender deference is frequently described as a key aspect of married women's lives in Russian households. Single mothers seldom miss this work.

Certainly, there are many reasons driving women to divorce, yet patterns are evident. As with recent research in other parts of the world where single motherhood is common, Russian women seldom leave men because of a lack of income. Instead, "old" problems of male drinking, domestic violence, and chronic infidelity, problems that have long caused divorce and have only worsened in today's Russia, continue to push most women toward divorce. Besides these three major reasons, women describe men who fail to contribute to the family by sharing their earnings, who refuse to work at regular jobs, or who cannot hold down jobs for any length of time. Lack of money certainly contributes to relationship stress, and material difficulties still plague many families, including those headed by single mothers. But lack of money is not responsible for the growth in broken families in Russia. Nor does a lack of money deter many women from becoming single mothers.

✎ Motherhood a Must, Marriage a Maybe

While divorce is the main route to single motherhood in Russia, there has been a huge increase in nonmarital births since the breakup of the Soviet Union. Even though the Russian state is concerned about the declining birth rate and has begun providing incentives for women to bear second or third children, most Russian women will have at least one child (and typically most still stop at just one) regardless of their life circumstances. Marriage is valued, but it is increasingly one option among several, even if it is still the idealized option for women without children. But motherhood, in contrast to marriage, is considered compulsory for women, offering women a promise of security and fulfillment that is increasingly illusory in marriage. Not only is motherhood compulsory, but many women report that the joys of children help to render material difficulties trivial, or at least they help to make those difficulties much more insignificant than they might otherwise seem. Motherhood is not only compulsory but is also compensatory for many Russian women.

Although just twenty-three women in my sample had never married, nearly one-third of mothers had experienced a nonmarital birth at some point during their lives (some had divorced previously, whereas others married and divorced sometime after a nonmarital birth). Thus, my sample closely parallels the Russian population as a whole, where about one-third of all births are nonmarital.[37] In about half of these cases, women were living with or seeing a man regularly before becoming pregnant and had planned on marriage eventually. After becoming pregnant, these women were left by partners who did not want children at that time, would not leave their wives, were involved with other women, or were insufficiently committed to them. Mothers describe men who left town after experiencing financial problems or men who treated them differently after learning of the pregnancy. Women prefer to have both a child and a husband but are unwilling to risk never having at least one child only because they lack a reliable man. Tamara, for instance, was disappointed that her timing had not coincided with her boyfriend's preferences. But she was twenty-nine years old and felt ready to have a child: "When I found out I was pregnant, at first I was in shock since it was unplanned. But I thought about it and resolved to give birth to the baby whether or not the father accepted the child. After becoming pregnant, nothing else mattered to me except the baby! I no longer cared about anything else. . . . I mean of course I would have really liked for things with the father to have worked out, to have everything be normal. To have a husband. But I was already twenty-nine years old so I never considered having an abortion."

Russian women still value marriage highly, but relative to the late Soviet period, marriage is seen increasingly as optional. Conversely, the experience of motherhood is considered fundamental to being a fulfilled woman. Men may come and go, but a mother will always have her child, insist single mothers of all kinds. Many women ultimately view motherhood as more important, dependable, and long-lasting than marriage. Compulsory motherhood, the belief that all women are biologically programmed to aspire toward having children, remains a critical part of how women feel valued in society.[38]

In Russia, the belief in compulsory motherhood is extremely strong. Perhaps it is because Russia has never had a grassroots feminist movement or because the Soviet state promoted motherhood for years as an important part of women's duties. But from factory workers to university professors, Russian single mothers argue that real women should have at least one child—or risk feeling unfulfilled. Only one woman of the ninety interviewed admitted that had she known of how difficult it would be to provide for her child, she might have acted otherwise. Vera, a thirty-eight-year-old gynecologist and unmarried mother, explained that women who say they do not want to have a child are held back by fear: "Somehow I just can't imagine life without a child. When women come to me for appointments, I never believe those who say they don't want to give birth. Every woman should become a mother, you know? Motherhood is simply a great feeling. . . . I never believe women who claim they don't want to have a baby. So maybe her personal life didn't work out, but that doesn't mean anything. Do you know why many women aren't giving birth? They're simply afraid of the difficulties. And there are many." Material difficulties are not considered insurmountable obstacles to having just one child. Instead, women take pride in their courage to face hardships. Children allow mothers to transcend the limitations of other disadvantages they may face. Of course, the social pressures on women to have at least one child are tremendous, with a child essentially considered the prerequisite for full-fledged womanhood. For most women, and especially for those single and financially strapped, bearing and raising a child in spite of limited supports from men or the state is a real achievement.

Besides a culture of compulsory motherhood, unmarried mothers describe motherhood as compensatory. About half of the unmarried mothers had expected to marry the fathers of their children, only to be disappointed by circumstances beyond their control. The other half pursued their dream of having a child even though they never really expected to marry their child's biological fathers. These women often had kin support or some means to support their children. Most still hoped for some support from biological fathers. But a minority spoke of fathers as little more than sperm donors and described a preference for raising their child alone. In Lara's case, she had been unlucky in love. She had once been engaged to be married, but she broke off the engagement after her fiancé started beating her while they were still living together. She saw no reason to further postpone having a child since she had met a viable candidate for a partner: "We'd been seeing each other for a while, and I saw in him a quality that gave him an advantage over other men. He is a smart person. . . . He's finishing up his degree now. I simply felt that I could have a child by this man. He doesn't smoke, doesn't drink. The child would be healthy. So I told him that I wanted to have a child and he didn't try to change my mind when I said I would do it. . . . I had decided that when I turned twenty-five I would have a baby no matter what." Although the father of Lara's four-year-old daughter is a purely biological one—he sees other women besides Lara and scarcely acknowledges his daughter's existence—Lara, believing that many fathers are unhealthy alcoholics, is actually thankful that her child has a healthy, intelligent biological father. Similarly, Alexandra spoke about choosing a man with whom to procreate, joking that in her case the man was basically a studhorse: "I was looking for healthy genes. So I looked at his physical and psychological qualities. He was Siberian, a former paratrooper. Very intelligent, educated, and goal-oriented. He had a lot of positive qualities." Adding that Siberians are considered healthier than other Russians, Alexandra said that she did the best she could for her child, short of giving him a real father.

Single mothers repeatedly claim that "like any normal woman, I wanted a family: a child and a husband," but for most having a child partly compensates for the lack of marriage and a husband. Becoming a single mother in Russia today is seldom, if ever, a woman's first choice. Yet at the same time, most women are happy to have not only part of the package but the most important, enduring part of that package: a child. More than a consolation prize, women consider a child the most essential part of being a woman and having a family. Women emphasize that in principle they know that two-parent families are best; but in reality the absence of marriage is no longer considered an obstacle to motherhood.

To be sure, women who never marry sometimes feel disappointed that their personal lives have not worked out as planned. But most of the lingering unhappiness, women believe, can be dispelled through having a child. Nina, a forty-seven-year-old professor and science fiction writer, described how having a child makes up for the lack of a two-parent family: "I've had all kinds of plans in terms of family life. I don't want to reminisce about them now. A lot of things didn't work out. But I still wanted a baby—that's all. A happy family life no longer seemed realistic at a certain point. But when Sasha was born, my other plans completely vanished. Finally I had a family, my daughter. I stopped feeling bad about not having a normal family. When she was born . . . well, she is the most important gift God gave me." Few Russian single mothers spontaneously speak of God apart from this life event—having a long-awaited child. Even mothers like Ludmila, who say they never cared as much about marriage and children as did many of their peers, positively glowed when describing how a child renders trivial life's other mundane worries: "My life became wonderful. Having a baby is the most joyous event that can happen in one's life. Other things don't really matter, whether there's someone else at your side, whether there's a father or not. She is so sweet and affectionate sometimes. And she's so active and full of life. When she says, 'mama dear' and hugs and kisses me at night, well everything else . . . is simply nonsense." Women decide to have a child on their own only after concluding that marriage, or at least marriage to the kind of man they could tolerate, is not possible.

Russian women often attribute a woman's desire for a child to a biological drive, diminishing the extent to which motherhood, like fatherhood, is always socially constructed and a choice. But women's reflections reveal the social pressures women also face to have at least one child. Unmarried single mothers readily admit that motherhood ultimately improved their social relations and self-confidence. It is generally unacceptable in Russia to dwell

FIGURE 4. A single mother and her new baby, her second child.
Photograph by the author.

on the burdens of motherhood; instead, most agree that it is a positive, transformative event, especially for women who give birth later in life. Yana, a
forty-year-old factory laboratory assistant who became pregnant by a married man at age twenty-eight after two failed marriages, described feeling
ready for a baby. But she also described wanting to fit in with her girlfriends
at work: "Maybe it was because of my age, I felt it was time. I wanted to
have a baby. Maybe the fact that all of my friends had children also influenced me. Whenever we got together they would end up talking about

children. I guess I felt a bit left out. . . . I wanted to have a child even though I imagined the difficulties, and I expected that I would be raising my child alone. I didn't count on having someone at my side."

Yana, like many women, described no longer feeling alone after having a baby. Even as an unmarried mother, Lara, too, discovered an enhanced ability to bond with her coworkers after joining the ranks of motherhood: "Even at work we can't forget about our children. Our conversations generally revolve around them. . . . They are the main joy in our lives."

Women are expected to experience joy and an elevated social status through having children. Some women do. In any case, emphasizing the difficulties of motherhood is not really acceptable. These social pressures are critical for understanding what motivates women to bear children in materially challenging circumstances, under conditions where they have little hope in getting much help from men or the state. Lucia never had much family support in raising her twelve-year-old son, but she described vividly how the transformative aspects of motherhood lessened the impact of material difficulties: "Materially life got harder. But you know, life also became completely different. You watch your child playing, and already you're in a different mood. Sometimes when I have a bad day, after some kind of unpleasantness at work I might have a headache, but he is like a little bell ringing with joy, and right away everything is fine. All problems disappear." Nina, the most well educated of the mothers interviewed, also argued that motherhood is both compulsory and compensatory. It is compulsory because a woman who does not become a mother is still pitied somewhat, even though Nina admitted that this is unfair. Motherhood is compensatory because it transforms one's perspective and improves one's self-image and social relationships:

> My life became more stable, more optimistic, only after giving birth. I felt like life had given me such a great gift, that I didn't have to get as upset if something else didn't work out for me. . . . Oh, my material situation didn't change that much. Of course I had to economize a bit more, but I think that even without Sasha there would have been other reasons to economize. . . . Of course, I felt like my relationships with others also improved. I felt more confident. I mean a person who doesn't have children, at my age; it seems to me that such a person is a bit disadvantaged. A woman. Be that as it may. Maybe I'm wrong. But she is damaged not because she is worse than others but because her life is worse. Inside herself. A child provides some balance to one's life. And people saw me differently, and were kinder to me.

Russian single mothers face many pressures in providing for their families. But alongside the inequality that gives women so many more responsibilities than it gives men in Russian society—responsibility for the family's survival, for caring for children and relatives, for working and "making something of themselves" in labor markets, and so on—mothers, unlike so many men, benefit from having multiple sources of identity and of meaning in their lives.

✒ Widowhood

Typically the situation of widows is set apart from that of divorced and unmarried mothers. Fewer widows live in poverty, many have some kind of an inheritance, and widows in no way choose their single status as the loss of a spouse is foisted on them. However, I found few differences between widowed mothers and other unmarried or divorced mothers. Although just seven women, less than 10 percent of my sample, were widows, most spoke in a similar manner of troubled marriages, burdensome husbands, and the challenges and unanticipated benefits of going it alone. Four of the seven widows had never divorced, while the other women had divorced prior to remarrying and becoming widows.

The descriptions women gave about how their husbands had passed away reveal much about the problems plaguing men in the post-Soviet era. Of the seven deceased husbands, one died in an alcohol-related car accident, two drank themselves to death, two died of heart problems, one died of a drug overdose, and one was a heavy drinker later murdered by the local mafia. I had expected widows to be somewhat reluctant to discuss marital problems they had experienced with late husbands, but this was not the case. Women were relatively dispassionate as they discussed their husbands' deaths, and most marriages had been troubled. Women seem to save their emotion instead for describing the passing of their own mothers, who had typically helped them a great deal during the early years of childrearing. Valya, for example, spoke at great length about her mother's death in 1999: "Ilyousha was in fifth grade when my mother died. . . . If my mom hadn't been around I would have had to go on an academic leave. But instead I gave birth and started my sessions two months later, spending a full month in Moscow. My mom helped me a lot with everything." In contrast, Valya had little to say about her late husband, stating bluntly: "Well, it's not like everything was simple or smooth. And I can't say I really loved him. Those feelings were never there. But I always wanted a child."

⚓ The Immateriality of Material Difficulties

Understanding what single mothers experienced prior to becoming single is important for coming to terms with how and why mothers dismiss many material challenges. Many Russian mothers are simply so accustomed to material difficulties that they are no longer surprised by them. Besides the hard times many women experienced while still married or partnered, most women grew up watching their own mothers routinely struggle to make ends meet in the Soviet-era shortage economy. Faina, for example, a thirty-two-year-old twice-divorced taxi driver and mother of two, was struggling to pay off a huge loan as a result of her involvement in a pyramid-type marketing scheme. Still, she considers her life as a single mother relatively simple compared with her efforts to support her family in the early 1990s, when she worked as a salesperson at an open-air market: "We women stood in the streets for ten to eleven hours. In winter I was standing there selling things in 33 degrees of frost. I only had cotton pants, short boots, a sweater, and gloves, but I managed to feed my family. My husband was an officer, but he didn't earn enough money to feed us." Although Faina had expected her husband to work side jobs to support the family, he did not. So she picked up the slack, remaining married until she discovered he was cheating on her with other women. She continued to face material difficulties, but they were not her central concern: "Probably the most difficult thing for me is not having enough moral support. But materially . . . well, I know that I can always earn money. It's probably just how I was brought up. And no one is going to feed my family for me. No matter what I will always scrape by."

Mothers like Faina who had struggled with providing for small children in the early to mid-1990s generally find life much easier now. Virtually every woman interviewed considered life in the Putin era (2000–present) a marked improvement in terms of stability. Ksenia, a factory worker and thirty-nine-year-old mother of a thirteen-year-old son, described coping with salary delays by selling produce at an open-air market for nearly nine years. She, too, was living with the father of her child at the time, but he drank and did not help much materially. She shuddered as she described her work at the market, remembering the extreme cold, the dirty environment, and the embarrassment she felt when going to parent–teacher meetings after work, her face ruddy from the cold, her hair windblown and fingers numb. She came home exhausted, finding it hard to summon the energy to spend time with her son. Given these experiences, she has little sympathy for Russians who see certain kinds of jobs as beneath them. Similarly, Kira, a special education teacher and divorced mother of two, also emphasized that her daily life, at least materially, had not changed as much as others assume: "My personal life, of course, is freer now. But there was no drastic change. Even materially, things were also difficult before because he didn't really earn much and what he earned he spent on himself, even though he also ate and we had to buy stuff for him. I worked a lot before and I work a lot now."

Not only are material difficulties no longer novel for most women, but for many they have simply become part of the routinized crisis that characterizes Russia. Women, in particular, also take pride in their ability to manage material difficulties successfully.[39] This pride is related to the Soviet legacy of encouraging "superwomen" to juggle work and home effectively (see chapter 3). Scholars of Russia have also argued that "This ability to make do with whatever life deals one is the essence of *po-russki*, or the Russian style."[40] In contrast to many accounts portraying Russia as perpetually in a state of crisis or chaos, Caldwell (2004) argued that Russia's stability is based on ordinary citizens' ability to cope with change. However, while Russian men may be highly adept at "making do" in other areas, the skill and resourcefulness that it takes to feed a family, in particular, are gendered. In Russia, the responsibility for ensuring a household's survival is led by women.[41] Women, regardless of marital status, are experts at ensuring that their children are well fed and dressed, that their home is neat and well provisioned, that they have enough money to provide necessities for their families, and that many other household management tasks and chores are completed.

Even women who faced rather severe material hardships report matter-of-factly about their ability to live on small salaries. Aleftina emphasized that she had become accustomed to dealing with material challenges on a daily basis, buying macaroni instead of potatoes, for example, because the latter are more expensive: "Everyone wonders, 'How do you live on your money?' Oh dear, I am just so used to economizing, I economize on everything, and of course, I try not to borrow money. It's very rare for me to ask for a loan. It's really very rare. . . . I try to buy products cheaply, and we do not buy meat. My kids are never hungry. . . . I've also never been hungry. But the quality of the food isn't always the best and I'm used to eating a lot of bread. I can eat nothing at all and be satisfied on bread alone. It's cheap, and still filling."

Though Aleftina struggles with material difficulties more than most single mothers interviewed (especially because she has little family support), for many other women, like Natasha, a thirty-eight-year-old art teacher and mother of two, the worst of their material difficulties are behind them. Natasha earns very little as a teacher, but she also edits photographs at a private retail shop, advises private café and restaurant owners on lighting, design, and décor for their new businesses, and occasionally sells her paintings to foreign clients. She takes pride in being able to provide well for her family. But she also described a particularly difficult time in her life, while living with her alcoholic husband in Ukraine:

> One time I was in a terribly difficult material situation. It was a year or two before my divorce. My husband wasn't working, and I earned very, very little. And one morning my kids woke up before me, quietly tiptoeing around and Loshka came to me and asked, "Mom, what are we going to eat for breakfast?" I got up and went to see what we had and there was nothing. Absolutely nothing. No reserves, no cereals, nothing. Not to mention bread. And I already owed a decent amount of money. And I felt then so helpless, it was terrible. I understood then that if I borrowed more money then my salary would go to pay back what I already owed, and then a knot would begin forming, a knot from which it would be impossible to escape. I thought: "what should I do?" And then I really cried. It was such a difficult moment. I can't let myself cry for a long time, it quickly passes. . . . I get tired of it! So I sat and thought: "What can I do, all the same I have to feed my kids, I have to borrow money again." . . . When I got a hold of myself, I thought, that's all, I'll go and borrow money, to hell with whatever may happen for I've got to feed my kids. At that moment my girlfriend came by and said, "Natasha, maybe you would consider selling me that painting of yours?" I hadn't planned on selling it. That painting was special to me. But I said right away, "Sure, I'll sell it to you." . . . There were times when I sold a bouquet of flowers given to me by students, just to buy bread. There have been all kinds of difficult things in my life. But now we don't have any of this, and my kids are relaxed. Everything is normal now.

Though more detailed than most, Natasha's story is nonetheless typical of accounts describing extreme material difficulties. Women talk about their hardships as experiences they learn from which make them even stronger. From this story and others, it is clear that although many women argue that men should concern themselves primarily with materially supporting their families, in practice women are ultimately responsible for family provision.

Part of being a good woman and a good mother is managing to overcome material obstacles and doing whatever it takes for your family, even if it means occasionally sacrificing one's own desires. Single mothers' dominant presentations of themselves as successfully self-reliant is a new development (see chapter 3). At least among a younger generation of women between the ages of roughly twenty-five and forty-five, it has become somewhat embarrassing to not be getting by economically or to speak excessively about one's problems; a new ideology that each individual is in charge of her own destiny has taken hold.

However much women face material hardships, their skills in adroitly dealing with them, rather than the hardships themselves, shine through. I probed extensively regarding specific hardship situations. When asked if they had run out of money for food, most said yes, explaining that they simply borrowed money from family and friends. Some single mothers have left behind the sphere of stable personal networks that routinely provided material sustenance during the late Soviet era, but most have not. Those women who no longer borrow money from friends or neighbors still rely extensively on family connections for employment or child care assistance.

Besides borrowing money, women rely on folk remedies for illnesses instead of buying expensive medicines. They borrow children's clothing and winter coats from friends with older children who have outgrown them. They help out at their parents' summer cottages on weekends and receive fresh vegetables and berries in exchange. Women also work extra jobs to supplement low salaries from their main jobs (especially if they work in the state sector), including tutoring students privately, selling handicrafts, and even sweeping floors for a few hours a week at their workplaces or nearby offices. Women work hard to make sure that their children are not deprived of the dance lessons, new backpacks, and colorful books that they feel many two-parent families can afford for their children.

In spite of material challenges, many women are not hesitant to emphasize all that they have gained postdivorce. Aleftina endured seven long years with her abusive husband in the country, bereft of relatives and extended family support, before planning her escape route. She thinks about every ruble she spends, and although warm and open, she faces serious material strain. Still, she feels lucky to be single: "I am my own mistress. And I also have such a character, well, I don't like when someone stands over me, orders me about. I like to be in charge of myself. I want to be free, a free woman. . . . I come home from work and I lay down. I want to rest awhile and I don't want anyone telling me what to do, ordering me around. Do you know how it is here, what kind of men we have? They love when . . . everything is done for them, they want to be waited on. . . . Maybe there are some who also help, I don't know, everyone is different, but I never met any of these men." In Aleftina's situation, the peace of mind she gained upon leaving her husband overshadowed any difficulties: "For me it was happiness to divorce—I'm free, I'm single, and . . . well, yeah, there are those material difficulties."

Some mothers emphasize the extra support they receive after becoming single mothers. Often this support comes from women's own mothers, their children's *babushki*, but other women joke about how people offer more assistance once they know about their single status. Kira emphasized that not much had changed since her husband unexpectedly left her: "Materially life hasn't gotten any worse, and in some ways it's even better because, well, my aunt started helping me out right away. I mean I'm a single mother with two kids, so help started coming my way. If someone knows my faucet has a leak, and they also know that I don't have a husband at home, well, it gets fixed. . . . Sure, I have a lot of support because everything thinks that I'm poor and unfortunate! Ha! Now I also laugh when I'm hanging out with my friends, for I say: 'but I'm the poor, unfortunate mother of two children, raising them all alone!' " Single mothers like Kira argue that, apart from the minority of good marriages, the poor and unfortunate women are the ones still putting up with burdensome, alcoholic, or philandering husbands for fear of being alone.

However difficult their situations may be materially at times, women focus on several positive aspects of their lives. Mothers describe developing increased self-confidence, achieving greater success at work, spending more time with their children, meeting new friends, and feeling like new, stronger women after getting through an initially arduous transition period. Kira, too, spoke of life becoming simpler after her husband left her. She can now relax more after work, particularly with her mother's help, and she no longer feels guilty about having two higher degrees or apologetic about the kind of work she does: "He never believed that I worked while at work. He thought I only rested there. . . . I would sit there and write my lesson plans until midnight, but he didn't consider it work."

More than any other benefit, women emphasize that their everyday household burdens (*byt*) were lightened considerably after becoming single. This is no small gain. Although convenience food products and Western-style grocery stores are more readily available in provincial Russian cities than in the past, many families cannot afford ready-made food items, and home-cooked meals are often considered superior. Except for a few higher-priced stores, many grocery stores in Kaluga require customers to follow a Soviet-style shopping protocol. Shopping, I learned firsthand, was time-consuming even for an individual and was that much more so for a family: First one selects items in a particular department (meat, dairy, sweets, etc.), noting the price; then one waits in line for the specific cashier taking orders for that department, telling her the cost of each of the items. Next one pays for the items and collects the receipt, bringing the receipt back to the department counter, sometimes waiting alongside other customers with receipts. Once acknowledged by the clerk, who checks off the items against the receipt, the customer can finally pick up the items and bag them. Furthermore, many households still do not have automatic washers and dryers, and most women depend on public transportation to do their shopping.

DeVault (1991) described some of the domestic paradoxes present in single-mother households, arguing that women bear more responsibility but experience the work as much less constraining: "women have nearly total responsibility by virtue of their status as sole caretakers, but, ironically, they also experience the gendered character of feeding work as somewhat less constraining than many married women. Although single mothers do all of the work of feeding, they experience less pressure to elaborate the work for male partners."[42] Single mothers generally find their household burdens reduced even when they lack the support of female kin nearby. While lower-income mothers emphasize the increased control they have over their money upon becoming single, women with somewhat higher incomes or significant kin support were more apt to mention what amounted to reduced gender deference. Because most women favor two-parent families in principle, some described their streamlined domestic lives in hushed, conspiratorial tones. Valya, a thirty-six-year-old economist and widowed mother, smiled sheepishly, as if her increased freedoms were a shameful secret:

> Oh, I'm afraid you'll judge me for saying this: but there are advantages. I don't have to submit to anyone, to adjust myself to anyone else. . . . I can allow myself to be the master of my own time. Regardless of the fact that I have duties, and things to do that no one else will do for me, that only I can do, still, when it's just me and my son, well, we might do something and then take some time to relax. We can let ourselves do the rest later, when we feel more like doing it. . . . I feel more free. I can choose who I want to see, and who I don't feel like seeing. If I don't want to see a certain person I can say, "no dear, no need to come by today," explaining that I'm not in the mood or that I'm busy.

Besides feeling that their household labors have been eased and their lives freed of burdensome husbands, mothers argue that the satisfactions they obtain from having children lessen the importance of any material difficulties they might face. In a context where political instability and economic unpredictability have until quite recently been accepted as part of Russian reality, children help to provide a sense of purpose, stability, and meaning. Faina, who has achieved a great deal in life since leaving her husband, nonetheless argued that children enriched her life in a way that her other achievements had not, making her life "like a holiday":

> Your children will always be loyal to you, no matter what they are faithful. . . . What else can I say? People come and people go, and we change where we live, we change our friends, but your children are a gift, something you will always have. . . . Because, well, looking after them is terribly interesting, it's such a process, it's stunning really, and I get such satisfaction from it. . . . My kids have made my life easier. After all, one's material situation is not the essence of life.

In some ways, managing material difficulties effectively in order to provide for one's family is simply a big part of what it takes to survive in the New Russia. But women, especially single mothers, are experts in this work. Pointing out the gendered aspects of household survival in Russia is not merely a matter of giving credit where credit is due. Without attention to how and why this work of ensuring a household's survival is gendered, with women being held accountable for it when push comes to shove, we cannot understand how Russians have really managed during trying times and why their families and their children are doing as well as they are in spite of various financial and political crises.

By taking the waved hand—this diminishing of material difficulties so common among single mothers—seriously, I do not want to minimize the significance of the challenges and real hardships that women face. However, given the continued growth of single motherhood in other industrialized countries, material challenges do not seem to stop the rise of single motherhood. We must delve deeper. Single motherhood simply does not make much sense from a strictly economic point of view. Indeed, single motherhood is somewhat more common in those countries where it makes the least economic sense, where state supports are meager and costs are high.[43] A narrow focus on material difficulties cannot help but miss several critical aspects of what it means to be a single mother. In spite of significant material challenges, single motherhood continues to appeal, at least as a last resort, to a steadily growing number of women. More women are willing to accept hardship as the price for freedom. Yet as free as single mothers may report feeling as women raising their children on their own, I argue in the next chapter that women are constrained in new ways in the post-Soviet era. Adhering to the dominant cultural code of single motherhood requires that women stifle complaint and focus on transforming their very selves.

✦ CHAPTER 3

"Where the Women Are Strong"
Navigating Practical Realism

> A Russian woman will stop a galloping horse and enter a burning hut!
>
> —Excerpt from a nineteenth-century poem by Nikolay Alexeyevich Nekrasov

"All mothers should learn to be more like Natasha. Always smiling, never complaining, and just look at her two boys! Where does she find all that energy?!" exclaimed Emma of her single-mother neighbor, Natasha. Indeed, Natasha's energy is infectious, and people feel fortunate basking in her glow. I got to know Natasha, a thirty-eight-year-old art teacher, freelance design consultant, and divorced mother of two teenagers, through talking and drinking tea with friends of hers in various homes. We chatted as we walked around the city, with Natasha typically in constant motion, moving from one job to another. She seemed to be, as Emma implied, the proverbial single-mother superwoman.

Although she has experienced her share of difficulties, she works hard to create a "normal life" for her family. Natasha had gone through an awful period when her alcoholic husband had fallen into a state of "utter degradation," and even though it took her six long years to leave him, Natasha reflected: "It passed. In general, I've learned to treat difficulties as temporary. As my grandmother used to say, 'There is no grief, there is only temporary unpleasantness.' That's because true grief is the loss of a loved one who cannot be returned. Everything else is just petty troubles that eventually pass."

Her ebullience notwithstanding, Natasha has her moments of doubt while keeping petty troubles at bay. She worries about her mother out in the countryside caring for her ailing, alcoholic father in spartan conditions; she wonders whether her lover will ever leave his wife (confiding that it is unlikely to come to pass); and she hopes her sons will qualify for a scholarship since she cannot pay for university tuition otherwise. Like most single mothers, she says she does not really count on anyone, declaring: "It's extremely rare for me to find things difficult. I rely on myself alone and I simply accept circumstances as they are." But in practice Natasha works relentlessly to improve her family's material situation. She earns little as an art teacher, but she feels that only the lazy settle for a low salary when they could instead do something to improve their circumstances. Natasha also tutors students, produces artwork on occasion to sell to foreigners, and built her reputation as a local interior design consultant from the ground up. She claims to no longer need much sleep.

Natasha is strong but not "naturally" so. She works to manage her feelings and project a positive presentation of self. The stereotypical view of Russia as a country "where the women are strong" naturalizes women's strength, which is considered as vast as the Russian steppe. This notion oversimplifies and renders invisible the cultural work that women routinely engage in to become strong. Such strength is even more important now than during the Soviet era, which had its share of superwomen. During the transition to capitalism, more is expected of single mothers, and the costs of failure are higher. Yet unlike Western working mothers, Russian single mothers do not merely laugh at the mythical "woman with the flying hair," the superwoman who seamlessly combines paid work and domestic work while making it all look easy.[1] Instead, most single mothers feel they have no choice but to look her squarely in the eye and strive to become more like her.

Single mothers are expected to step up, without complaint, to compensate for systemic weaknesses. In so doing, they draw on the broader cultural discourse of strong women and weak men to make sense of their feelings and actions. But they frequently go on to describe how they have had to harden their emotions, hold back tears, and stamp out traces of self-pity so as to become the kind of women who have what it takes to make it in the New Russia. They aspire to treat problems as "temporary unpleasantness" and difficulties as "petty troubles." In so doing, they demonstrate their cultural competence and skill in managing with dignity a double transition—both to post-Soviet conditions and to life as a single mother.

Such cultural work to transform the self—managing one's emotions, trying to feel the right feelings, thinking differently, and focusing on attainable goals—paves the way toward success, or at least a successful presentation of self, for single mothers.[2] Single mothers work to create the socially necessary selves needed to get by in what most see as a man's world of market capitalism. Because of a lack of options, most women make a virtue out of necessity and embrace a fatalism that demonstrates their own cultural competence despite abandonment by the state and by most men. This self-reliance is shaping a new discourse of feminine heroism. Given failed relationships with men, single mothers face additional pressure to somehow compensate, to not only survive but to show they can thrive for the sake of their families. As one mother put it, "Well, my personal life didn't exactly work out. But that doesn't mean other aspects of life can't work out in my favor. I can still create a good life for myself, and for my child."

This chapter shows how and why single mothers are constrained to become strong and to present themselves according to a dominant cultural code that I call *practical realism*. As they work on themselves, single mothers generally accept a neoliberal ideology of market capitalism, which promotes self-reliance to improve one's circumstances. Women like Natasha learn to steel themselves in order to better manage life's challenges. Getting a hold of oneself over time, learning from one's own mother and other women to treat difficulties as temporary, women adapt until it is almost second nature. Women also discipline other women to conform to practical realism. Concerning others struggling, Natasha advises: "One should never give in to feelings of despair. You just need to get a hold of yourself, control yourself, because nothing is final."

✐ A Neoliberal Ideology of Self-Reliance

A neoliberal ideology of self-reliance is widespread among single mothers.[3] This worldview promotes the idea that independent individuals should exploit opportunities in the market, without depending on the state or anyone else. Neoliberalism, an ideology as well as a form of modern governance and power, encourages decentralized responsibility and the personal cultivation of autonomy and discipline. Neoliberalism has become the dominant discourse in Russia. "Personal responsibility for one's actions serves as the main 'moral disposition' of neoliberalism, along with 'ethical practices of work on the self.'"[4] Of course, other discourses, from Soviet to Orthodox Christian, are also available. The contemporary dominance of neoliberalism has not entirely replaced existing practices but rather has been grafted onto them, making them more efficient.[5]

Single mothers do sometimes remark that the state and men should do more to help raise the next generation of children. Yet they rarely dwell on this for long. Instead, most women are fatalistic about their chances of getting significant outside help, speaking mainly in terms of "taking what they can get." Women feel as if they have to do everything on their own, so they transform this challenge into a badge of honor. Mothers of all kinds proclaim, "I fully realize that no one but me needs my child" (though many worry that the state will need their sons for military service after they turn eighteen). Presenting oneself as reliant on others or dependent on institutions is almost unthinkable. The rapid spread of neoliberalism is shaping new forms of personhood in Russia, involving both discourses of self-reliance and efforts to improve one's life chances. Given the vacuum left by the shrinking state and unreliable men, to most women the idea of making it on their own is somewhat appealing, especially considering their lack of alternatives.

Although trying to make it on their own is the dominant strategy among today's single mothers, other strategies are possible. But strategies of trying to land a rich husband or resurrect some of the state guarantees on which their own mothers relied are far less common. Of course, material and sentimental logics frequently overlap in practice, so that trying to marry a rich man may be connected to other strategies to improve one's chances in the market.[6] Yet although the case of Russian women marrying Western men is an important angle from which to analyze Russia's gender crisis and the dearth of "real men" many women perceive, it is worth remembering that most women remain in Russia. Even in this era of globalization, most people do not migrate, and migrants always differ from those who stay in place. So while a few single mothers reported attending a social with Western men in Moscow or considered corresponding with European men on the advice of others, contrary to the assumptions so frequently and often recklessly made about Russian women, few single mothers are really counting on these kinds of strategies on a daily basis, even if they do not rule them out entirely.[7] Instead, most women seek to acquire dignity by trying to make it on their own.

New ideologies may be even more appealing to people, and more visible as culture, during times when people feel adrift and their lives are unsettled.[8] As Zoya put it, "I'm a single mother-lone wolf. It's kind of romantic even, just me and my child against the world. Here in Russia women are strong. . . . I don't need anyone else. I can handle anything that comes my way." Getting to feel heroic counts for something. Women declare that the state owes them nothing and they owe nothing to the state, a discourse that aligns with neoliberalism. In her ethnography of normalized crisis, Olga Shevchenko points out that the discourse of autonomy in Russia produced "an illusion that individuals, indeed, *could* manage their business entirely on their own, and thus created fertile ground for precisely the kind of neoliberal politics that they detested."[9] The effects of neoliberalism, however, are experienced in distinctly gendered ways.

↶ Practical Realism: A Gendered Cultural Code

Neoliberalism affects Russians differently depending on gender, marital status, class, age, race/ethnicity, levels of social support, and other salient axes of inequality. Differences abound, too, among single mothers in varied situations. Still, the commonalities are striking. Neoliberal ideology compounds the particular pressures single mothers face to "make something of themselves," forming a distinctive pattern of discourses and practices. Because of these dilemmas in common, mothers conform to, or display a keen awareness of, what I call the dominant cultural code of practical realism. By "practical realism," I do not mean to suggest that single mothers are in actuality always practical or realistic in outlook or that mothers necessarily believe in or even value being practical or realistic. Instead, practical realism is a gendered form of neoliberal ideology, the main cultural code of single motherhood. Practical realism has cultural power because single mothers of all kinds present themselves according to this code so that their actions make sense to others.

Even though what is expected of "good mothers" conflicts with "ideal worker" norms under neoliberal market capitalism, forcing mothers to navigate competing cultural schemas, single mothers in Russia often garner considerable respect as mothers by providing well for their families.[10] Yet this new form of personhood demanded of women, a new kind of habitus required of them in Bourdieu's terms, constrains single mothers considerably.[11] The code works from the outside in, shaping the kind of publicly acceptable selves women present to others. A useful analogy is how American voluntarism shapes how people present themselves to others in the United States. Many Americans do not necessarily feel autonomous, yet "people understand that their own action will not be properly assessed if it is not presented as the result of free choice by an autonomous individual actor."[12] In a similar way, some Russian single mothers do not feel as practical as they feel they should be, and some are not exactly realistic when they overlook the many sources of help they rely on in raising their children. But most women are constrained to present themselves according to what I will show are the main tenets of this cultural code. Cultural codes, in this case practical realism, both facilitate and constrain single mothers' behavior.

If single mothers were constrained by stigma and limited choices in the Soviet period, today single mothers are constrained by the dominant conception of successful single motherhood. Even though many single mothers consider themselves freer than their own mothers were, modern subjects can be even more constrained than their predecessors.[13] As Jane Collier argues in her study of the development of modern subjectivity in a Spanish village, documenting a shift from "following social conventions" to "doing what one wants to do," justificatory discourses of free subjects are not necessarily freeing; indeed, they can be even more limiting.[14] As women discipline one another to become stronger and transform their lives, those who fall short are painfully aware of doing so. To elaborate further the cultural code of practical realism, I first present evidence from a couple of evenings spent with Sveta and Alyona, two single mothers, and then delve into various facets of practical realism in greater detail.

✒ Sveta and Alyona

After several months back in the United States, I paid a return visit to Sveta, a thirty-five-year-old former factory worker living with her daughter, Masha, in a dormitory room on the outskirts of the city. Instead of cleaning houses around town, Sveta had begun working as a nanny in a private home. This was a big step-up in status from "talking to dishrags all day." She had managed to save enough money for Masha's eye operation, bought a new television and wall unit, and had gotten a phone installed in her apartment. She continues to sell Amway products and cuts her neighbors' hair for extra cash because she hopes to buy a small apartment of her own in ten to fifteen years.[15] Sveta strives to maintain a positive outlook, and she is open to whatever might give her strength. She sometimes lights candles at icons in a nearby church, and once I accompanied her to collect medicinal spring water at Tikhonova Pustyn′ monastery outside of Kaluga. Sveta believes that thinking differently itself can turn one's life around. She strengthens herself to deal with life's challenges by reading self-help books every evening, absorbing the translated works of Andrew Carnegie and Joseph Murphy. She reminds herself that she controls her own destiny.

Sveta did not exactly choose single motherhood, but she feels better off than several of her married girlfriends who put up with lazy, drunken, or abusive husbands for fear of going it alone. When Sveta was twenty-eight years old, she got pregnant unexpectedly and gave birth to Masha. She married Masha's father, but the marriage did not last long. Her requirements for her future husband would strike many as modest enough—she hopes to meet

FIGURE 5. A large gathering of Russian pilgrims, mostly women, collecting curative spring water at the fifteenth-century Tikhonova Pustyn´ monastery outside of Kaluga. Many Russian women are open to whatever might help them cultivate the strength so frequently expected of them. Photograph by the author.

a nonsmoking, clean man who does not drink heavily and who would love her, spend time with Masha, and help provide for the family—but she believes most men are either married already or just out for a free ride.[16]

During my visit, Sveta eagerly shared her recent accomplishments with me and her friend Alyona over vodka and snacks. Along with her new job, Sveta recently had many suitors, which she sees as a consequence of her improving material prospects. One of the guys she sees now and then *dlya dushi* (literally "for the good of one's soul," meaning "just casually" here) suggested they move in together. Sveta scoffed at the idea, noting that he had simply eyed the brand-new refrigerator her boss had given her, her new television and stereo, and the work she did painting and decorating her apartment and wanted to be supported in style, with her taking over his cooking and cleaning. Sveta said she would consider living only with a man who had either his own apartment or a decent job. A man should bring something useful to the table, she feels, especially because men seldom help out much with child care or housework.

Sveta's friend Alyona, a thirty-nine-year-old mother of a deaf girl, Rosa, was also doing better financially than when I first met her, having quit her low-paying factory job for work at an upscale nail salon.[17] Although officially married, her husband left the family three years earlier after his gambling debts led them to be evicted from their apartment. He lives with his new girlfriend in a distant city. Angry though she is, Alyona is ready to forgive him if only he would face up to his responsibilities and return to support the family. In the meantime, Alyona has her own mother's support. Her mother babysits for Rosa, which gives Alyona some time to spend with her boyfriend, Dima. Alyona insists there are no long-term prospects with Dima, but for now she welcomes his attentions and he helps her a bit with money and fixes her car when needed. She feels somewhat guilty about seeing him since he lives with another woman and his two-year-old daughter, but she admires his work ethic ("it's rare to find real hard-working men these days") and likes how feminine he makes her feel.

Before the end of the evening, Sveta's neighbor Inga stopped by, and Alyona led us in one of several toasts. "To Sveta, for being such a great hostess [*khoziaika*]! The men out there don't know what they are missing!" Inga retorted, "Oh, please! The men do know what they're missing but they don't care. We don't have real men in Russia, we only have bastards [*svolochi*]." Sveta insisted, "No, that's not true. Some guys I know are devoted to their families, they would never leave their wives . . . but unfortunately there are not very many of them." Alyona explained that her husband's failure to face his responsibilities is very typical for Russian men. Sveta and Inga nodded solemnly in agreement: Russian women, all three began to explain at once, are stronger than men and thus better able to adapt to life's challenges. This was a refrain I heard continually, from all kinds of Russians.

Sveta and Alyona are not unusual in attempting to become stronger and think positively. But despite fatalism about men and the state, they are far from fatalistic when it comes to improving their material circumstances. The women also keep several options open rather than supporting any abstract principle as the solution to their problems. When women do slip away from the tenets of practical realism, they tend to correct themselves, or others correct them. During a subsequent gathering with the same group several weeks later, Alyona gave in briefly to lamenting her situation with her former husband: "I still cannot believe that he really left us. He didn't even call for Rosa's birthday last month! After Rosa was born, when we were visiting all those doctors together, I thought we would be together forever, no matter what. How can he be living with another woman, and another woman's child, when he has his own daughter right here? And what man will want me now, with an invalid daughter who cannot speak?!" As she fell away from practical realism, turning from fatalism about men to active complaint, others encouraged her to think differently. Alyona had violated the "feeling rules" of practical realism, for she was not supposed to admit to feeling abandoned or unloved. Her situation may have been harder than that of most women because of her daughter's disability, but that was no excuse, in the eyes of others, for departing from practical realism. Sveta admonished her, exclaiming, "You are wrong! You need to think differently. I can give you some psychological books that will help you to think differently about your life and work and help you to make things different. It's up to you. You need to think, 'I am worthy. I have the best, prettiest, most charming daughter and any man in his right mind would be lucky to have me as his wife.'"

Practical realism, however, is not always so explicit. Typically practical realism is instead simply taken for granted among single mothers. I witnessed this cultural code most clearly in group interactions, as women disciplined each other to stay on track when anyone dared to veer away from its tenets. Most single mothers learn to perform the emotion work that helps them to feel the way they are supposed to feel; emotion management is a precursor of success.[18] There is no room for self-pity; instead, successful mothers are expected to work hard to change their situations if they find themselves unhappy, taking personal responsibility for their own well-being.

☛ Becoming Practical Realists

In practice, the four facets of the gendered cultural code of practical realism blur together. Here I discuss them separately for analytical purposes. As women become practical realists, they focus on thinking positively and becoming strong, accepting a negative discourse on men and the state, improving their material circumstances, and keeping several options open. A neoliberal ideology of self-reliance under capitalism has only strengthened this gendered cultural code of practical realism, leading most women to see few options besides working harder to embrace it.

☛ 1) THINKING POSITIVELY, BECOMING STRONG

There is a long legacy of framing women's strength in terms of their endurance and capacity for suffering. The Soviet discourse of gender reinforced these ideas of women's "natural" endurance and expertise in caring for others. What is new today is the perception that a woman can also be strong by taking care of herself.[19] Like most Russians, single mothers describe women's strength as natural at first. Inessa, a thirty-five-year-old divorced accountant, observed: "A person gets used to things, especially a woman. And a Russian woman, well, she can probably get used to anything at all, she can adapt to any situation." Women refer to sayings from folklore to describe women's strength: "I am a horse, and I am a bull. I am a woman, and I am a man."[20] Nevertheless, being strong in the post-Soviet context also requires work on the self.

Single mothers feel they must embody strength to teach their children how to survive in today's Russia. Mothers worry about how to shape their sons into "real men" who will later become responsible for their own families rather than letting women shoulder most of life's burdens. Yet although mothers want their sons to both respect women and be responsible, there is a sense that there is only so much mothers can do with sons given a lack of male role models. However, mothers of daughters are adamant that they must teach their daughters how to survive by remaining strong in the face of adversity. Some wish their daughters could be traditional, family-oriented women in intact marriages, but counting on this scenario strikes most as foolhardy. Yelena, a twenty-six-year-old divorced bookkeeper, reflected on raising her five-year-old daughter: "I want my daughter to be independent, and strong. Morally strong. All kinds of things can happen in life. We women are very emotional, our hearts are vulnerable. But all the same in this life we have to work on becoming stronger. So that everything doesn't affect you. Or at least you cannot show how much things affect you. I will do all I can to make sure that she can survive on her own in any situation. She can't be dependent on anyone." In contrast to what Yelena perceives as women's natural state of being, involving emotion and vulnerability, life under market capitalism requires distance from feminine characteristics. Whatever their desires, women must manage their feelings and cultivate strength. The rules of the game have changed; projecting practical realism means faking it to help you make it.

This new requirement that women be able to take care of themselves coincides with the neoliberal ideology of self-reliance. Being weak under market capitalism can have dire consequences for one's family, including ending up homeless or destitute. Yet the odds of employment are stacked against women across the life course. Nearly every woman I spoke to described how hard it is for mothers to find employment when they are of childbearing age, have young children, or are over forty. Mothers bristle at this limited window of opportunity, even as they try to strategize around it. Evgenia, grateful to have a job even though she felt capable of more than was demanded of her in repairing meters, explained: "At first women aren't needed because they might soon have children. If the girl is young employers say, 'You're going to get married and have children soon' and that's a problem. Then later a woman is raising her children and employers say: 'You've got kids and they're going to get sick, so why should we hire you?' And then after women turn forty they are old and no longer needed . . . but I'm over forty and I'm still seething with life!" Should women fail to become strong enough, they risk falling into the pitied category of Russians who are "needed by nobody."[21] Evgenia, like most single mothers, resists attempts to make her a "nobody" on the basis of her age or qualifications. She wishes conditions were otherwise, but she sees few options apart from working on becoming even stronger.

Women also summon the strength necessary to adapt to a man's world. Jobs have become only more sex-segregated since the onset of market capitalism.[22] As Lena put it: "Of course, a woman and her child should be more protected in our rather tough world. It is a man's world right now. Women have no choice but to acquire more masculine qualities in order to make their way in this world." Yet in trying to conform to standards of masculine ideal workers with no caregiving responsibilities, women describe feeling alienated from themselves.

The gendered feeling rules of post-Soviet single motherhood require suppressing one's emotions. Larissa was one of several mothers who described an inability to cry, at least when facing real-life troubles. Single mothers argue that women should be able to occasionally cry and should have "strong shoulders" to lean on. If Russia lacks "real men," it is also difficult for women to become what they see as "real women." Women feel that their femininity is undermined by the very masculine qualities to which women like Larissa attribute their success. "I have a masculine character. . . . What I mean is that I don't give up no matter what, I will find a way out of any situation no matter how terrible the circumstances might be. I never lose heart and I never cry. I can watch TV and start to cry, read a book and start to cry, but when I face real-life troubles I will never cry. Of course, probably a real woman should cry. When she has an argument with her husband she should let her tears fall, and then her husband should feel sorry for her. But I can't."

Single mothers have become inured to controlling their emotions, becoming estranged from the part of themselves that might want a good cry now and then. It is no accident that the qualities that single mothers say come naturally to them—being constantly in motion, never needing to cry, never getting sick, relying on themselves, and so on—are also precisely what is demanded of them in neoliberal Russia. After a four-hour interview interrupted by phone calls, homework help, and dinner prep, Nadia concluded, "Having a masculine character, as long as you have a feminine appearance, is really helpful these days."

Besides suppressing feelings, women try to reduce what they need. Anya was one of a handful of women who tried for a time to earn more money by working at a job coded as masculine. Her boss had been reluctant to hire her, but Anya surprised him by becoming more like a man, proud that she had developed the ability to ignore things that other women might complain about: "In our society we don't exactly have equality between women and men. Let's just say that equality is a somewhat relative term here! Employers prefer men. . . . People believe women are sufficiently capricious, that they demand all kinds of special conditions. So men cannot be themselves, they can't relax, they can't use foul language, and so on. But I let them know that I wouldn't tire anyone with my demands. They could swear and say anything to me. I wouldn't mind at all." Even when it comes to a work environment free from sexual harassment, women are doubtful about what they can manage to get given the current status quo in Russia. Whether or not Anya actually minded the extensive daily use of *mat* (obscene language), for her becoming stronger meant accommodating an all-male collective while stifling any demands of her own concerning the work environment.[23]

More frequently, women reduce their needs by developing exceptional abilities to go without sleep, to never get sick, to enjoy moving constantly, or even to instantly "become sober," showing no impaired judgment or other side effects of drinking alcohol, when circumstances demand it. They develop what Hochschild described in a very different context as a "conception of themselves as 'on-the-go, organized, competent,' as women without personal needs. Both as a preparation for this strategy and as a consequence of it, supermoms tended to seem out of touch with their feelings."[24] Sveta, for example, attributes her love of constant movement to her personality, rather than her lack of options: "I'm the kind of person who is constantly on the move, I can't sit still. I'm constantly moving, I've always got something to do, some problems to solve. . . . I've been on the go for so long and I've gotten so used to it that I don't really consider anything difficult. . . . I know that I can't count on anyone else. I'm alone, you know? No one is going to do my laundry, make me something to eat, or look after my child. I'm relying on myself alone, my own strength." Sveta's narrative is reminiscent of Natalia Baranskaia's late Soviet novella *A Week Like Any Other* [*Nedelia kak Nedelia*] (1969), in which the Soviet supermom heroine is constantly running everywhere as she carries out her many responsibilities, mostly unassisted (even though she is married). In Sveta's case, however, she cannot count on even the occasional help of a partner, and she scoffs at the idea of the state doing anything on her behalf.

Women who fail to think positively and transform their lives are often blamed personally for their failure to adapt, even by other single mothers. On one of our walks, I told Natasha about the challenges my neighbor was having. Natasha warned me against getting swept up in sympathy. These women, she argued, were simply not trying hard enough. The issue of "juggling work and motherhood" is an invented problem, which thinking positively could solve: "If someone says, 'Oh, look at you, you're poor and unhappy,' you will start to believe it. But I don't consider myself unfortunate. One time my mom said to me: 'Why do I have such unlucky daughters?' I said, 'Mom, how can you say that I'm unlucky? I've always been lucky in work, and I'm very fortunate with my children. It seems to me that in my life, and my career, everything has worked out. The fact that my husband and I are divorced doesn't matter, it's only a trial that has given me greater strength. And in many ways it's also turned out to be good fortune!'" After becoming single, the more fully women can manage their emotions and embody the strength expected of them, stifling any complaint, the more dignity they acquire. Through becoming strong and thinking positively, single mothers become practical realists. Yet women are allowed, and even encouraged by one another, to be fatalistic concerning men and the state.

2) Accepting a Negative Discourse on Men and the State

Most women feel that there is little to be done about the general state of the gender crisis in Russia. I encountered this fatalism so often that it started to seem normal to me as well. Once I accompanied a group of girlfriends, mostly single mothers, to the local *banya* (Russian sauna) to celebrate Margarita's birthday. While lying around in the steamy room, a few of them gently teased me about how hard and indeed boring it must be for me to be alone in Russia for so long, mainly talking to women. "Zhenya, are you spending time talking to our Russian men too, I hope?" one woman queried with a smile, while others giggled. I started to launch into my interview plans, but one woman interrupted me. She warned me that I would have to be prepared to find only a few good men in Russia. Another woman cut in with: "No wonder her husband back in America isn't jealous! After all, we hardly have men to speak of, especially in Kaluga!" Everyone laughed. A third woman then piped in. "Have you heard this one yet? A foreigner asks a Russian man, 'Do you have children?' And the Russian man replies, 'Well . . . my wife has two!'" Once again, everyone chuckled knowingly. Margarita then turned to me and said, "That's pretty much all you need to know about our men!"

Women draw on a broader gender discourse of Russia's weak, infantile men as well as a newer discourse of a weak state as they conform to practical realism. The weakness of men, in particular, is referenced routinely and ritualistically. Though other Russians (including men themselves; see chapter 6) also engage in disparaging men, the discourse takes on new meaning among single mothers. Single mothers engage in it to fortify themselves to deal with the challenges they face and to demonstrate their competence. Participating in this ritual allows women to build solidarity with others, let off steam, and focus their efforts on improving other, more controllable, aspects of their lives. Women likewise consider meaningful support from the state rather unlikely. Russians, including women whose narratives were more dramatic, relieve stress and establish solidarity with others through *crisis talk,* "a cathartic ritual through which the tensions of everyday life" are "lived out and transformed into narrative."[25]

Crisis talk has a distinctly gendered component, and this variant of crisis talk is widespread among single mothers. Through disparaging men and the state, women become savvy post-Socialist subjects. They demonstrate to others that they will not be taken in by men's promises or the state's proclamations—as much as they might be tempted to believe in both from time to time.

However, single mothers' fatalism—the feeling that they have little power to change the Russian status quo—is selective. Because women have to become strong to take care of themselves, they can hardly permit themselves to succumb to fatalism completely. Their general stance, in line with what Shevchenko observed as Russians' "blend of self-reliance and fatalism," tips toward a belief in their own abilities to make it against the odds. This fatalism about men and the state is also tightly interconnected.[26] There is no institutionalized way to meet a good man, nor is there any way to act that people believe will make a significant difference in how the Russian state supports mothers. As the state has withdrawn many supports for mothers, women have adapted by lowering their expectations for what the state might do, often becoming blatantly apolitical, while raising their expectations of men. Women want men to be reliable family breadwinners and are only further disappointed when their expectations concerning men are not met.[27]

Ritualized joking was more common in groups of women, but most single mothers are careful to qualify and make exceptions to what they see as the general rule of weak Russian men. However, even when women notice the exceptions, it seldom changes their assessment of the big picture, as if the reality of the problem of weak men and a weak state was so self-evident that attempts at explanation are futile. The dominant perception is that the state does not care about women or children and that most men are unreliable. Similar to what Jennifer Patico observed in her research among Russian women marrying Western men, many women consistently argue that "the few desirable Russian men—the ones who are not alcoholics, abusers, or unfaithful"—are "already married."[28]

Women engage with this negative discourse to varying degrees, but to refrain from participating in it entirely, as a single mother, is to display naïveté. The discourse on weak men, of course, is not a statement of fact; instead, it is a discourse of gender relations in a state of normalized crisis. At the same time, Russia has alarming statistics on male alcoholism and premature male mortality, and intimate partner violence and male infidelity are normalized in everyday life. Thus, accepting the negative discourse on men and the state appears useful for many single mothers in making sense of their lives. These rituals of disparaging men and the state strengthen women's feelings that they can count only on themselves or on other women.

The prevalence of this negative discourse is also noteworthy because today newer discourses, in which men are competent breadwinners, are available. After all, many Russian men are reliable enough to hold most positions of leadership in politics and business, with President Putin frequently cited by women as embodying a decent man's sober reliability. The Russian media, too, has been idealizing nuclear families in which men earn enough money to support stay-at-home wives and children while still remaining strong leaders and fathers in their families. Nevertheless, "the new family ideal in which the man plays a key role does not as yet match reality."[29] Women describe a critical mass of men who should be reliable but are not. Among single mothers, the Soviet-era negative discourse on weak, irresponsible men is dominant and has been infused with new meaning. Women discipline one another to remain within this discursive frame, making other frames for women's thoughts and actions almost unimaginable. Speech genres, after all, are "not merely a way of speaking about the world but also a way of *acting* in the world."[30]

The major strand of this discourse reinforces the unreliability and weakness of men as the status quo. Lada, a thirty-year-old factory worker with a four-year-old daughter, wishes she earned more money and hates being so dependent on her own mother. Yet she still feels proud of doing her best as a single mother and hardly feels at fault in this regard given the state of Russia's men: "Today everyone knows that women simply cannot rely on men. When a woman can't count on a man to take care of the family she goes it alone. . . . We have very few men who are really reliable, men you can count on. Men now depend on women. People know this!" The idea that men live at the expense of women and depend on them is derided as shameful. Still, women repeat the idea that men in many cases are figuratively "sitting on women's necks," (*oni sadiatsia na sheiu zhenshchine*) or free riding on women's hard work in families. Because some women have a better chance than before of earning good money, women feel there are more men than ever seeking to free ride on women's work. The Soviet state compelled men and women to work. But now people are free to refrain from working, if they can find adequate support.

Beyond the idea of men depending on women, the negative discourse on men is a ritual that repeats key phrases. A burdensome man, for instance, is invariably lying on the sofa (*na divan*), the spatial location of male dominance in families. Gulnara, a thirty-five-year-old divorced mother and sales clerk, explained: "Here in Russia, working men come home, lie on the sofa, eat, and watch television. That's it! But women have the laundry, cleaning, cooking, and always all of that. How does that saying go? 'A woman's road is from the stove to the threshold' [*zhenskaia doroga ot plity do poroga*]." There is some fatalism about men's place at home on the sofa. Women are not happy about the situation, but since women see men as unable to be reliable breadwinners (men's main responsibility according to women), wishing for them to also do more at home seems futile. Oksana, a twenty-six-year-old mother pressured by her own mother to marry a rich New Russian after she got pregnant by him, described a husband who had barked commands at her from the sofa.[31] After he beat her one time too many, she filed for divorce from her hospital bed, where she spent two months recovering. Given the severity of the other ordeals she endured while married, like most Russian mothers Oksana accepts that household work somehow "always falls on the woman."

Some women, especially women with higher education, do make exceptions for the kind of man they would consider sharing their lives with in the future. "He should help me, so that I don't have to do everything," Oksana clarified. But other women, like Lada, are unwilling to make even these limited demands on a future partner, absolving men of all "women's work." As long as a man is a reliable breadwinner, he need not bother with the dishes. Lada would be willing to settle for any kind of "help," however narrowly defined: "Even if he were just a simple man, a man who didn't help me at all, he could at least do men's work around the house. Even if he just hammered nails, did the household repairs, and figured out where to get the parts needed to make the repairs. Just solving these kinds of problems would be something." The problem of Russia's men for single mothers is not really that men do not do enough at home (although the unequal division of domestic labor contributes toward relationship breakdown) but the wider belief among women that too many men cannot be relied on. If they could only find someone reliable, some women are ready to "trade power for patronage," accepting subordination and a greater workload at home in exchange for compensatory benefits.[32]

Fatalism concerning men is part of why Russian women typically stop far short of demanding relational equality. In *Soviet Women*, Gray argues that while women in other countries are "struggling for freedom to," Russian women, who have been juggling paid work and second shift responsibilities for decades, are "struggling for the freedom *from*."[33] Other scholars argue that Russian women unwittingly contribute toward men's disengagement from the household by accepting primary responsibility for running their households while expecting men to do little more than "help." Because serving as subordinate assistants is unlikely to appeal to them, men remain on the sidelines.[34]

Many Russian women do seem to accept primary responsibility for running their households while expecting men to help. However, a more complete explanation of why women are more concerned about getting men to help rather than aiming for equality in domestic labor must grapple with just how entrenched gender discourses are in Russia and with the crisis of cultural imagination concerning relations between women and men. In other words, most women will not expend energy wishing for what they think they cannot ever manage to get. It is not that Russian mothers do not want a partner to share breadwinning, home, and child care responsibilities with them. Instead, the idea of men doing much more at home beyond "hammering nails" (the phrase repeatedly used to describe men's main work at home) or perhaps at the very most "washing dishes" (the phrase used to describe men helping with "women's work" at home) is almost unfathomable. Most women cannot imagine Russian men equally sharing, or even taking significant responsibility for, child care and housework. Because it seems unattainable, wishing for it violates the tenets of practical realism.

Single mothers are focused instead on getting whatever help they can from men, in the absence of much state support. Practical realists focus on what seems feasible given limited options. Yet perpetuating the negative discourse on men ends up reinforcing women's low expectations of men and ensuring that the status quo of gender relations stays in place.

Women are even more fatalistic about the chances of the Russian state doing much to help mothers. Recent research has highlighted Russians' lack of trust in broader social institutions, including distrust in the law, police, and government officials, but this lack of trust is experienced by single mothers as an abandonment relative to the supports their own mothers had. "Russia doesn't care about children the way it used to," Galya explained. "Sure, they care about raising the birth rate so the Russian nation doesn't die out and all of that. But they don't care about giving kids a real childhood. Nor do they care about helping mothers."

In terms of child support, in particular, women feel they have no choice but to negotiate with former spouses informally since they are not protected by the law. Of course, women are in a double bind because by not filing for support, women then have no recourse to the court, and the support of their children depends entirely on the good will of fathers—reinforcing women's feelings of uncertainty and instability vis-à-vis men and the state. Zoya, for example, explained that she had no choice but to accept an informal arrangement for child support with her former husband. He pays what he can, when he can, and only if and when he is so moved: "He threatened that if I took him to court he would arrange things so that he'd be officially earning the lowest possible salary. Here a woman can get less than two dollars a month for two kids! But in reality the guy might be earning 10,000 rubles or more [approximately $333]. All of this is done on the sly. Everyone knows that the laws here do not protect women." Fathers can easily obtain certificates (with the help of a few friends and connections) showing that they have very low salaries, so many women feel there is no point in filing for support at all. Even if a woman does take a man to court and wins, entitling her to one-quarter of her ex-husband's pay, it is often almost pointless because "Most Russians work on false contracts, which record only a symbolic sum as wages; up to 90 percent of the real figure is paid in cash."[35] Natalya, a thirty-three-year-old economist, was pregnant with her second child when her husband started to earn much better money. He insisted that she get an abortion, she refused, and he soon left her for a younger woman. But she has not filed for any child support: "Getting child support is complicated in Russia. . . . I don't know how it is in America, but here people conceal their real income to avoid paying taxes. So there are official salaries and unofficial salaries. And people try to show that their official salaries are very low. So if I were to file for child support, I would get very little. . . . There's really no point. So I just take what I can get, and I remind him about his duties as a father from time to time."

Women carefully weigh the costs and benefits of filing for official child support. Many worry that although their husbands provide only sporadic support, like $30 at the start of the new school year for books or New Year's gifts, they might lose even this tangible support if they turn to the courts, which they do not trust anyway. A willingness to seek official support signifies a total lack of trust in a former partner. Women choose between settling for informal, often minimal and sporadic, support from their child's father or getting what they call "crumbs" from the state. Women hope to at least leave open the possibility of a personal appeal to fathers for their child's winter boots or holiday extras.

Most women experience their dealings with the state as humiliating even beyond child support. Although it has since expired altogether, the child allowance in 2004 of 70 rubles ($2.30) or 140 rubles ($4.60) for never-married mothers was a paltry amount even for low-income women. Mothers consider the subject of the child allowance or state benefits unworthy of discussion, calling the allowance, and the state's attitude toward mothers, alternatively insulting, humiliating, or else just laughable. Rimma, a divorced thirty-six-year-old mother of three who is officially unemployed but makes traditional dolls and folk crafts to sell at local festivals, needs the money. Yet she finds it too humiliating to prove it to the state: "My husband will want an official divorce only when he decides to marry that woman, but basically for now he just left me. I don't have any certificates showing what he earns. . . . Collecting all those papers is hard, all those certificates . . . oh dear! All of that to get only 70 rubles for each child! I think that I'm healthy enough to work and earn that money myself rather than running around everywhere humiliating myself. And then those awful lines. The whole situation makes me jittery."

Interactions with the state cause humiliation, and most mothers hardly need more aggravation. The Russian child allowance made very little difference to the standards of living of families with children.[36] It made the most difference to households headed by never-married women, but even for them it comprised only 6.5 percent of total income.[37] Women are not counting on much tangible support from the state, or from men, anytime soon. Participating in these rituals of disparaging men and the state collectively reinforces the sense that mothers can count only on themselves.

3) IMPROVING THEIR MATERIAL SITUATION

"Love comes and goes, but one always needs to eat" (*Liubov' prikhodit i ukhodit, a kushat' khochetsia vsegda*), pronounced Anna, a thirty-three-year-old divorced accountant, as she poured tea. She had only recently started "to look at things in a more mercenary way." Although single mothers do not see material difficulties as the main story of their lives, at the same time most feel more in control over their chances of improving their material circumstances than they do about life's other aspects. Similar to Bourdieu's "choice of the necessary" among working-class French people, it is hardly surprising that single mothers feeling abandoned by the state and by men need to prioritize providing for their families themselves.[38]

However, this focus on improving their material situation goes well beyond simply surviving. Women want to succeed and thrive. Both survival and success are slippery, relative concepts, with no objective definition across contexts. In Russia, especially given the recent onset of market capitalism and various crises, success involves a significant material component. Women want to earn better money to give their kids opportunities and protect against future instability. Success in market terms is increasingly considered part of good motherhood. Even though the kind of success women seek may seem modest—women are not necessarily comparing themselves with successful men (who most likely are not single and do not bear primary responsibility for children)—for most, being a successful single mother remains within reach.

Besides putting food on the table, mothers are aspiring to buy their own apartments, save for a child's higher education, and earn more. One mother reflected: "I'm not fully successful yet, but I'm trying. At least there's a chance I can get a better job." Two mothers were planning a joint trip to Moscow to work, leaving their children with their own mothers in Kaluga and returning home on weekends, to determine whether by doing so they would be able to save more money (salaries for professionals in Moscow are two to four times higher than the salaries in Kaluga).

But in spite of increasing numbers of women on the move in Russia and the former Soviet Union, whether from small city to capital, or east to west, most single mothers hope to remain in Kaluga. They strive to find better-paying jobs, or they take second or even third jobs that they can do at home, such as private tutoring or making handicrafts or art. Many mothers work extra jobs near or at their main workplaces, such as taking on a shift as a cleaner for an hour before or after work for the extra cash. For mothers working in lower-paying, female-dominated state-sector jobs, these extra shifts are almost de rigueur to make ends meet.

Even in this "man's world," there is nonetheless an ideal of success for women, and this ideal of material success is considered more attainable for single women. Women who own businesses, for instance, are admired in Russia, even among women who do not have the time, connections, or capital to go this route themselves. Ksenia, a divorced mother, showed me on article in *Marie Claire* one afternoon, entitled "The Poor Rich." The story featured a woman, Olya, whose high school sweetheart husband changed for the worse once he started earning better money, and although she had a child with him, she had no choice but to divorce him because he worked all the time and no longer cared about her, the kid, or even sex. Ksenia saw the story as a cautionary tale for women: "Here's a woman who was afraid of material difficulties at first, but who didn't let that stop her. She became successful on her own terms, through starting her own business. Now that woman feels sorry for those who still think a rich man is the ticket to happiness. Olya will never be dependent on any man again!" I asked if she knew women like Olya. She replied, "Well, there aren't that many of those women here in Kaluga. There's probably more in Moscow. But at least they exist!"

Just as other ideologies, such as the American dream, are illusory rather than accurate representations of reality, so there are fewer examples of wildly successful single mothers than women's narratives imply. Yet even though entrepreneurs are associated with masculinity and toughness in Russia, "the share of women among the group 'individual entrepreneurs' in 2007 was 41%," hardly an insignificant number.[39] In any case, these new ideologies of feminine success and independence in Russia influence ordinary single mothers. As long as a few seem to embody the dreams such ideologies represent, others may be able to find something worth pursuing, and the ideal of a woman becoming an independent business owner with a child of her own and a steady stream of boyfriends is alive and well among today's single mothers. It might not have been their first-choice life since it departs from the nuclear family ideal. But it is a solid runner-up, a pretty good life all the same.

Some scholarship on the post-Soviet period has emphasized that women do not want to work outside the home anymore and are eager to be housewives and mothers, letting a strong, breadwinning man lead the household. These claims are greatly exaggerated.[40] Women may want to work less, but they are strongly committed to paid employment. Single mothers argue that women who stay at home become degraded and less interesting, letting themselves go, whereas work stimulates women to be at their best. Even President Putin in his May 2006 demographic speech alluded to this idea of the "degraded housewife": "I think that the state has a duty to help women who have given birth to a second child and end up out of the workplace for a long time, losing their skills. I think that, unfortunately, women in this situation often end up in a dependent and frankly even degraded position within the family."[41] Participation in the labor force has long been critical to Russian women's sense of identity, and it remains so.

Lena explained that although it would be nice to meet a man doing well financially, she cannot count on it. Furthermore, she added: "I want to earn good money myself, through my own hard work. Then it can really be my own." Women direct their energies toward work more than when they were married or partnered, too, in large part because they are freed from much domestic drudgery, a kind of work they associate more with husbands than with children. They also feel that they must somehow compensate for less-than-ideal private lives. Many feel that improving their material situation is within their grasp. And it does not hurt that this strategy garners them respect and status as single mothers.

Considering the lack of trust pervading gender relations in Russia, most single mothers put their energies into improving the conditions of their lives. Of course, some women have more opportunities than others. Lida, a professor in Moscow, earns more money through her consulting side jobs than most women could ever manage to earn in Kaluga. But the untrustworthiness of men and the need for women to earn their own living in her view transcends even class differences. Lower-earning single mothers, too, learn that they can rely only on themselves and that this means relying on one's job. Lida explained, "A man can decide to support you in the manner in which you've become accustomed. Or he can decide that he no longer wants to support you. He might fall in love with another woman, or find a lover. Women eventually learn that a stable job is better than the dubious support of a man." Women with higher education were more likely to feel confident about developing their own means of support. But single mothers of all kinds speak of developing their abilities to succeed on their own.

Although few were as explicit as Nadia, a lawyer with two higher education degrees, several women described wanting more of the market, not less. "It's a good thing capitalism has come to us," Nadia explained. "We only need to make sure that it develops further. Because right now we no longer have socialism but it's not real capitalism yet either." Just as women count on motherhood as a positive force in their lives, more so than they count on any man, so single mothers have little choice but to accept the marketplace. They do so in spite of the odds women face. Survey data have shown that "Women are disadvantaged on the labor market to the extent that, relative to men, they have *higher* rates of layoff and voluntary employment exit, *lower* rates of employment entry and job mobility, *higher* odds that their new jobs are low-quality positions, and *lower* odds that they are high-quality."[42] Many women still feel somewhat optimistic about their labor market chances, perhaps because standards of living have been steadily improving due to high oil prices since 2000.[43]

Through striving to improve their material situation, women actively manage uncertainty, conforming to practical realism. Even though women had more supports in the late Soviet period, most mothers believe that women have more income-generating opportunities today. When I spoke with Lilya, a forty-nine-year-old unmarried librarian, about why she thought women seemed freer today, she explained: "Well women, of course, always earned less than men back then. It's somewhat different now, women have a chance to earn more. . . . Back then women always earned less." Single mothers value this chance for a better life, however slim. Even though there are far greater inequalities between the richest and poorest Russians today than there ever were in the Soviet Union and most women, on average, still earn considerably less than men, the extent to which single mothers support a new ideology of hard work and potential success under market capitalism is undeniable. Women still want socialism in terms of subsidized housing, education, health care, and child care. But many also want more capitalism.

Concentrating on achieving economic independence and improving their material prospects earns single mothers dignity. As Roxana, a thirty-eight-year-old schoolteacher and private tutor reflected: "Today if a woman is providing well for her children, no one cares if she is single or not. But if she cannot provide for them adequately, then people will begin to judge her." Moral worth is linked to marketplace success. Through accepting a neoliberal ideology of self-reliance and success, planning their career moves, and saving for their next major purchases, mothers strategize mostly in terms of getting ahead on their own.

4) Keeping Options Open

Conforming to the tenets of practical realism also requires that women refrain from getting too attached to a single set of strategies. Apart from valuing self-reliance and independence, single mothers instead remain open to several possibilities for their lives, maximizing potential opportunities. Flexibility and adaptability are hallmarks of successful single motherhood. Mothers do have cherished ideals about family life, and many still hope to realize them in time. But as single mothers, most remain open to various forms of support or opportunities. This openness toward several options may seem contradictory at first, but it is an important part of the adaptability that women are expected to master. Some mothers describe how much they enjoy their newfound independence and freedom after divorce and a few moments later express a longing to meet a man who could be a real leader in the family, who would take charge of major decisions and relieve them of some of their responsibilities. Some women will claim in one breath to want nothing more to do with a man who had left them for someone else while in the next breath admitting they could possibly forgive him. Others argue that marriage is nothing more than a stamp in one's passport guaranteeing nothing, but moments later they will say that if they fell in love with someone trustworthy they would consider a real church wedding, with a white dress and all of the trimmings.[44]

Rather than imposing order arbitrarily on discourses and practices that seem contradictory on the surface, we should accept this ambivalence as an integral part of single motherhood. One can appreciate freedoms, for instance, while still hoping to meet someone with whom to share the workload and endless responsibilities. Furthermore, cultural worlds have internal contradictions as well as coherence, and coherence itself can be somewhat thin.[45] As sociologists of culture have noted, "It may be much less important for people to have a coherent worldview than to have enough different beliefs to adapt to most contingencies without losing the conviction that somehow the world makes sense."[46] Given the state of permanent crisis that most Russians, including single mothers, find themselves in, remaining open to a range of possibilities makes sense.

For instance, women often remain open to several possibilities in terms of moving in with a man who might help provide, marrying officially, or just making do with boyfriends or lovers from time to time, including those men with seemingly few prospects as long-term partners. Ludmila, a forty-two-year-old unmarried mother and hair stylist, had lived with her lover for a time but got fed up when he could do nothing for himself, even things like heating up food in a microwave. When he came home drunk after hanging out with work buddies, he expected to be waited on. She considers living with him too burdensome on a daily basis, but Ludmila enjoys his weekend companionship. "We get along pretty well. Perhaps I love him even. But just on Saturdays and Sundays." Although Ludmila remained open to meeting a more reliable man, becoming a practical realist, in part, means settling for what one can get in the world as it is, not as one would ideally want it to be.

Mothers frequently shift their stance even within the same interview, showing a willingness to accommodate a future partner and his preferences. When I first asked Valya, a divorced mother, about whether she would ever consider remarrying, she replied: "I would never rule it out. I don't rule anything out because life can change at any time." Later, however, she said she much preferred the ease of cohabitation over official marriage. While some women feel that official marriage has more stability and seriousness, many others prefer cohabitation because it avoids legal entanglements and is easier to get out of if things do not work out. Mothers also worry about officially remarrying especially because an official husband would then acquire rights to live in or inherit her apartment, even after divorce.

In addition, women leave their options open through professing traditional beliefs about gender, even when these beliefs seem to contradict how women live. Scholars have long been perplexed by Russian women who reject feminism and full equality yet in many other ways live out some of these feminist principles, by being strong and independent at work and at home, managing the family budget, and divorcing men who become too burdensome. In Russia, feminists are stereotyped as man-hating lesbians or as those seeking to irrationally deprive women of the few pleasures they are entitled to as compensation for their other burdens. At best, feminism is associated with women receiving a distressing lack of compliments and gifts.[47] As the Russian commentator Larissa Lissyutkina has argued: "Russian women reject feminism, political correctness and the entire discourse of sexism because they do not see how these things can be of use in the environment they inhabit."[48]

Nevertheless, women's willingness to embrace more traditional ideas about gender is selective and often partial. Many women desire more male support and sometimes seem willing to accept some level of symbolic domination by men in order to improve their chances of getting some support. Practical realists hedge their bets when they keep several options open. We need to move beyond binary oppositions of traditional and modern, to see women focusing on what is most useful in dealing with their specific life challenges. Some single mothers say something very traditional about gendered responsibilities, such as how being feminine and domestic should be the main priorities for women, affirming normatively traditional ideals, but then a few moments later they will describe how much they love going to work and how they were anxious to return to work after maternity leave because they were "going crazy being confined within four walls." Quite commonly women argue that men should be the real leaders in their families, making the most important decisions (i.e., women are not flexible in terms of men's duty to be strong, reliable breadwinners), but then they will say something similar to a sentiment expressed by Vera, a head clerk in the local government and divorced mother: "I'm an Aries, and we are often single. Maybe I need a man who I can respect, obey, and who could really keep me under his thumb. But on the other hand I would never put up with firm leadership over me! I am also a leader and I want my opinion considered." Perhaps some Russian women cannot conceive of finding a man who would take over some major responsibilities without also requiring gender deference from wives.

Similarly, Sasha, a twenty-nine-year-old unmarried child care worker, explained that men should be leaders but not dictators. Respectful leaders take over some responsibilities, consult with their wives, and share tasks equally. Sasha's comments reveal a belief in equality in spite of men's symbolic domination: "A man should be the leader of the family, the head. He should take some of the responsibility for the family, for raising the children, upon himself rather than putting it all on the woman's shoulders. At the same time the woman is the neck—wherever the neck turns the head follows. She should listen to him and he should listen to her. He shouldn't force his opinions on her but should instead consider her desires. . . . We have equal rights and things should be 50/50." The Russian saying that "the man is the head of the family, but it is the neck that turns the head" (*Muzhchina—glavoi sem'i. No kuda sheia povernet, tuda sootvetstvenno i golova tozhe*) captures the idea that women have long been the decision makers, the ones ultimately responsible in their families. Few women consider parting with this tradition, even though they would gladly hand over some responsibilities and work to a reliable partner.

This issue of faster-changing women and slower-changing men is hardly unique to Russia and is common in the West, particularly concerning the second shift of housework and child care.[49] Russian women's comments, too, suggest there is a disconnect, a gender gap, between what women feel they should be able to expect from men in family life and what men feel responsible for contributing. Because of this gender gap, women and men who allude to strong male breadwinners may have different strategic aims. Rotkirch notes that "Soviet-style gender traditionalism often implied a normative *longing* for a certain kind of fixed, stable relation, thought of as 'natural' and 'normal.' Men longed to be able to control women's reproductive and professional behavior; women longed for emotional and practical support from men."[50]

Of course, mothers who pay lip service to tradition do not necessarily conform to traditional practices in their own lives. Indeed, women speak so much of wanting a normal family and arguing that two-parent families are best that it demands further explanation. Many women present themselves as traditional women who are simply forced by Russian circumstances to become more modern in forging ahead as single mothers. Galina, a thirty-two-year-old salesperson and twice-divorced mother, confided: "I would really like to live in a normal, full-fledged family. . . . I've always wanted a normal family, it's very important to me." Single mothers describe families consisting of mother, father, and child as "normal" or "complete" (*polnyi*) families, implying that families departing from this model are somehow not normal or are "incomplete" (*nepolnyi*). Galina wants to live in a "full-fledged family," a *polnotsennuiu sem'iu*, which implies a superior family of full value. Single mothers argue that they are just like everyone else, but the way things are in Russia does not allow them to fulfill their ideal family dreams. Yet at the same time women conclude that it is "better to have no father at all than a bad one" (*luchshe nikakogo ottsa, chem plokhoi*). Putting up with any man no longer secures women much respect, and this is significant change. Nina, for instance, upheld traditional family values but at the same time argued: "Complete families, especially happy families, are very good, but they are so rare. You probably know this from spending time here. It is better that there be no father at all than a father who isn't any kind of a father anyway, the kind that a family is better off without."

When life is experienced as constantly changing and unpredictable, being ready to cope with unpredictability by leaving several life options open takes center stage. However, even though most mothers attempt to conform to practical realism, working to become strong and focusing on what they can control, some women are acutely aware of falling short.

✒ Falling Short

Superficially, Regina, a thirty-six-year-old mother of two, seems like Natasha's opposite. Both single mothers must navigate practical realism, but Regina finds it harder to present herself according to the tenets of practical realism. Her habitus seems almost stuck in the late Soviet period. Although they are friends of the same age and class background, both divorced with two sons, Regina never finished her college degree and she is having a tough time establishing herself in a career or, as she put it, "making something" of herself. She recently began writing children's books but has no steady work. Her well-to-do New Russian former husband is unusual for supporting their kids financially, but his support is erratic and conditional, and he reminds her frequently of her dependence on his largesse. She worries her sons are absorbing his views when they are showered with video games, multiplex movies, and other outlays of cash during biannual visits to papa and his new wife in Moscow. She is somewhat distracted, too, by a stream of quirky characters, both men and women, who seem to burden her life further as they gulp her tea and chomp biscuits around her kitchen table, sometimes asking for loans in addition to a willing ear.

Regina worries about her future, longing for the security and guarantees of the Soviet period, when "everyone was needed." She cannot ignore the homeless guy in the stairwell of her building and throws him spare change whenever she can. "Back then there weren't any nobodies," Regina reminisced. "Life was not perfect, but there was some justice. There is no justice now. And no one is socially protected." Regina has more income on average each month than Natasha or many others, but she has to plead with her former husband repeatedly for the money, which goes mainly toward her apartment rent and her kids' private school tuition.

Single mothers presenting themselves as Regina did, departing from the tenets of practical realism, are rare. Even when the façade of strength falls away momentarily, women seldom question that they have to be strong and get a hold of themselves to adapt to life in Russia. Mothers departing from practical realism crave closer and more authentic friendships, want to meet a man to love rather than settling for occasional liaisons with married lovers, and explicitly describe themselves either as stuck in a Soviet way of seeing the world or as not normal. Evgenia, for instance, feels insecure: "I don't do things normally because I'm afraid of a lot. My mom had no time for me. She was as beaten down as I am."

In spite of practical realism's dominance, mothers do vary as to how skillfully or thoroughly they adapt themselves to it. Ultimately, many women besides Natasha and Regina are differentially situated and equipped to deal with pressures to demonstrate that they have made something of themselves, that they are worthy of their children's admiration, and that they are doing just-fine-on-their-own-thank-you. Women like Natasha have internalized facets of practical realism, making it all seem effortless. Regina and other mothers like her have not. Regina is painfully aware of falling outside of expected norms in terms of her accomplishments (she wonders, what has she really made of herself besides having two kids?), her behaviors (shouldn't she just step over that homeless man in the stairwell, like everyone else?), and her feelings (why is it so hard to think more positively and keep self-doubts in check?). These mothers are not necessarily the poorest of single mothers, for failing today means more than not earning enough money. Failing involves being unable to summon an outward display of confidence, pluck, optimism, and strength expected of single mothers, qualities that garner them respect. Regina explained: "A good mother should be even-tempered, calm, confident, and probably strong as well. This is especially so if the mother is raising her children alone! Unfortunately, my kids are growing up without this sense of confidence. If I were stronger they would feel differently. . . . I'm torn between the home, my personal life, taking care of them, and trying to make something of myself and I cannot do everything at once. . . . I am nobody, and Alexei doesn't let me forget it. And they feel this, the fact that I am nobody."

Failing to summon the proper way of being in the world means more than failing as a breadwinner. For single mothers, it means feeling like a failed mother. Scholars are correct to point out that Russian men have few alternative arenas for self-realization apart from paid work and that men seldom have a place in the home apart from breadwinning. Women, however, have an alternative source for self-realization in the home and with their children, which allows them to develop identities in multiple realms. But however critical this gender difference, in today's Russia single mothers are also expected to prove their dignity through paid work and providing well for children, in order to qualify as good mothers. With limited supports, this task, in spite of the strength many women are forced to summon, is far from straightforward.

For Regina, life in the New Russia means inequality and insecurity. Taking care of children and the home with little or no help while simultaneously being expected to earn good money and "become somebody" are formidable pressures. Moreover, these pressures are rarely recognized as such, whether by others or by women themselves. Instead, people consign these struggles in juggling myriad tasks to mere problems in women's heads that might be solved by thinking or acting differently. Indeed, navigating a range of pressures without complaint is expected of Russian women: they hardly earn extra credit for it. People are quick to notice, however, when women fall short.

Rather than attributing women's struggles to systemic weaknesses and a lack of adequate supports, "failures" among single mothers are increasingly treated as matters of personal deficiency, making women feel at fault as individuals. Lada, a factory worker and unmarried mother, earns little money but has a difficult time seeing other options. Going back for a higher education seems impossible with all the housework she does on behalf of her own parents, who are still working to put food on the table. She hopes to get a better job when her daughter starts school, but for now she resigns herself to feeling uncomfortable about her status. "Our situation is not normal," she adds, noting, "I'm supposed to be able to earn good money. Maybe there is something wrong with me, but I just don't see how it is possible."

Mothers taking on personal blame for systemic failures, whether a lack of well-paying jobs or inadequate child support, are not exclusive to Russia. This happens routinely in other societies where neoliberal ideologies hold sway, most notably the United States. Notwithstanding regular platitudes and pronouncements about the dignity of motherhood and how much we care about children, in reality mothers—at least if they are single and poor—must prove their dignity through paid work. Through a most peculiar alchemy, domestic work considered noble when performed by married, college-educated women on behalf of their families becomes the height of laziness and irresponsibility when poorer, less educated, and especially women of color do it.[51] In Russia, too, given the competing demands mothers navigate, it is hardly surprising that single motherhood fosters considerable ambivalence, encouraging women to leave a range of options open and making it difficult at times to cherish their "freedoms."

Most Russian women who briefly depart from the cultural code of practical realism correct themselves and fall back in step through adopting the right attitude. Women are routinely reminded by others that they are ultimately in charge of their thoughts and actions. Even when women touch on moments of vulnerability in their lives, they quickly move on to describe "getting a hold of themselves." Ira, a taxi driver, paused before explaining what she has found hardest since her divorce: "Is it hard to be alone? Only sometimes. When I start to feel frustrated and start thinking and feeling sorry for myself. But it soon passes. I make myself calm down and get a hold of myself."

Women who fall short in conforming to the dictates of practical realism prove how constraining, and truly exhausting, this code of successful single motherhood can be. Conforming to the code successfully, after all, requires making it all look effortless. In order to make it in the New Russia, a single mother is expected to be strong, capable of multitasking, flexible, adaptable. The majority of single mothers make a virtue out of necessity by trying to become even stronger versions of Soviet-era superwomen. Yet the stakes for success are much higher in capitalist Russia, with costs of failure more dire. A married mother acquaintance told me, "It is no longer proper to admit that you have problems. It's personally embarrassing to have problems nowadays. Before connections and who you knew mattered a lot more. Today if you are not making it, most people think you only have yourself to blame." Single mothers experience these pressures acutely.

Although single motherhood is not stigmatized as it was in Soviet times, single mothers are still seen as "having been somewhat unlucky" in their private lives. They have fewer options for alternative identities and thus feel the need to become practical realists more profoundly. The consequences for failing to get a hold of themselves are more serious for single mothers given the state's toothless set of state protections for women. Regina feels a bit like a misfit from the late Soviet period, dealing with a brand-new world she had not asked for while feeling ill equipped to learn the new rules. And beyond survival, her dignity is at stake.

Surprisingly few single mothers challenge the rules of the new game. Many call for more, not less, capitalism. Single mothers would also like the social protections of the late Soviet period, but that possibility seems very remote to most, given all the other more immediate challenges in front of them. Although Russian women have long been required to adapt, mothers may find it more manageable to work on transforming the self rather than tackling the systemic change that might better accommodate their responsibilities as workers and mothers. Russian women are experts at making a virtue out of necessity, embracing reliance on the self as a kind of heroism. Given a lack of real alternatives allowing for more systemic change, theirs is an ironic heroism.

In working to transform their thoughts, feelings, and actions, women hope to change their lives and their destinies. To conform to the gendered cultural code of practical realism, women think positively and work on becoming strong, accept a negative discourse on men and the state, work on improving their material circumstances, and keep several options open. Practical realism has become widespread among single mothers not only because of the historical precedent of women holding households together but also because the rise of a new neoliberal ideology of independent self-reliance encourages this way of thinking and being in the world. Certainly, there are aspects of practical realism that seem more utopian than practical, as women embrace a self-reliant ideology in spite of needing supports (as chapter 4 will show), but women feel compelled to conform outwardly to the code, a kind of gendered ideology, whether they believe in it or not. There are certainly similarities here, too, to Soviet superwomen. But making it in the New Russia allows for even less weakness and no complaint, and women are not really counting on the state or even on a "real man" to come to their aid.

Mothers believe, or try to convince themselves, that they can make it on their own, relying on themselves in lieu of men or the state. Yet we will see in the next chapter that most cannot. Single mothers can make it without a man in today's Russia. But few can make it without their mother.

⤷ CHAPTER 4

It Takes a *Babushka*

Single Mothers' Youth Privilege and Grandmother Support

"No one helps me," Vera pronounced. We sat in her cozy living room, walls adorned with Persian-style carpets, drinking tea and enjoying freshly baked *pirozhki*, which her sixty-five-year-old mother, Antonina, had brought out from the kitchen.[1] Even after a few months in the field, I still found declarations like Vera's unsettling. I witnessed repeatedly how much Russian grandmothers help their adult children. Such support might include homemade pirozhki or, more frequently, borscht simmering on the stove top, but it often encompasses much more—from walking grandchildren to and from school, helping them with homework, planting and harvesting fresh produce from the family's *dacha* (country land plot), canning fruit preserves and pickling vegetables, making a rent payment, shopping, cooking, cleaning, and offering moral support. Even this list is far from exhaustive. It is difficult to overestimate the breadth and depth of support that most Russian grandmothers offer their adult daughters and their children, especially after daughters find themselves single.

Grandmother support of adult daughters in the New Russia is hardly a tangential detail of family life. It is a long-standing, if underappreciated, institution. Understanding Russian family life requires analyzing, and theorizing, the contours of this intergenerational support system. Notwithstanding the cultural dominance of nuclear family ideals, in practice, extended households, especially those with a supportive grandmother, are just as common.[2] The support of grandmothers is changing, but this support has become even more important during the post-Soviet transition to market capitalism. Single mothers vary in terms of how much they express gratitude for their own mother's support, but taking such wide-ranging support for granted is most common. Grandmothers do not take the support of adult daughters for granted in the same way or to nearly the same extent. This chapter explains why, by making visible both single mothers' relative youth privilege and grandmothers' unpaid, often devalued, care work.

Given the spread of neoliberal ideologies and the pressures single mothers face to do gender by conforming to the code of practical realism (see chapter 3), Vera's brandishing of self-reliance is not unusual. Discourses of self-reliance demonstrate personal competence and autonomy in postsocialism, and this demonstration may be especially important for single mothers.[3] So I probed further, asking Vera: "But your mother?" She replied: "Well, my mother helps in that she gets around 30 U.S. dollars a month after working for forty-seven years. But I get double that from my salary." Money is a big part of what counts as tangible support under market capitalism, but even this vexed me. Child care and extracurricular activities are no longer entitlements for Russian citizens, and in a world where care work has a price tag, wouldn't a grandmother's contributions become even more appreciated? I pressed on: "Does your mom ever help with dinner or around the apartment?" Vera explained: "Of course, yes! She does, and she watches Kostya for me. Sometimes I don't manage to get the cooking or the washing done in time. . . . In principle I could do everything myself but my mom loves me and she feels sorry for me. [laughter] She always helps me, she never refuses."

The idea that "of course" grandmothers provide extensive support to self-reliant single-mother daughters as a natural expression of their love and empathy for children and grandchildren is a traditional belief in Russian culture. And of course, many grandmothers do support their adult daughters, especially after their daughters find themselves as single breadwinners with kids. But love and empathy are only part of this story. Cultural pressures combined with unequal power relations in the wider society also shape intergenerational negotiations for support between grandmothers and single-mother daughters. To borrow a concept from research on husbands and wives over second shift struggles concerning the division of housework and child care, an "economy of gratitude" is also at work among grandmothers and single-mother daughters. The economy of gratitude shapes not only who does what but how women feel about it, including which contributions get counted as gifts and which ones get taken for granted.[4] I focus on the intersectionality of age and gender relations to unpack these relationships of power between single mothers and their children's grandmothers.

The support of grandmothers, affectionately called *babushki*, is neither automatic nor unproblematic.[5] Framing the contributions of grandmothers as such oversimplifies and obscures power relations that shape women differently depending on their age, primarily, but also on their social class.[6] As values change with the onset of capitalism, more women are coming to prize autonomy and self-fulfillment, with fewer embracing the traditional babushka's self-sacrificial duties.[7] Nevertheless, grandmothers are often constrained by tradition and economic necessity to provide assistance to their adult daughters, irrespective of their personal desires.

In the post-Soviet period, according to Tartakovskaya, "gender relations are in flux and old certainties have dissolved."[8] The state has pulled back supports for working mothers significantly, and cutbacks in state subsidies for child care and children's afterschool activities have burdened parents, and by extension grandmothers, with new responsibilities for caring for children. Uncertainty in older age predominates, with youth being valued more than ever, especially for women. Because the state no longer ties men to families as it once did through housing policy and the strict enforcement of child support, single mothers are more frequently turning to their mothers to compensate for a lack of other forms of support. At the same time, more grandmothers now work after retirement to supplement their meager pensions, complicating the cost in time and money of providing kin support. Men are important but still minor figures in this story of single-mother families; grandmothers perform starring roles.

Given the many societal changes that have placed additional burdens on families, single mothers and grandmothers have a very difficult time managing without one another's mutual support. Because intergenerational relationships face multiple pressures, relations between grandmothers and adult daughters are frequently strained and conflicted.[9] Yet more grandmothers are trying to set some limits on their support, especially in middle-class families.[10] Some want to feel a bit more appreciated; others want to enjoy their work or even a bit of leisure in older age. Age and gender relations intersect, producing different sets of opportunities and constraints for single mothers and grandmothers. The two generations of women are held accountable for "doing gendered age" differently, with labor and marriage markets tipping the balance in favor of single mothers. Single mothers benefit from youth privilege in these negotiations, finding life much simpler with their own mother's help.

This is no simple story of oppression: grandmothers do love their daughters and grandchildren, and most want to help them. And some single mothers do express gratitude for the multifaceted support that grandmothers provide. Yet, considering the pressures wrought by the transition to capitalism, combined with the retrenchment of state supports that older women experience more acutely, many grandmothers are also resigning themselves to their perceived lack of choice in doing whatever they can to help single-mother daughters.

↝ Extended Mothering and the Transition to Capitalism

Grandmothers have long made extensive contributions to Russian family life. Although babushki contribute to heterosexual married households as well, most evidence suggests they do even more for single-mother households. After Russia experienced a catastrophic loss of men during the Second World War (see chapter 1), several generations of men and women were raised without fathers present. Soviet families resembled African American families in that mothers often became responsible for primary breadwinning, while grandmothers took over responsibility for housework and child care. Even when fathers were present, everyday life was supported by extended mothering.[11] Women developed intricate networks for carrying out predominantly female care work; these networks were critical as women provisioned their families in a shortage economy and performed household labor in addition to wage work. Although normative in many non-Western contexts, extended mothering contrasts with the ideology of intensive mothering that predominates among U.S. white, middle-class households. Unlike intensive mothering, in which mothers lead childrearing that is "child centred, expert-guided, emotionally absorbing, labour intensive and financially expensive,"[12] extended mothering is authoritarian, family-guided, socially integrated, and based on informal networks.

Extended mothering also represents one of the major continuities in Russian history, and grandmother support, in particular, has long provided stability during periods of rapid change.[13] Even prior to the Soviet era, Russian families lived in extended family households while working both inside and outside the home. "Hierarchical networks between women—in-laws and servants—were an integral part of daily coping," notes Anna Rotkirch, and women "were used to their fathers and husbands being away fighting, drinking or at seasonal work. And even if present, they were not automati-

cally reliable sources of either income or support."[14] Regardless of grandmothers' desires, extended motherhood made their contributions necessary.

Yet much of what we know about grandmothers relies heavily on anec-
dotal evidence and stereotypes about the older generation of Russian women.
For instance, one dominant portrayal suggests that even though some Soviet
women chose to work after retirement, most freely chose the babushka role,
seamlessly fulfilling their expected family functions without complaint: "The
babushka, in effect, takes full responsibility for her daughter's home, freeing
up both daughter and husband to participate unhampered in the work
force. . . . Women freely choose the babushka role as a form of work, rather
than continuing to work outside the home. This voluntary assumption of
the babushka role is, in part, a reflection of the love that frequently transcends the generations."[15] In her absorbing portrait of Soviet women, Gray
(1989) refers to a grandmother who explains that caring for her grandchild
was not even a decision but simply an impulse, a return of love for what her
own mother did for her.[16]

In spite of these portrayals of grandmother support as unproblematic, even
before the onset of perestroika older women had begun associating retirement with leisure rather than babysitting and housework. Responsibilities were
foisted on grandmothers because of inadequate child care facilities and minimal assistance from men with chores.[17] A "crisis of the grandmother's role
in the family"[18] may be emergent, but I found that babushka support in
families continues, especially in single-mother families, with grandmothers
helping their adult daughters with child care and household tasks. Even
single mothers who initially present themselves as going it alone frequently
rely heavily on a babushka's support, at least during critical moments of
transition in their lives.

The responsibility for ensuring a household's survival is gendered, and
in Russia it is led by women.[19] The grandmother frequently transmits these
critical cultural capacities even though her key role has been overlooked in
the Russian case and internationally. A gap between discourse and practice
also obscures the grandmother's importance. Women spend a lot of time
talking about how hard it is to find a man and having to go it alone, but in
practice many single mothers routinely turn to their own mothers for everyday support. Because they turn to their own mothers so routinely, single
mothers may have less of a need to talk about this support explicitly. There
is more to talk about when such support is somehow missing or threatened
by conflict.

The state is likewise relatively silent about the centrality of grandmothers in families.[20] Yet the number of mothers living with children and

grandparents increased during the 1990s, with one-third of children in single-mother households living with at least one grandparent.[21] In my sample, 40 percent of children were living with a grandparent, almost always a grandmother. Whether children live with grandparents or not, grandparents care for nearly 50 percent of Russia's preschool-age children and provide more pragmatic help to their adult children than vice versa.[22]

Single mothers are expected to provide well for their children by achieving some success in the "masculine" endeavor of primary breadwinning. In practice, this means that mothers must find child care at all costs. Grandmothers, much more frequently than grandfathers, contribute most to families in this regard.[23] Because of the large gender gap in life expectancy (with men's life expectancy now sixty-two years and women's seventy-four), more pensioners are women than men. Women retire earlier than men, at age fifty-five (age sixty for men), and nearly one-fifth of all pensioners work after retirement, often contributing earnings and a pension to their children.[24] Besides fathers dying earlier, there are more estranged fathers as there is typically little paternal involvement after divorce and "unlimited self-sacrifice primarily is conceived of as a female and motherly quality."[25]

After reflecting briefly on getting to know Russian grandmothers as linchpins of support in single-mother families, I describe three major themes that emerged from my observations of and conversations with babushki: single mothers' youth privilege vis-à-vis babushki, shaped by labor and marriage markets; the association of feminine self-sacrifice mostly with older women; and, finally, the cross-generational conflicts that threatened women's mutual support system.

✒ Fissures in Supportive Webs

Although I became aware of the importance of babushki early on in fieldwork, it took more time for me to learn about the many tensions and conflicts in grandmother–adult daughter support networks. The dominant stereotype of a good babushka has long been one of boundless love and support, so grandmothers admitting to feelings of being underappreciated are almost breaking a taboo. Mutual support occurs, but single mothers and grandmothers feel differently entitled to various forms of support. Höjdestrand, too, pointed out that "There is a deeply ingrained idea that parents should sacrifice themselves for the sake of their children and help them in all possible ways, while the reciprocal duty of adult children to care for their parents is less pronounced."[26]

Over time I witnessed single mothers eating at their mothers' homes routinely, even if they lived separately, sometimes barely clearing away their plates
before bounding off to another engagement. I overheard grandmothers curtly
say to their daughters, "You haven't yet asked if I am free to watch Igor on
Saturday." Because I seldom showed up at anyone's home without at least
some fresh fruit, if not sweets, and was genuinely appreciative of the hospi-
tality women offered, grandmothers sometimes openly wished their daughters would also spend time with them and appreciate their efforts rather than
treating them as on-call babysitters.[27] Some single mothers requested that I
meet them in parks for interviews because they wanted to be able to speak
freely without their own mothers eavesdropping or correcting them at every turn. Several single mothers gritted their teeth when I brought up the
subject of babushka support during interviews, explaining that they wanted
a normal family and that two women trying to control one household is akin
to asking for trouble. Following these clues, I sought to understand more
about how mothers and daughters negotiate conflicts and divide paid and
unpaid labor.

At first some older women were skeptical about social research, but frank
conversations increased over time. When I first interviewed Emma, for instance, her mother, Yelena, came to the door, querying about the purpose
of my visit: "Do you really think you, an American, someone who is not
even a mother, can begin to understand the lives of today's single mothers?"
These questions were not the norm, and over time feelings of distrust dis-
sipated, but it took some effort to remain unruffled in these cases. I answered
truthfully, explaining that even if total understanding is elusive, a partial understanding struck me as well worth the effort given all that women are experiencing during the transition to capitalism. My earnest desire to hear their
stories gradually led most women to share considerably with me. For instance,
during a return visit with Yelena after several months back in the States, she
launched into how angry she had been after Emma had decided to bear a
second child recently without a father around. "Zhenya, can you imagine?!
Sure, she wanted a daughter and I love children, but she never consulted with
me. . . . My health cannot handle this!"

I interviewed thirty grandmothers in all, though I learned much more
about conflicts from a larger number of grandmothers informally, after the
recorder had been turned off.[28] Through participating in several networks
of grandmothers and adult daughters—there was one grandmother with
whom I spent time talking over tea at least twice a week and several others
every few weeks—I was also able to observe how intergenerational relationships change over time. In spite of a slower start, and even though

grandmothers were frequently as busy, if not busier, than their single-mother daughters, grandmothers were clearly appreciative of my interest in their experiences and recollections. Most had more complaints than their daughters did about how the support system functions in Russia, with more grandmothers feeling somewhat taken for granted and hoping to eventually enjoy the fruits of leisure, relationships, or work. Several grandmothers treated me like a daughter of their own and opened up their homes to me, offering advice and companionship. My discussions with Russian grandmothers and extended observations among several grandmothers over time offer a unique perspective on Russian family change.

☛ Single Mothers and Relative Privilege

☛ Marina, Valentina, and Katya

Marina, a twice-divorced, forty-seven-year-old factory worker and grand-mother to her daughter Katya's two-year-old son, Ilyousha, lives with her own mother, seventy-two-year old Valentina, a retired lathe operator. Marina glowed as she described her wonderfully supportive work collective. Apart from a brief experiment trying to earn slightly more money "doing boring work" at a private firm where no one cared about her, she has enjoyed working at her factory for nearly twenty-five years, describing it as her second family in spite of the abysmal pay. She is nostalgic about the past, when factory workers were valued and considered more important than "people getting rich from selling overpriced imported junk." (I was thankful my token of gratitude had included a box of Babayevsky's "Inspiration" [*Vdokhnoveniye*] chocolates, a favorite from her youth, rather than an imported variant.)[29] Apart from her friends at work and the chocolates, Marina's eyes similarly gleamed when talking about her boyfriend Volodya of many years, a married man whom she loved even though he could never leave his wife. Other details of her life emerged over a series of conversations, from the bittersweet (mainly, the unfaithfulness of her first husband, which broke her heart) to the humiliating (the abuse she endured with her second husband). Concerning Volodya, she remarked: "I like how I feel when I'm with him and he makes me laugh. And in my life, I have learned to be happy with what I can get."

Even though Marina's twenty-six-year-old daughter, Katya, lives separately in what used to be her grandmother's one-room apartment, Katya enjoys the practical and financial support of both Marina and Valentina, especially in terms of help caring for Ilyousha (who spends equal time living in both

homes, according to Katya, but spends much more time living with his grandmothers, according to Marina). Lacking a higher education, Katya feels her
best shot at success lies in developing her photography skills. Both Marina
and Valentina disagree and would like Katya to take any kind of regular paying job. But Katya yearns for a job that would allow for *samorealizatsiia* (self-
realization).[30] Katya knows she must earn money, but she feels entitled to
develop her talents in a way her mother does not: "My grandma comes over
to help me with Ilyousha. She tells me to go and look for work. . . . But it's
impossible to earn enough money to raise my son in Kaluga. The salaries
are better in Moscow, and there are more jobs where I could realize myself.
But I'm faced with two extremes. I can either raise my son and have no money
or go out to earn money while leaving my son to be spoiled by his babushki!"
All kinds of work done by babushki on behalf of grandchildren are at times
reduced by single mothers to "spoiling." Currently without a job, Katya spends
less time with Ilyousha than the two older women she refers to as her "parents." Her grandmother cares for Ilyousha while her mother works all day at
a factory job. Marina routinely buys Ilyousha's diapers, walking thirty-five
minutes to work each way to save on bus fare. Katya realizes that without
babushka support she would have to work at "awful" jobs rather than pursuing her dreams. She added, tellingly: "Parents give you power."

Katya has no regular income, so her power in relation to her "parents" is
due to her relative youth and family status. As a younger woman, she feels
entitled to have fun and pursue her dreams, whether in terms of building a
career rather than taking any job or spending time with a boyfriend who
might be able to help the family in the future. This privilege was evident
one evening when Marina had invited me over for dinner. After waiting nearly
an hour for Katya, we eventually began eating without her. Marina and Valentina confided that unfortunately Katya gave them "nothing to boast about"
as she refused to hold down a regular job and instead wanted to rely on their
sacrifices. Two hours later Katya burst into the room proclaiming, "I'm fam-
ished!" and began digging in to the dishes warming on the stove top. Katya
spoke about the challenges of starting a photography business while still finding time for her new boyfriend, but the family's daily survival clearly depended on both babushki. Marina wished her daughter would not be so
impulsive, spending her last ruble on a taxi ride or coffee drink.

Because she cannot count on the state, Marina feels unprotected and quite
vulnerable given her age, gender, and class standing. Katya, economically
dependent on her mother, still has substantial bargaining power, a power
exacerbated by Marina's worries about her elderly mother's health and her
own future. Marina earns little, trying to believe in her daughter's potential,

and perhaps eventual, success. She hopes Katya will meet a new man or get lucky as a freelancer, so she stifles her complaints and supports her daughter. Sometimes she even blames herself for Katya's impulsiveness. Her second husband was quite impulsive, she admits. Probably she should have divorced him sooner.

◆ Youth Privilege in Labor and Marriage Markets

Although Katya has substantial bargaining power in relation to her mother and grandmother, any advantages she has are relative only to the experiences of older women. Russian women are in no way generally privileged in gender-segregated, often discriminatory labor markets, where many women work in the lowest-paying sectors and find it hard, even with higher education, to find work according to their specializations. There is also great variance as to how privileged women are in marriage markets depending on education, age, appearance, and other factors.

Nevertheless, I use the language of privilege to get at aspects of social advantage that are accorded to individuals on the basis of group membership. So beyond how individually privileged a particular woman may be, an institutional kind of privilege grants advantages to some women but not others solely on the basis of membership in a particular age category (socially perceived age). In relation to grandmothers (and in relation to those mothers lacking babushka support), single mothers with babushka support are encouraged and even expected by society to adapt to masculine ideal-worker norms on the job by doing whatever an employer asks in terms of extended hours or travel and to keep their options open concerning marriage or relationship opportunities. Grandmothers feel pressured to stifle their own interests and desires more frequently, doing gendered age by performing unpaid care work for adult daughters.

Many grandmothers enjoy their work, but it is even harder for older women to find good jobs. Most employers prefer younger workers, especially in the private sector. Russia complies with many formal commitments to gender equality, but at the same time women's everyday experiences tell a different story—one of stereotypes, discrimination, and pervasive sexism.[31] An emphasis on youth and beauty, too, is much more pronounced for women than for men; Zdravomyslova notes that "advertisements, television programs, and glossy magazines are 'aggressively sexualizing' the common idea of women's roles in society, and reinforcing traditional attitudes."[32] Discrimination against mothers and potential mothers (i.e., the vast majority of Russian women) is open, widespread, and unchecked.[33]

Natasha, an art teacher who works several freelance jobs to make ends meet, clarified aspects of this gender and age bias in employment: "In Russia we don't exactly have equality between women and men. . . . All the same employers prefer men. . . . And if a woman is over forty, well, she's no longer needed." It is striking that nearly every woman interviewed commented on employers refusing to hire mothers of young children and preferring women under forty. Private employers do not want to pay for sick or maternity leave, so women feel pressured to demand nothing and advance quickly to gain access to somewhat higher paying sectors of the economy. Even when child care is available, employers do not trust that women will not take sick leave when children are too ill for group care.

The major way to circumvent aspects of the discrimination against mothers is to have someone else, typically a babushka, available to care for children. Many single mothers cannot work unless grandmothers provide child care.[34] Women report that employers routinely treat them as problem employees unless a babushka is available and willing to act as an on-call mother substitute. Single mothers with babushka support are able to better approximate masculine ideal-worker norms, which presume access to unpaid caregiving at home.[35] Many women assume that the early career-building years should be prioritized for single mothers regardless of grandmothers' preferences. As Vika explained: "Sure, my mom wants to keep working. But she can take time off and not have it hurt her in the same way that calling in sick would hurt me. Mostly she has agreed to take a sick day if Anya wakes up sick. There's no other way." Although the "mostly" here suggests some ambiguity concerning negotiations, Vika is secure enough in her own job and class position to assert her youth privilege, and the bargaining power it holds, relative to her mother's job. These interactions between women do not happen in a vacuum. Institutional arrangements favoring younger workers naturalize Vika's views that her own job matters more. Many Russian grandmothers, it bears mentioning, are only in their late forties or fifties, given earlier childbearing in Russia in relation to the West.

In the single mother–grandmother relationship, single mothers routinely report feeling "like a man," working more hours and doing less care work at home. Olga reflected: "Employers will take the worker who doesn't have any problems with kids. Luckily my mom can cover for me." Buffered against potential disruptions, women describe feeling freer to concentrate on their careers with a babushka's support at home. Masha reflected: "I suppose I haven't experienced discrimination because I have someone with whom I can leave my child—my mom. . . . I trust in her 100 percent and she'll look after my son even better than I can at times. And we get along very well. She never hindered my professional growth or job searches." Ideal grandmothers are expected to help without hindering, to support without nagging, to provide guidance while still showing deference to adult daughters as their grandchildren's mothers. However, patterns of mutual support do shift over time. When Masha was finishing school and at home with her baby son (age ten at the time of interview), her mother worked outside the home and helped to support Masha and her grandson financially. She retired only after Masha returned to work.

Babushki are considered ideal mother substitutes, even though the pattern of babushka support varies somewhat by class. As family members, single mothers and babushki tend to share the same class background, making age more salient as an axis of difference and inequality. Still, it is easier for middle-class or married grandmothers with access to more income to consider cutting back on work after retirement. Masha, for instance, admitted that she was "lucky" to have such serious babushka support. She explained that she has girlfriends whose own mothers are not able or do not want to spend so much time with their grandkids. Her mother is married and had a solid career as an official in local government, making it more possible to shift into retirement without holding side jobs.

Yet in spite of these assumptions that the work of younger women matters more, most grandmothers continue to work after retirement.[36] Many enjoy working and are not eager to stop working at the early age of fifty-five. But even when babushki work for pay, they provide daughters with support. Grandmothers take sick leave to help daughters when needed and face less societal pressure to be economically successful in their jobs. Single mothers are expected to work on becoming better primary breadwinners and are seen as more autonomous because of their relative youth.[37] Thus, social expectations concerning age category, family status, and gender prioritize the careers of single mothers, making it difficult for grandmothers to challenge these norms.

Mothers in the private sector are more likely to argue that it is impossible to succeed at work without babushka support. But mothers in the lower-paid state sector also see a babushka's support as essential. Yuliya, a librarian, reflected on whether she would face discrimination if she had to suddenly look for work: "No, I wouldn't. If I didn't have her [babushka's] support, then yes, I'd face discrimination. . . . Therefore, I'm a little bit protected. And I can let myself work more in general. This is a big advantage. I have an entire detachment at home—my grandma, great-grandma, and my sister!" Yuliya, who earns more money in her freelance evening job writing term papers for students than she does as a librarian, still feels that a babushka offers protection. This feeling of being "a little bit protected" is even more important considering the lack of state protections and employment rights that so many women routinely encounter. Access to a babushka's support allows Yuliya to work into the evening, devoting additional time to supplementary breadwinning and improving her longer-term economic or career prospects.

While still busy with work of all kinds, single mothers with babushka support also have more time, relative to grandmothers, for friends and leisure activities. Grandmothers help married mothers as well, but married mothers face additional gender constraints as wives serving husbands in heterosexual households. Like single mothers elsewhere who experience the gendered character of household work as less constraining,[38] in contrast to married women, single mothers experience a major reduction in household work and gendered rituals of deference. This reduction is amplified further when grandmothers take over much of the second shift work. Sonya has an apartment one block away from her mother's, but she still prefers to live with her mother most days: "My mother has many household problems on her hands. That is, she buys groceries, makes dinner, cleans the house. And so for me things are simpler. I have a child who is fed and looked after, but for many women it is a matter of coming home, making dinner, and all of that." Women seldom seriously consider that a male partner might help significantly with household work or child care. At the same time, few women seem to consider that a grandmother might have other plans apart from contributing toward an adult daughter's household work and child care.

Some women initially present themselves as equal partners on a team with their mothers. But after further observation, I learned that youth privilege, too, shaped these intergenerational negotiations. As Emma memorably put it, "Mama and I share one household, for she couldn't survive on a pension of 800 rubles and I couldn't survive without her help as a nanny. Therefore we united and we're together, and we share everything with each other. We have a kind of communism!" Her mother, too, seemed to agree with this portrayal but only provisionally. During subsequent conversations, after Emma had her second child with no father in the picture, the weight of unequal care burdens and responsibilities troubled her more deeply. Grandmothers are often responsible for more repetitive and time-consuming work done on a daily basis. The "family myths" of egalitarianism in spite of unequal sharing that are so common in heterosexual families in the West are also apparent in Russia's intergenerational relationships;[39] a "leisure gap" between single mothers and grandmothers persists, based on age and gender. Grandmothers do gendered age by spending more time in the kitchen and with grandkids (or feel they should), whereas single mothers feel more entitled to visit with friends, exercise, or take care of themselves.

In part because grandmothers experienced more state supports when raising their own children, they feel more dependent on their daughters today. This feeling of dependence is somewhat diminished for those grandmothers with more class resources or income to fall back on. But most babushki are worried about daughters who must cope with challenges such as state cutbacks, insecure and infrequent child support, and new market pressures. Lusya argued: "Vera works all the time. I mean I worked hard all my life, too, but at least I got child support every month and I knew I'd have something to eat. She's got it worse." Another grandmother added, "My daughter is doing what she can, it's different now that jobs are not guaranteed for anyone. I think she is trying her best. What more can she do?"

Galina and her mother, Ruslana, for instance, expressed satisfaction with unequal arrangements, even though Ruslana bore responsibility for more arduous forms of work at home. Galina reflected: "If I lived alone, then things would be difficult. But my mom and I have a common household where I handle all of the child care—my mom doesn't really help me much with Liza—but she does all of the laundry, cooks, and handles everything else." Showing off her long manicured nails and the family photos she spent many evenings carefully cropping and editing, she proclaimed: "My friends wonder how I find the time to do it all. But my mom makes it possible!"

Ruslana also worked full-time, but she knew her health would eventually decline, leaving her with only her daughter to depend on. At the same time, she argued that Galina worked a lot at her computer, in addition to bringing work home sometimes and getting up in the middle of the night with Liza. So the arrangements were mostly fair, in her view. Of course, unequal relations based on gender and age are frequently internalized and naturalized, especially when broader institutions strengthen various forms of youth privilege. In any case, it was not that Galina's income gave her power, for Ruslana earned a decent salary. Instead, Galina's perceived potential for higher income, based on assumptions about her relative youth and supported by labor (and marriage) markets, shaped women's negotiations and expectations.

Most women feel they cannot rely on the state nor on any man. Yet at the same time, besides her daughter's income potential, Ruslana confided that Galina was young enough to have a chance of meeting a decent man, with access to a man's higher salary that the family could use. Thus, Ruslana ceded authority to Galina in childrearing, but she still watched Liza often so that Galina could attend social functions and activities, such as her ballroom dance club meetings.

But Ruslana's help had some conditions. She had pressured Galina to divorce her second husband, threatening to withdraw her support of her daughter should Galina continue living with such a "worthless bum," a man who was out drinking often and cared little about Galina's pregnancy. Ruslana reflected: "What choice do I have? I worked my whole life for nothing, I have not even a penny to show for it. And what if I get sick? I cannot expect anything from the state. I can only count on my daughter." Ruslana laughed when I asked about her free time. Gesturing toward the stove top, she said: "That's my free time. I'm done with men." The state's retreat from supporting women as worker-mothers has left a vacuum that many grandmothers feel obliged to fill, both for their daughter's well-being and for their own. Working-class grandmothers feel this obligatory duty more intensely, but given the uncertainty that is part of daily life in Russia, many middle-class grandmothers feel similarly dependent on their children.

Marriage markets, too, however unfairly, place a premium on relative youth. In this context, single mothers, especially those under forty, feel entitled to pursue more social outlets than older women. Grandmothers are expected to facilitate these possibilities for daughters through providing child care. Some babushki also have boyfriends, but these men typically are married and the relationship seldom involves much practical support. One grandmother reflected, "Ksenia still has time to get her private life in order. . . . For me the chances are probably slim." The younger generation of women directly benefits, in terms of leisure, by the invisibility older women acquire as "sexual castoffs."[40]

Even when grandmothers want to relax, daughters' social calendars are prioritized. Grandmothers sometimes seem to be fighting an uphill battle in trying to carve out time for themselves beyond time spent with grandchildren or on housework. Toward the end of fieldwork, I invited Tatyana, a middle-class, working grandmother of pension age, to a local concert. She had told me about how much she enjoyed Party activities and socializing while raising her two kids, yet now she seldom went out apart from going to work or to the market. I wanted to return the generosity she had shown to me, but planning just one night off proved rather complicated. We enjoyed an evening out, but she felt more stressed about "clearing the date" with her daughter than I had anticipated. This was so even though Tatyana cooks for her daughter's family almost daily (while living separately but nearby) and watches her granddaughter most evenings so that her daughter Olga can study or spend time with her boyfriend, Mikhail. Mikhail occasionally helped out at the dacha, so Tatyana felt the family might benefit further from his continued support. Because of family status and age, older women are expected to sacrifice more for the family's well-being.

✎ Grandmothers: The Reserve Army of Feminine Self-Sacrifice

The story this chapter tells is far from inevitable. But while it is certainly possible for a grandmother's unpaid work to be considered of equivalent value to market work, in Russia this rarely occurs. Earning money has increased in importance during Russia's transition, so single mothers who fail to give much credit to a babushka's efforts reflect broader societal values that consign unpaid care work to grandmothers on the basis of age and gender. In married heterosexual households, mothers are expected to do gender by taking on more of this devalued care work. Unwittingly perhaps, many single mothers accept the value of primary breadwinning over care work, leaving much of the latter to their children's grandmothers and obscuring the significance of grandmothers' contributions.

With few exceptions, single mothers assume that a grandmother's unpaid work is a natural result of feeling sorry for daughters and loving them; others are quite candid about their mother's lack of alternative options. Svetlana, a single mother working in a male-dominated profession as a taxi driver, minimized her debt to her mother, Alla. Alla spent most of her time caring for Sveta's two children and cooking and cleaning for the family. Sveta highlighted her mom's lack of options as well as her love: although Sveta complained considerably about her mom's forceful personality and domineering nature, she shifted her tone when I asked why her mother helped her so much, given all of these conflicts. Sveta replied: "Well, she doesn't have much choice. She sees that there's no one else. And of course she loves them very much."

The gendered transition to capitalism playing out in Russia is very much dependent on how much the unpaid care work of society continues to be gendered from below, with grandmothers in most cases continuing to shoulder much of society's unpaid care work.[41] With cutbacks in state support for families and child care and single mothers' need to maintain a foothold in the workforce, the pressures grandmothers face to provide unpaid "help" are tremendous. Grandmothers are expected to derive their own sense of value primarily from conforming to ideal babushka expectations, but this is oc-

FIGURE 6. A grandmother helps her granddaughter get ready to go home after her first dance recital. Photograph by the author.

curring in a society where paid work has more value and status, for women as well as for men. In Russia as a whole, pushing the unpaid care work onto Russia's older generation of women postpones some of the thornier societal issues of who should be responsible for how much care work and why. In addition, it further entrenches care work as "women's work" in families.

In spite of this dependence on babushki, there were some single mothers among my informants, mainly those in Moscow, who hired nannies instead. Salaries are much higher in St. Petersburg and Moscow, and both of these more cosmopolitan cities feature more developed markets for child care. Women prefer in many cases to hire nannies to maintain their independence,[42] but the practice of turning to nannies extensively for child care is not yet widespread in provincial Russia.

Masculine values of autonomy and independence are prioritized in newly capitalist, neoliberal Russia, among women as well as men. Single mothers must earn money. But many also tend to distance themselves from the self-sacrifice associated with traditional femininity in Russia (even if they conform to other aspects of traditional femininity). Values of feminine self-sacrifice and selfless caregiving are mapped on to the bodies of older women. Older women are pressured to offer their unpaid labor to their families because of their age and because of age-related assumptions about family status. Single mothers do perform care work, value their children, and spend time with them. Yet at the same time, single mothers are keenly aware that their social value and worth as single mothers under market capitalism comes from economic success in what is often described by women as a "man's world" of work. Through earning money or attempting to do so, they prove their worth as good single mothers—not anyone's burden or a social problem. By focusing on breadwinning, single mothers demonstrate that they are competent women adapting well to postsocialism, even "on their own."

Many mothers present themselves as able to do everything single-handedly, when in practice a babushka makes this supermom strategy possible. Freedom is conceived of as more limited for older women, especially grandmothers. Grandmothers may want to care for grandkids and help adult daughters not only out of love but also because they find they are valued primarily for this kind of care. Constrained to perform unpaid work because of their age and family status and fearful about future implications of the state's retrenchment of support, some grandmothers do feel as if they have no choice but to help.

Single mothers without babushka support offer additional insights into this dominant pattern of taking babushki for granted. These mothers speak most poignantly about their child's lack of love or luck. Regardless of their material situation, these women often report feeling truly single because they lack the support that so many others take for granted. Twenty-five percent of mothers in my sample lacked babushka support.[43] A mother's unexpected death, illness, or residence in a distant city generally deprived these mothers of this critical social safety net, and these women palpably felt the lack nearly every day. Particularly in the post-Soviet era, when many people are experiencing the present as more insecure compared with a more stable and secure Soviet past replete with social guarantees, babushki signify a longed-for stability and probable support. A babushka's support helps single mothers feel even more secure than they do having a good job with a decent income. After all, as many women note, a job under market capitalism can be lost at any time. Single mothers without babushki, keenly aware of their disadvantage in this regard, are more verbally appreciative than other mothers of the Russian grandmother's contributions to the family.

For example, Zhenya, a neighbor of two working-class single mothers interviewed, has been taking care of her sick mother for several years. She chose to remain childless in large part because she feared raising a child without a babushka's assistance. Whenever her friend Alyona sang the praises of her boyfriend's attentions one evening, in terms of making her feel special and boosting her self-esteem, Zhenya reminded Alyona that her own mother deserved more gratitude. Alyona's mother, after all, often watched Alyona's daughter, grew vegetables for the family at her dacha, and cooked home-made meals—she truly deserved Alyona's gratitude. Because roles were re-versed in Zhenya's case (she was caring for her mother rather than her mother supporting her), Zhenya was more aware of the wide-ranging support that babushki provide. In talking about grandmothers' contributions to adult daughters, one night Zhenya proclaimed: "In this country as long as you have your mother, you're fine. A mother is the closest person a woman can have. She is one of your own, not a stranger as a husband can be, and only one of your own will not abandon you in a time of need."

Women who lose a mother unexpectedly after having counted on her sup-port feel vulnerable, insecure, and even guilty over their child being deprived of an essential part of growing up. Even though Tonya is poor and supple-ments her income by renting out a room in her apartment, she explained that she had been much more concerned about her daughter being deprived of time spent with a babushka when she decided to give birth alone. Wor-ries about a lack of material support paled in comparison to worries about having no mother at her side: "I was afraid of being alone. I considered the fact that I didn't have my mother at that time, I only had my old grand-mother. . . . Mothers here are very busy! Growing up I spent a lot of time with my babushka, talking to her. Yuliya doesn't have a babushka. I'm al-ways running around, cooking, going to the store. Therefore, she hasn't been very lucky." Unlike many women who feel compelled to bring at least one child of their own into the world whether or not there is a reliable father around, raising a child without one's own mother, for most, seems much more daunting. However much the lack of a father in the family departs from so-cietal ideals, it is hardly ever considered a tragedy. A lack of support from one's own mother, however, most often experienced when one's mother is deceased, ill, or lives far away, is almost always considered a monumental loss for women personally but also for their families and children. Women worry about how to raise children without a babushka's love and support. Single mothers seldom "choose" to bear children without counting on at least some support from their own mothers. Even if a minority of women later go it alone without babushki, many have counted on babushki during a limited, if critical, period of time when they were finishing a degree or acquiring additional skills to prepare them for supporting their families.

Considering the import of what is considered a babushka's love, self-sacrifice, and care, single mothers draw distinctions among mothers on the basis of the extensiveness of babushka support, diminishing the significance of marital status and even income in the process. Evgenia, for instance, links her insecurity at work to her lack of babushka support; her mother died in Siberia shortly before Evgenia's wedding: "Some women really like going to work. And they are calm . . . but you know which ones are calm? The women who generally like working have a babushka. In these cases, of course, you're at work, but you're at ease knowing that babushka is at least looking after the kids, making sure they get home. . . . There's an adult at home. It's a big deal." Just as single mothers assume that most babushki help their daughters, and vice versa, so they also assume that most husbands do not help their wives much beyond the traditionally male task of primary breadwinning. In this way, the amount of babushka support a mother can rely on greatly influences her expectations and career ambitions, in a way that husbands, given the rather low expectations women have of them, do not.

The presence of a babushka provides emotional and social supports that, while difficult to quantify, are just as (if not more) significant as material support. Like many women, Oksana described how her life changed with the breakup of the Soviet Union in familial rather than in political terms. For outsiders and for many Russians, the collapse of the Soviet Union was a huge, life-altering event. Yet for many women, other events were arguably more important to them, especially personal events such as a divorce or the loss of one's mother. These kinds of events sometimes trump even the Soviet Union's dissolution. Indeed, how a woman experienced this dissolution event in 1991 has a great deal to do with the amount of support in her life at that time. Oksana reflected: "In 1991 my mom died. For me *this* is the event of 1991. . . . The loss of support, well, it's impossible to even explain." Oksana contrasted her experience with that of her single-mother friend Lena: "When Lena is with her mother, well you can see how [Lena's mother] is all about her grandchild, how she'll provide support anytime."

Oksana, by any objective set of criteria, has access to more material resources than Lena, one of my closer informants. Still, Oksana longs for the kind of babushka support that Lena relies on daily. Russian single mothers are more aware of being really single when their own mother or other female kin support is not available, and this awareness is magnified by their sense of having been abandoned by both men and the state. When all else fails in Russia, typically it is one's own mother whom one can almost always expect to count on.

Given the cultural pressures women face to be strong and to demonstrate personal competence, single mothers in Russia do not frequently express vulnerability in the interview context. But vulnerability was clearly and poignantly expressed by single mothers lamenting the absence of a mother in their lives. Ludmila, a forty-two-year-old hairdresser and single mother who gave birth while unmarried only to unexpectedly lose her mother shortly thereafter, spoke about how much her mother's encouragement and promised support had shaped her decisions to have a child without a reliable man nearby. With the backup financial support of a successful brother in New York and an established clientele in Kaluga, Ludmila, like Oksana, is doing much better materially than many of the other single mothers I came to know. Yet because of the lack of babushka support in her and her daughter's life, she admitted to feeling quite vulnerable: "For me nothing is especially difficult. But simply because my daughter is small I don't have enough . . . well, she needs a babushka. She doesn't need a papa, for she kind of has a papa, I mean at least she knows that he is her papa. But she doesn't have enough of me. There isn't enough of me, as a mom. Because I am always out making money in order to support her well, so that she won't need for anything. Therefore, I don't spend enough time with her. She has no babushki to spend time with her. And because of this I worry a lot. I feel sorry for her when she goes to bed alone. She doesn't have enough kindness." Despite material success, Ludmila considers her family more insecure than most; it lacks a stable base that a babushka helps to provide. In contrast, many of the poorest single-mother families with babushka support function surprisingly well, with neither mother nor babushka feeling, as Ludmila does, that everything is on her own shoulders. Single mothers long, too, for a man's "strong shoulders" to lean on, but this strength is what women frequently seek or fantasize about in men, not something they feel confident they will necessarily find in reality. But having one's own mother around to rely on in times of need is critical for single mothers, both practically and emotionally.

Several mothers were at least able to benefit from a grandmother's support temporarily, and this, too, makes a tremendous difference for most women. The temporary support of a babushka enables women to pursue higher education or skills leading to a better job later on. Mothers making do without babushki pursue two main strategies to compensate for their lack— they cultivate babushka substitutes and work to make relations with them familial, and they emphasize the importance of their child's independence from a very young age. Ludmila, like most mothers in her situation, finds life hard without a babushka, but she eventually found an older woman to take over some of the tasks a grandmother provides. She stressed the emotional closeness of the relationship: "I now have a babushka who lives in our hallway. And she loves my daughter very much. She really helps me."

Other mothers place more emphasis on the independence and self-sufficiency of their children, teaching them to be self-reliant, responsible helpers. Nadia, for example, explained that although the state nurseries do not enroll children under one year of age, they made an exception in her son's case when they saw that "he could do everything for himself." Like Nadia, Zarya's children were home alone because she had few other choices while they were young, but she emphasized the independence she sought to foster in her kids: "I always trusted them, and they felt that I had confidence in them. Because of this, they somehow behaved responsibly." Single mothers have long been expected to prioritize primary breadwinning in addition to care work.

A babushka's support represents a kind of unsullied-by-the-market, idealized form of care. Babushki are expected to satisfy children's emotional needs for love while providing practical support to ease the burdens of working mothers. More work is given to grandmothers as a neoliberal state makes cuts to the supports that women count on in raising their families. A grandmother's own desires are rather invisible in this story. In spite of grandmothers' love and devotion, many feel pressured to comply with entrenched social expectations relegating babushki to unpaid second shift work on behalf of their adult daughters. When grandmothers do try to set some limits on the help they provide, many have a difficult time doing so. Both institutions and the force of cultural traditions shape the micropolitics of women's negotiations for mutual support.[44]

✎ Navigating Conflicts

Most grandmothers are beginning to express a desire to take more time for themselves, but working-class grandmothers feel somewhat less entitled. Age and gender relations are shaped by other axes of inequality, especially class. The transition to capitalism, however, diminishes some of these class effects because so many families consider the post-Soviet future unstable and unpredictable.[45] Rather than forming distinct groups of grandmothers, older women tend to vacillate between new discourses of femininity emphasizing self-fulfillment and older discourses foisting unpaid work on grandmothers. Grandmothers are increasingly trying to set limits on their support, but it is a struggle for many. Yana described this process of negotiation: "Let's assume she says, 'Mama, take Seriozha today,' but I say 'I can't.' Of course this happens at times! I can't say that I'm such an ideal babushka, that I do everything. No. But I can see for myself how she is doing, and if it's really needed, then naturally I help. But if she simply wants to rest, well then . . . no, I raised you, enough, you raise your own kids yourself. But generally we don't ever resent each other." Yana attempts to set limits on her support, but she still shows awareness of dominant cultural and institutional ideas framing the "ideal babushka" as one who does everything. Values of self-fulfillment are ascendant in Russia, and more grandmothers seek to pursue their own interests. But grandmothers struggle because these newer values of feminine self-care and leisure are expected to apply more to younger women.

Babushki sometimes differentiate between grandmothers who sacrifice themselves for the sake of adult children and those who care for themselves. Frequently, grandmothers who put some limits around their sacrifices are admired. Luba underscored the necessity of boundaries: "When my granddaughter was born, I clearly said to myself, yes, I'm a babushka. But not constantly. . . . I also have my own plans!" Luba admired babushki who did not lose themselves in their contributions to family: "Natalya Ivanovna took in her grandson at her own expense and now the parents are complaining. . . . And then there's Aleftina Mikhailovna—oh, how I admire that woman! She helps out only when she considers it necessary. She takes care of herself as a woman should—she reads, dresses well, devotes time to herself. But when she has free time, then sure, she says, 'I'll go buy some groceries for them.' That is, when it's not to the detriment of her own life." Luba aligns herself with a growing number of babushki who help adult daughters but also put some effort into taking care of themselves, insisting that their support be treated as a gift rather than taken for granted.

Nevertheless, grandmothers speak of enforcing limits more often than they do so. Cultural discourses often change faster than practices. In other cultural contexts, such as the United States, for instance, divorce culture—where marriage is optional and contingent and divorce is always an option—has given women some negotiating power vis-à-vis husbands. Hackstaff makes the important point that many women use aspects of divorce culture to achieve relational ends and to improve existing marriages.[46] But in Russia no culture of divorce exists between grandmothers and single mothers. Although women describe conflicts, the practice of withholding support or severing ties because of these mother–daughter conflicts remains rare.

Most conflicts occur when daughters fail to prioritize breadwinning sufficiently and take their youth-related privileges too far. Grandmothers complain about daughters spending insufficient time with children or too much time with boyfriends. The amount of care work women are expected to perform varies by age, but single mothers are criticized at times for unduly burdening babushki. Svetlana praised her mother, Nina, as a woman who can "do everything" but felt her own job entitled her to more leisure: "I seldom see the children. Babushka is the one most occupied with raising them, because I'm forced to earn money. . . . I have to relax and get rid of tension. I can't do this at home because there's always noise with the kids! My mom always shouts and screams at everyone. . . . But she knows everything so she's very serious support. . . . But she would like me to spend more time with the kids. We fight a lot over this." As to whether her mom wanted to spend so much time caring for her grandchildren, Svetlana dismissed the very question. Single mothers, especially those doing fairly well, are allowed to consider their own needs and desires in a way that older grandmothers are not. This leisure gap became obvious when I spent time at the family dacha. Svetlana slept in, and together we picked up a cake, arriving at the dacha shortly before Nina served a homemade multicourse lunch. After lunch, swimming, berry picking, and a brief siesta, Svetlana dressed to go out with her boyfriend for a while before work.

Meanwhile, Nina, after sweating over the stove top much of the day, spent the afternoon washing up, weeding, and supervising her grandchildren. Nina shrugged her shoulders, explaining: "Svetlana is in a better position now to earn money. So what can I do? I think she is doing the best she can." Later on, however, Nina grumbled: "Svetlana has no idea what mothers without support face in this country." Nina, who had raised her kids without any babushka support (her late husband had been a "useless alcoholic"), knew the struggles of unsupported motherhood firsthand. Svetlana's access to babushka support buttressed her already existing youth privilege.

Youth privilege, re-created daily in the process of doing gendered age, is real, strengthened by dominant cultural beliefs and institutional arrangements. However, relative youth is not always experienced as privilege at the individual level, especially for lower-class women lacking higher education. In a few cases, babushki become breadwinners while single-mother daughters manage the second shift. This division of labor was defined as temporary and aberrational. In other rare cases, single mothers chose to go without babushka support because of the difficult conditions accepting it demanded. Typically these grandmothers lived farther away, involving time and distance to get support, or grandmothers had competing commitments.

I was struck by how Lada, a thirty-year-old filter operator, feels guilty about not being able to earn more money; her inability to appropriately do gendered age makes her feel ashamed. In an interesting reversal from the usual division of labor between single mothers and grandmothers, Lada spends most of her time while not on the job occupied with never-ending housework. Because her parents earn decent money, she does all the work of the home, from hand washing laundry to doing repairs, and it is physically and mentally exhausting. She tries to frame the situation as temporary, yet she does not really see a way out of it as improving her educational credentials would take money and time she does not have.

Although better off economically, Inna is unusual in that her ex-husband, a wealthy New Russian, pays for her apartment and gives her a monthly allowance. She has difficult relations with her former husband and she hates feeling so dependent, yet at the same time she does not have to rely on her own mother as much as other women do. This provides some relief as she and her mother have such strained relations. Her mother, Raisa, is especially frustrated by Inna's generosity with non-kin and judges Inna for it: "Inna's husband sends her money for the children, but she has all sorts of dependents who attach themselves to her. We quarrel over this. We have constant disagreements over the way she lets herself waste her money and time. She spends her money not only on her sons but also on others. . . . Of course, she feeds and keeps her children, but she doesn't sufficiently carry out her duties." Raisa pursues interests of her own (a church group, taking private English lessons, etc.), yet claims she is ready to sacrifice for her grandchildren. But it is clear that Raisa has her own set of demands for Inna, and her help is contingent on Inna fulfilling these demands. Because Inna can survive on child support from her wealthy former husband, she resists pressures from her mother to change her lifestyle, reconciling herself to less support. Her mom, too, can survive thanks to her own father's generous military pension.

Though they might otherwise support one another more extensively, each has different ideas of what counts as support, and each woman is disappointed in how the other lives her life. Raisa feels that her traditional gift of self-sacrifice in raising Inna should merit a return in the form of Inna devoting all of her time to her kids and keeping money in the family. Inna longs for a modern gift of a mother willing to support her without micromanaging her life. So here the relationship suffered, and Inna was able to make do without as much support from her mother as some had. Still, Raisa serves as a kind of backup support should something fall through with the child support from Inna's former husband. Indeed, in spite of what Inna described as her mother's limited support, when I invited Inna and another friend to join me in Moscow one weekend, she was able to leave her children with her mom.

Even without her mom's support, Inna feels like a failed mother because she does not have a successful career as others expect her to have on the basis of her age and family status. Doing gendered age for single mothers means doing well in the market economy. Inna is struggling, with strained relations with her own mother and her former husband compounding her pressures. Her mother, Raisa, has her own elderly father, a senior-level war veteran, to care for at home, so she does not worry much about the attenuated support she offers her own daughter. In Russia, single mothers are generally privileged by their youth relative to grandmothers. Yet at the same time some women like Inna and Lada, finding success elusive, hardly feel privileged by the pressure, indeed the expectation, to be superwomen.

Russia's transition to capitalism is gendered, but age relations also shape family and gender dynamics, with single mothers benefiting from youth privilege. The silence of the state and much scholarship about age relations should change. Moreover, we cannot understand individual well-being in Russia without focusing on intergenerational support and older women. Grandmothers are shoring up Russian families, teaching many skills needed in the post-Soviet world.[47] Although grandmothers may love their children and want to help, they also feel constrained to prove their value by contributing unpaid caring labor, with scant recognition. Meanwhile, the state and society are free riding on Russia's older women, who not only work long days after retirement but who are called on to replenish a deficit simultaneously essential and devalued—feminine care and self-sacrifice.

Age relations systematically shape gender and class performances, with working-class grandmothers feeling even more constrained by age as a result of the state's retrenchment. This case study is only a starting point for understanding how age and gender get done in families of all kinds that rely on extended family support. Bengtson (2001) and other leading family researchers note that we must look beyond the nuclear family when asking whether families are still functional. Russia's single-mother families provide an example of families—despite the two-parent nuclear family ideals of women in these families—of women supporting one another reasonably well in the absence of much help from men or the state. Yet the health and stress levels of grandmothers are affected by these increased pressures to help, as the state and society continues to free ride on their labor.

Beyond how critical this grandmother–adult daughter support system is for women's well-being in Russia, the case has several implications for gender relations. Although women are constrained to do gendered age while remaining accountable to institutions and prevailing cultural beliefs about gender, age, and family status, the very success of women's support systems may reinforce men's more marginal family status. Western men, for instance, may have increased the amount of child care and household work they do over time not only as a result of feminism but also because of weak networks of relatives and minimal state supports for families. With Russian grand-mothers pressured to do gendered age through care work, men may feel as if their more active support is merely optional rather than essential.

Youth privilege is implicit in many families beyond Russia, part of pro-cesses that maintain gender inequality, particularly when buttressed by insti-tutional practices and cultural beliefs about which women are entitled to leisure or career fulfillment. Unpacking these age and gender relations should yield additional rich theoretical insights. While it is possible for single mothers and grandmothers to begin to value the equal sharing of paid work and care work, and to undo strictly gendered notions of who does what, structural factors in gendered labor markets often discourage change. The Russian state has withdrawn many supports for families, and while there is some evidence that political leaders recognize women's burdens, the state does little to ease them, leaving families to manage.[48] In the West, too, many good jobs are built around a masculine ideal worker who is available around the clock with no domestic responsibilities. Even when women can afford child care, the devaluation of care work and lack of societal and state support for it continues. Attention to age relations and older women should be part of remedying the devalua-tion of care work.

Women themselves frequently accept the devaluation of unpaid care work common in the broader society, having internalized wider assumptions. Per-haps they do so unintentionally, but in any case this still perpetuates age and gender hierarchies about what counts as work, where status lies, and who should handle the bulk of the work at home. Yet even when women want to change the status quo, to argue for their right to leisure or growth, with-out changes in policies or markets it is difficult to change gender and age arrangements that devalue "feminine" unpaid care work. It may also be dif-ficult to revalue care work without more men doing it.

Making the unpaid labor of Russia's older women, its babushki, visible is worthwhile. Certainly, the contributions of Russian grandmothers to families deserve to be recognized more fully. But this story of single mothers and grandmothers also reinforces the idea that care work must be recognized and revalued at the institutional level. Otherwise, older women are fighting an uphill battle, and single mothers are complicit in validating paid work to the detriment of "feminine" care work. Youth, after all, is by definition short-lived, its privileges precarious. Many single mothers are left to make do with-out any babushka support. And even "luckier" single mothers will eventually find themselves accountable for doing gendered age differently, faced with the bottomless expectations and more marginalized status of Russia's older women.

Although single mothers in Russia benefit most from the support of grand-mothers, given the marginalization of many men in households, grandmothers are often needed in married-mother households as well. Marital status is assumed to shape the lives of women forcefully, setting married mothers apart from those women labeled as single mothers. Yet I learned that this chasm between single and married mothers in Russia is not nearly as wide as the broader literature assumes. Most research still assumes that single mothers have it harder than married mothers. Certainly some do. But many do not. Given the pressures of Russian family life under capitalism, the lives of many mar-ried mothers bear an uncanny resemblance to the lives of single mothers. The Russian case of family change blurs the boundaries between single and married mothers, with many married mothers at times feeling single, or al-most single, as they manage home, work, and children without the kind of support they would like from partners.

↝ CHAPTER 5

Blurred Boundaries

Married Mothers and the Specter
of Single Motherhood

> Sometimes I'm even envious of those women
> raising their kids alone. Sure, it must be difficult,
> especially materially, but it seems to me that their
> lives are calmer and more peaceful. I'm envious of
> their courage. . . . Of course, it was probably difficult
> for them, but they managed to get a hold of
> themselves and divorce.
>
> —Olga, thirty-four-year-old married mother of two,
>   factory worker

Climbing the stairs to their fifth-floor walk-up
apartment, I literally bumped into Sergei, Olga's husband, in the narrow stairwell. Returning from work, he was stumbling and his speech slurred. His
breath reeked of alcohol. When Olga heard us and opened the door, she
managed a weary smile, directing me toward a table in the living room set
with tea and cookies. At the same time, she began whispering and guiding
her husband into the kitchen, reminding him that he was supposed to go
over to his friend's place and that dinner would not be ready for two hours.
He pleaded with her to let him stay at home, dropping down onto a kitchen
chair. Sergei sat there sulking, scowling at a small kitchen television.

I had met Olga and Sergei at least once previously, but I suggested, considering the circumstances, that we reschedule for a better time. Olga would
hear nothing of it. The situation felt awkward, but for Olga, a petite, soft-
spoken woman with shortly cropped blond hair, this was clearly, apart from
my presence, a fairly ordinary day. Olga treated Sergei like a wayward child
whose behavior was annoying but had nevertheless ceased to surprise. As it
was a beautiful summer evening with a slight breeze and their kids were away
at an overnight camp, Olga suggested to Sergei that he meet his friend Boris
for a stroll or a smoke as planned, but Sergei declared that it was his house

and he would remain in it. He emerged periodically to tell us he was getting bored and to ask whether we were done talking yet. Olga shooed him away dismissively each time and continued talking.

When Sergei eventually joined us in the living room, he proudly showed me the family's photos, paging through a few albums until he found their wedding photos. "Life was pretty grand before kids," Sergei declared. Glancing at the album, Olga's expression was blank. She mused: "I should not have married so young. I still wanted to hang out with my girlfriends and dance and have fun." Her face brightened only when she showed me photos from a recent excursion to St. Petersburg she took with her daughter, a trip heavily subsidized by her factory's labor union. Olga and her family get by on an extremely tight budget, living month to month, with little left over for holidays and trips, even within Russia.

Olga's life is one of quiet desperation. During the interview, she stoically described feeling stuck in an unhappy, burdensome marriage for just one reason. Sergei, who works at her factory as a milling machine operator, earns twice her salary. Were it not for her husband's paycheck, Olga "would have divorced him long ago." She cannot fathom saving enough to rent a separate apartment on what she earns, especially considering the costs of two children. And if she perhaps had ended up with one child instead of two, she wondered aloud (interjecting to tell me about her neighbor Diana, who divorced her husband recently and seems much happier), she might have mustered the courage necessary to divorce her husband.

Vodka, however, is cheap. In spite of his drinking, her husband still contributes a significant amount of money to the family. Sergei usually drinks five days a week, generally on workdays. Most of the factory men drink; the bosses look the other way because good specialists are hard to find. He has been violent toward her in the past but usually when drinking to the point of utter oblivion. Thankfully, this has not happened in a few years. Olga had a lover for three years, a married man who helped her materially, but once it really sunk in for him that some of his money would end up subsidizing Sergei, they went their separate ways. She hopes life will at least remain stable, even though stability is hardly a given in Russia.

Although Olga's mother lives on the other side of town and suffers from failing health, her mom is her main source of practical support. When their son was seriously ill, her mother took over at home and cared for their school-age daughter. When the kids were little, she came over daily to serve a hot lunch and help them with homework until Olga got home from work. For moral support, Olga turns to her best friend, Alla.

Olga feels single in many ways. In feeling single while married, she is hardly an anomaly. Other married mothers routinely arrange for their own mothers to care for children in their own absence or illness, attributing this to men's irresponsibility. Others worry over the poor health or drinking habits of husbands given that men die so early, preparing themselves psychologically in advance for the possibility of becoming single. Still others feel lonelier than ever while raising a child single-handedly, especially if they suspect a husband's philandering or other signs of indifference. Feeling isolated is more likely when mothers lack extended family support or when their husbands contribute only a small portion of their salaries toward the family's needs.

Single motherhood is hardly a self-evident category describing a subgroup of women. Instead, single motherhood is a falsely homogenizing category given the diversity of women who end up single and the differing income levels and support systems of single mothers. But single mothers are also not uncommon even among the partnered. Beyond the officially single, there are many quasi-single mothers: married mothers who are solely responsible for their family's welfare.[1] Even mothers who do not consider themselves quasi-single know other mothers who are. Some feel single as they work to hold their families together, to maintain a semblance of partnership for the children or because they fear life outside of marriage for a woman with children under neoliberal market capitalism. When we look beyond the statistics, which can end up reifying differences on the basis of constructed categories, distinctions based on marital status are not necessarily meaningful. Single motherhood functions as a metaphor in women's lives. In particular, it is a metaphor for how supported or unsupported women feel as mothers, regardless of marital status.

Resignation is the dominant mood among married mothers in Russia. Few exude the confidence and determination that most single mothers do. Most single mothers, even though they also feel resigned on occasion, overwhelmingly present themselves in terms of moving forward, becoming stronger and more confident, focusing on concrete goals, and learning to take better care of themselves as well as their children. Of course, it goes without saying that there are happily married women in Russia, and these women have their own distinct stories to tell. But part of what is most distinctive about contentedly married women in Russia is their very conviction that they are exceptionally lucky. The contentedly married with whom I spoke describe hitting the jackpot with their husbands, feeling as if they should not talk about their happy home lives with too many other women at work, fearing resentment.

They know their situation is rare, and considering the pressures on families during the transition to market capitalism, the resigned group is likely larger, with many married mothers resembling Olga. Although married mothers do not necessarily dream of divorce to the extent that Olga does, many still resign themselves to living with less-than-ideal circumstances at home, thankful to have a bit of extra income or proud that they have managed to hold their families together in spite of difficulties. But married mothers can hold their heads up high only if husbands refrain from having serial affairs, withholding money from the family, or drinking to the point of public embarrassment. There are plenty of marriages where these patterns do not recur. Yet there are plenty more where such patterns are painfully prevalent.

Given Russia's culture of divorce, it should not be surprising that the specter of single motherhood also affects most married mothers. As in other countries where divorce affects close to half of all marriages, marrying, especially in the post-Soviet period, is increasingly optional and contingent, with divorce a reliable option.[2] Some women are more affected than others, but many married mothers, too, are influenced by the ubiquity and normalcy of single motherhood, regardless of the state of their marriages.

My approach to married mothers is somewhat unconventional. I take single motherhood as a norm in Russian society and then consider how the lives of married mothers may share some features in common with single mothers. In family scholarship, marital status remains a primary basis for dividing mothers into groups, with married mothers assumed to be the "normal" group of mothers while single mothers (even if implicitly) require more explanation as departures from a norm. An unchallenged assumption is that single mothers heading families of their own differ dramatically from married mothers in two-parent families. Some studies assume that women who divorce are different from other women to begin with, whereas other studies frame the experience of divorce or relationship dissolution as decisive in changing women. Whatever the reason, distinctions of marital status dividing women persist.

Marital status distinctions among women may indeed be valid for many questions but certainly not for all of them. There is much to learn about the character of ordinary women's lives from probing the similarities among women with varied marital statuses,[3] all the more so during times of transition and family instability. In Russia today, differences of marital status mean much less than many assume. Rather than extrapolating about mothers on the basis of marital status differences, we should probe whether and how marital status matters, especially where families frequently function matrifocally. Russian women routinely suggest that marital status does not really matter all that much. It seldom offers guarantees, protections, or even status for women in the post–Soviet period, and women's views on this should be taken more seriously by scholars. Ethnography can illuminate the blurred boundaries between single and married mothers.

The de facto predominance of matrifocal families in Russia, in spite of nuclear two-parent family ideals, complicates any easy assumptions about the primacy of marital status in women's lives. If we set aside the issue of how family breakup affects children and examine the experience of single motherhood as an increasingly common phase in many women's lives, we learn that many of the challenges single mothers cope with are shared by a wider group of married mothers. A more thorough understanding of what it means to be a single mother requires examining the contours of married women's lives, whether we are considering the happily married, the quasi-single, or the many resigned mothers in this larger group of women.

✎ Potential Single Mothers

Considering Russia's culture of divorce, its history of marginalized and absent men alongside the centrality of grandmothers, and the challenges that the transition to market capitalism poses for so many families, single motherhood is becoming more prevalent as a prototype of family life. This is not to say that Russians do not value marriage. Most Russians marry, quickly and relatively early.[4] But divorce has long been an accessible option, all the more so in recent years given lessened stigma surrounding all forms of single motherhood, and many married mothers have at some point considered divorce. Most married mothers also know single mothers as friends, colleagues, neighbors, and relatives.

Families were fragile in the late Soviet period, as evidenced by high divorce, but families are more fragile than ever today. Since the collapse of the Soviet Union, the reduction in state supports, loosened constraints tying men to families, and new pressures of market capitalism have combined to increase the strain on families of all kinds. More so than before, a larger number of Russian mothers are potential single mothers. This reality is obscured if we examine single and married mothers separately, as if they were two different species.[5]

Furthermore, single mothers seldom compare their lives with the lives of men or with the lives of the small minority of women without children in Russia. But they do compare their lives with the lives of married mothers, whether it is a comparison with their own experiences as married mothers (for those who divorced) or with the married mothers they perceive around them. Many married mothers think that they should, just in case, be able to manage on their own. They frequently feel like single mothers, more or less raising their children on their own, without sufficient involvement from their children's father. As they work and care for children and a home, married mothers often receive the most practical support from their own mothers nearby. Finally, like single mothers, whether they include their husbands among Russia's weak men or exclude their husbands as exceptions to the general rule, married mothers in Russia share the negative cultural discourse on men and the state so common among single mothers.

Previous chapters have examined how single mothers must make do with lives that depart from the two-parent nuclear family ideal. Many married mothers, too, routinely make do with, and resign themselves to, family lives that bear little resemblance to what they desire. Beyond Russia, women in many industrialized countries are changing rapidly, and their expectations of men are changing as well. Most scholars agree that women, on average, are changing more quickly than either men or the state. It may be that the incentives for women to change are greater because of the money and status associated with masculine domains. Perhaps there are insufficient incentives for men to rush into traditionally feminine, and devalued, domains of housework and child care, at least without a broader social movement demanding it. In any case, when women are changing faster than men and the state, societies are stuck with an uneven and stalled revolution in gender relations and family life.[6]

At the very least, some of the presumed differences between single and married mothers, especially in today's Russia, where extended family supports frequently trump marital status in shaping women's lives, are more accurately differences of degree rather than of kind. In a fragile family context, there is a fine line—rather than a wide chasm—separating the lives of single and married mothers.

Studying the Center: Married Mothers

To illuminate distinctions of marital status permeating mothers' lives, I interviewed twenty married mothers raising children under the age of eighteen at the time of interview, covering most of the same interview themes as with single mothers.[7] I talked to about a dozen more married mothers informally over time about topics overlapping with formal interview themes. Mothers were officially married (rather than cohabiting with a male partner) and in their first, still intact marriage. Using my existing networks, which included both single and married women, I created a snowball sample, never interviewing more than two women from the same network. Many of the women in my personal networks who recommended married mothers for me to interview had no connection to my research on single mothers. While the sample is neither random nor representative, I sought a range of age, income, occupation, and educational levels, and there is no reason to believe that the sample is somehow unrepresentative of married Russian mothers living in midsized cities. Using personal networks allowed me to gather richer interview data, gaining the trust of mothers.

Field notes and observations were essential for fleshing out the interview data. For example, as we saw in chapter 2, single mothers repeatedly claim that they feel freer since they no longer have to wait on husbands, a finding reflecting the starkly unequal gender division of household labor in Russia.[8] Through interviewing married mothers, I witnessed many everyday aspects of marital relationships, which provided several important clues, such as when Olga shooed Sergei into the kitchen and admonished him as one might a small child. When I interviewed forty-two-year-old Lida, she explained that her husband thinks women should mainly cook and clean but that he has gotten somewhat better in terms of his chauvinism over time. Yet during our interview, her husband arrived home much earlier than expected. All conversation abruptly stopped. Lida scrambled madly to heat up the borscht, cut bread, and prepare a second course as her husband sat silently at the kitchen table, waiting to be served while flipping through the newspaper. He began speaking to his wife only after his soup and cutlery had been placed in front of him. Conversation turned to questions about America, and although I ended up joining the family for dinner at their insistence, Lida and I finished talking another day. Field notes capturing these interactions illuminate further not only the lives of married mothers but the meaning of single motherhood—especially single mothers' accounts of dramatically reduced gender deference as a key advantage to life as a single mother.

In most cases, informal observations supported interview data. The vivacious and outgoing Masha presented herself as the happiest of mothers mostly because of her good fortune with her husband; informal interactions corroborated her words. I witnessed the joking camaraderie in her household and the appreciation she and her husband had for one other's contributions. Masha's husband joined us for a brief toast but then went to play with the kids and help them with homework. During a tea break, she pointed out his handiwork throughout the apartment (e.g., a wooden shelf here, the installation of a new light fixture there) while he effusively praised her good design sense and the intricate needlework hung prominently on several walls. I also saw her husband out with their two young kids alone (not the most common sight in Kaluga) while out running my own errands.

Furthermore, I lived with families (both married and single-mother) during fieldwork. Compared with the calm that pervaded most interviews with single mothers as well as time spent living with a single mother and her child, the married household featured more yelling, tension, and conflict. I am not suggesting that one married couple household is in any way typical of the diversity of families in Kaluga, but observations there did coincide with what I was learning in interviews, solidifying some patterns. The father in the family notably did not appear to drink heavily or have affairs—indeed, he was considered the ultimate family man by his wife—and while he worked full-time to financially support the family, the mother did almost all of the work of raising their daughter and maintaining the home, from helping with homework to cooking meals, shopping for the family's food and clothing, canning fruits and vegetables for winter, and doing household chores, even though she was also employed as well as studying part-time. While demanding a great deal of his wife's care, this father was still at the margins of the family's life, connected mainly through his economic contributions to the household.[9]

Surprisingly, too, it was somewhat difficult to even find mothers in intact marriages to interview. Many of my acquaintances thought they knew married women with minor-age children, only to learn that several women had been married for a short time previously, that others had been separated for a time, or that a married woman's child was from a previous relationship. Sometimes women told me they were married, but after further probing it turned out to be an unregistered marriage. These experiences only further corroborate the increasingly fluid nature of marital status in contemporary Russia.

Single Motherhood as Metaphor

Tamara, a married mother of a nine-year-old daughter, was not sure where she fit in my study design. She let me know right away that although she is technically married, her experiences might fit better into the category of single mothers. She explained: "Practically speaking, I feel like a single mother. Because I'm with my daughter from morning till night, and I've been with her on my own from the very beginning. My husband never really took part in raising her." She was in more of a rush to marry than he was since they were living in Estonia at the time, and although she wanted a child and he agreed, he already had two children from two previous marriages.

The meaning of single motherhood varies for women, many of whom do not even consider themselves single mothers at all depending on the level of kin and social support in their lives. Mothers without any support from their own mothers for one reason or another, regardless of income, tend to feel more single than single mothers who can count on a babushka's support. Tamara, though officially married for several years, feels single most of the time and thinks of divorce often because of her husband's frequent absence and disengagement from child rearing. She spent the summer with her daughter at her mother's place in a small provincial town about fifty minutes outside of Kaluga, but her husband never visited them. "Not even once," Tamara added. Marriage itself does not mean much anymore for Tamara, and she is not certain that it ever did. But she has to think of her child. Her husband provides additional income her daughter needs; and her daughter loves her dad.

State policies and historical circumstances shape the importance of marital status in women's lives. Whether the boundaries between single and married women are more or less permeable, the boundaries shape, too, how single mothers feel. Although it is seldom conceptualized as such, marital status serves as a social marker akin to other categories of difference, such as race, class, gender, sexuality, and age. The meanings surrounding marital status are fluid and constructed by states. Despite the postwar demographic crisis in Germany, for instance, in which there were many more women than men, the East German state did not treat surplus women as a major social problem and narrowed the difference between single and married women. West Germany did the opposite, creating and reinforcing distinctions based on marital status.[10]

The postwar Soviet state favored a more mixed approach. The Soviets de-emphasized the differences among various kinds of single mothers (e.g., between widowed mothers and the unmarried) and sanctioned adultery to increase the birthrate. But at the same time, the postwar Soviet state maintained firm boundaries between married and unmarried women. Only officially married women could count on financial support from the fathers of their children, freeing fathers who sired children with unmarried women.

There are some remnants in Russia of the Soviet status differences whereby having been married (if not actually being married) is considered higher status than having never been married, but a great deal has also changed. In today's Russia, both the state and society blur distinctions between married and single mothers. Rather than concerning itself with marital status, the state is focused on solving what it sees as the national demographic problem: the low birthrate.

Recent policies in Russia attest to the state's efforts to collapse differences in marital status while providing new incentives for the childbearing of wage-earning working mothers. Since 2007 the state has been offering increased benefits for all mothers who give birth to a second child. Most of these benefits take the form of a "ten-thousand-dollar voucher that they can apply toward housing."[11] Although it is the largest baby bonus in the world (relative to income), many Russians find it lacking as it pays for only a small portion of the costs of child rearing and cannot cover even a minimum down payment on a home. These recent policies do more than flatten distinctions of marital status; they also continue to marginalize men in families and further naturalize the idea that "women bear the main burden of bearing a child and bringing it up."[12]

The state is somewhat involved in trying to shape families through its explicit pro-natalist policies, but it still considers the balance of work and family a woman's issue. It does not mention fathers and men in family policy; mothers and "young families" are mentioned instead. Yet the state does not single out the rising number of single mothers or nonmarital births, even though it could easily do so and many other states have. This state involvement in trying to shape women's childbearing decisions still does not negate the more general pattern of the state's retrenchment in tangible supports for women and children since the Soviet Union's collapse. At the societal level, too, differences between women of varying marital statuses are much less important than they were in Soviet times. Ordinary Russians routinely say that marriage is not a guarantee of anything but literally is instead a stamp in one's passport, just as marriage was marked in internal passports during Soviet times.

Besides the permeable boundaries between single and married mothers at the state and societal levels, the continuing importance of social networks and connections in shaping Russian women's identities also keeps boundaries between single and married mothers permeable. Numerous scholars have demonstrated the significance of social networks, connections, and *blat* in daily life in Russia, with most arguing that social networks continue to shape people's lives, though perhaps to a somewhat lesser extent than in Soviet times, in the post-Soviet period. For example, in Caldwell's (2004) study, Muscovite soup kitchen recipients did not see hunger as a problem in Russia; rather than material scarcity, hunger had more to do with whether one had access to adequate social networks, and eating at the soup kitchen meant one must have access to important networks. Caldwell argued: "Thus, the word *hunger* is better understood as a marker of the extent and durability of one's social wealth as expressed through networks, whereas *aloneness* is the idiom through which concerns with material poverty are articulated and understood."[13]

In a parallel manner, single motherhood is not necessarily seen as a problem today in Russia, or at least it is not seen as a problem of women. Many single mothers are respected and admired as long as they support their families and adopt the dominant code of practical realism. However, "singleness" and "aloneness" are idioms through which all kinds of mothers reflect on the circumstances of their family lives and, specifically, how supported they feel as mothers raising children in today's Russia.

Even in strictly material ways, the lives of married and single mothers in Russia are more similar than most assume. Scholars of Russia have argued that "women who live with male partners, but who are responsible economically for their households, face problems much like those of lone mothers."[14] Kanji (2004) challenged stereotypes of single mothers as the poorest of the poor in Russian society, highlighting the high levels of income inequality among different kinds of single-mother households. Kanji emphasized that "Leaving 'woman-maintained' households out of the picture results in underestimation of the number of children living in lone-mother or 'quasi-lone-mother' households."[15] In the case of post-Soviet Russia, the blurred boundaries between single-mother and married but "woman-maintained" households is particularly relevant in light of scholarship arguing that Russian women, whether married or single, continue to manage households' "survival strategies."[16] While Burawoy, Krotov, and Lytkina make a stronger claim that women frequently direct and manage their households in terms of earning money, other scholars concur that women are responsible for managing budgets in households, "so the burden of providing for the household from the meagre resources available tends to fall to the woman."[17] Indeed, depending on how money is distributed in married-couple households, many married mothers have less control over their family's well-being than do single mothers.

✎ Dilemmas of Divorce

Divorce culture shapes all kinds of marriages. Fourteen of the twenty mothers in my sample had seriously considered divorce at some point during their marriages. Many single mothers, too, had talked about feeling like a single mother for years before filing for divorce or breaking up with their child's father. Some married mothers are envious of single mothers' courage to divorce, especially because women often find that their lives improve post-divorce, after a rocky transitional period.

Married women's reasons for considering divorce mirror closely the reasons given by single mothers. They consider divorce because of a spouse's alcoholism or heavy drinking (six women); financial problems (notably, not a husband's lack of a job but his unwillingness to stay at a job or to contribute more than a small portion of his salary toward the household while spending more time and money away from home) (four women); chronic infidelity (three women); and a husband's refusal to allow his sick mother-in-law to live with the family (one woman). Frequently the reasons overlapped, as they did with single mothers, such as when a woman's alcoholic husband did not help at all with the children or home or when a woman found out that her husband, who spends little time at home, was also involved with another woman.

Married women generally concur with the negative discourse on men so commonly used by single mothers, but it helps them to instead stay married or discourages future entanglements with men. For single mothers, using the negative discourse on men helps women to conform to the practical realism expected of them, demonstrating their competence as single mothers. But for married mothers, if men are unreliable, then it is highly doubtful mothers will be able to find anyone better than their current husbands should they divorce. So if married mothers (or their children) gain any benefits from remaining married, even in spite of considerable problems, accepting a negative discourse on men makes sense. For example, Tamara had used the negative discourse when explaining why she married in the first place. She did not love her husband and marriage meant little to her, but she wanted a baby and sought Estonian citizenship for her daughter. She used the negative discourse on men to explain why she married when she did: "I was afraid of ending up without a child. I was already getting on in years, and I would have had to find someone else with whom I could have a baby if I hadn't met my husband. Here in Russia it's not so simple! Many men drink, many cheat, many smoke. To find a guy with whom you can have a healthy baby, that's really a challenge."

☛ Narrowly Escaping Divorce

Though I had expected married mothers to be somewhat reticent to discuss divorce, most had a lot to say on the subject. Lusya, a thirty-six-year-old married mother who operates a small secondhand clothing stall at a local market, sighed, exclaiming: "I constantly think about divorce. I had the chance to get out before but now it's hard. And basically I've decided to just leave it be for now. It would probably be easier for me to live alone, even with our child. I don't think he'd completely forget about his child, he'd help some materially. Psychologically it would be easier to be alone." Lusya's comment that "psychologically it would be easier to be alone" confirms that much has changed since the late Soviet era, when unwed motherhood, and to a lesser extent divorce, still carried some stigma. Apart from her husband's paycheck, Lusya is raising her daughter alone. Her husband is on his third marriage with kids and was already the father of three kids from previous marriages when she got pregnant with their daughter. Psychologically, Lusya elaborated, it is hard being married when you keep expecting, or at least hoping, for support to come your way since that is what people still expect married women to have; at least when a woman is single, she mused, she knows she is truly on her own. For Lusya, the partnership marriage is merely a mirage. "For some reason even today I still feel single. I don't feel married because I am always handling difficult situations by myself."

In addition, Lusya has not divorced because her daughter, in spite of her husband's absence from 7 a.m. until 11 p.m. most days, still looks forward to seeing her father. Lusya's husband is involved in "some sort of business," but she also has no idea what he really does, much less what he earns. She always has to ask him for money since her earnings from the clothing stall are so modest. She feels alone, and the idiom of single motherhood helps her in making sense of her situation.

Although Lusya still lives with her husband, other married women have husbands who are away more than half of the time. Sonya's husband drives a taxicab in Moscow, and Irina's husband is a cargo pilot spending at least half of every year overseas. Distance may put significant stresses on marriage, but in these cases women saw distance as redemptive, even beneficial for the marriage. Their economic circumstances were quite different, with both women getting little money from their husbands, but Sonya had a more difficult time making ends meet in her husband's absence. However, she had more control over the money she spent in her husband's absence and could stretch it further because kids and women, in her view, do not require luxuries many men expect, such as meat at every meal. Unlike Sonya, Irina earned enough money herself to support her kids, so she did not worry as much about when her husband would next return home. Both women argued that distance from their husbands allowed them to preserve their marriages. The women showed some pride in their ability to preserve their marriages, against the odds.

A forty-two-year-old chemist-turned-cosmetologist with two teenage sons, Irina frequently feels like a single mother in her marriage but still identifies as married because she has managed to hold some semblance of a family life together. Moreover, she is proud that she has adapted to the new economy, even though this meant leaving her first love of chemistry several years ago for a more lucrative field, cosmetology. She now earns enough money to support her family single-handedly. She had really only considered divorcing her husband several years earlier, when he was drinking a lot. Now that her husband is away much of the time, she has no plans to divorce him: "My husband is a pilot. I married him right away, and I've had one marriage from the very beginning. The marriage has been preserved . . . well, I can't say for sure, but I think it's only because my husband is often away on business trips. It's probably simpler this way." Irina's comment about things being simpler with an absent husband echoes what many single mothers say about feeling that their lives became simpler after a divorce or breakup.

Married women like Irina who have seriously contemplated divorce describe a crisis point in their marriages and then explain how and why they managed to turn the crisis around, if not completely, then to the point where they could still remain married. In Irina's case, after her husband lost his job as a pilot in the mid-1990s, he had started drinking heavily and refused to work at jobs he considered beneath him, jobs where he would not be wearing "a white shirt and tie." Fed up with his drinking, which affected the family seriously (e.g., he ordered her and the kids to serve him when he came home drunk late at night), Irina literally threw him out one night. She described putting him outside with a suitcase of clothing and calling his mother to pick him up and take him away. He returned after three days, promised to stop drinking, and went to work as a cabinetmaker. Within a few months, a friend's husband got Irina's husband a new job as an overseas pilot. He has not entirely stopped drinking, but during the six months a year when he is around, he manages to keep it away from the family. This is Irina's main condition. In terms of infidelity or spending money outside the family, she imagines both likely. "There are worse problems in the world than an affair here or there," Irina remarked, noting that with the kind of travel and time away her husband spends on the job, she prefers to simply refrain from asking questions.

In these narratives, women tell of narrowly escaping divorce and being forced to take circumstances into their own hands. Women work hard to domesticate men, whether this means managing men's drinking or keeping other problems away from the family, and some take pride in their ability to do so. After all, it is due to women's skill in keeping their men in line, according to these narratives, that the "structure" of the two-parent family, if not every aspect of the ideal, is preserved.

While some married mothers work on managing men's drinking or other habits, others speak of preserving their marriages mainly for the sake of their children, whether it is giving children access to more economic resources or enabling them to have the example of a two-parent household. Varvara, a thirty-seven-year-old manager for her husband's business, is married with two teenage sons, and although she lived better materially than most respondents, married or single, it was a difficult interview. Her husband has been openly cheating on her for the past six years, and she finds this humiliating given her position of near-total dependence on him. She tries to rationalize his behavior with the explanation that maybe it is simply that men have sexual needs different from those of women, but her husband cheats openly, to the point where others in their upper middle-class business circles know what is going on. Varvara admires the courage of single mothers, though some might be a bit "hasty" in ending their marriages compared with the perseverance of married mothers. She believes that growing up in an intact family is important for her boys; she wants them to have a two-parent family model, even if she knows it is not the fully functioning model her heart desires.

For women like Varvara, staying married takes tremendous emotion work. She conceals her husband's affairs from her sons, but with some difficulty. In her efforts to remain married, she uses elements of the negative discourse on men, pointing out that many husbands, especially in Russia, are so much worse than her own. She tries to feel differently about the infidelity that is so hard to accept. Because her husband has a chronic skin condition and cannot relate easily to women, perhaps he really needs sex more than she does, Varvara wonders, her voice trailing off a bit. Her husband is more easily drawn into relationships with women; other men might just arrange quick one-night stands to satisfy their desires, but for her husband, perhaps, it is all more complicated: "I try to give him a break because he cannot meet women easily and this is why he probably ends up having these long affairs. He has a lover constantly, and he gets something from her that he doesn't get enough of from me. So be it. Because there are other men who just go to prostitutes, that's also a variant, you know? But he doesn't feel he can do this because of his skin condition. So I'm trying to make peace with the situation. It's not always easy."

Varvara's experiences and her attempts at normalizing a husband's behavior, which she finds painful and even abhorrent, provide some context for what single mothers perceive around them. Both single and married motherhood involve a series of difficult trade-offs for many women. To assume that one group of mothers is selfish or another group self-sacrificing demonstrates a profound ignorance for what real women encounter in relationships, especially given Russia's fragile family and insecure work context alongside a resurgence of neotraditional and patriarchal ideas. Varvara still cannot believe that the man to whom she is married went to live with his lover for seventeen days a few months ago and during that time never once asked about the children. She wonders aloud whether the sex could have been so amazing to the point where he would forget his own children. But then she shifted gears and said: "But he's a reserved person. I think. . . . No, I'm *sure* that in his soul he was very worried." The ambivalence that single mothers frequently feel about the advantages and disadvantages of their marital status is shared by many married mothers.

Reminiscent of many single mothers, who argue that their children help them in life, Varvara, too, takes refuge in compulsory, and ultimately compensatory, motherhood. Motherhood compensates, in part, for the lack of a loving husband. Varvara described why she became a mother in a manner similar to how many other women did: "One always wants to have someone close. Recently a famous actress of ours, a single mother of two sons, said: 'I gave birth to people who will love me. Because a man will love you today and change his mind tomorrow.' . . . When you have children, they will love you just as you love them." Tellingly, Varvara's account even compares her own reasons for having children with the reasons of a single mother, once more blurring marital-status distinctions. Many Russian women feel that this unconditional kind of love is found more frequently between mothers and children. Varvara corrected herself and added, though sounding as if she were not yet entirely convinced: "well, perhaps this love can exist between some *parents* and their children."

Like Varvara, other married mothers describe efforts to make peace with situations that involve putting up with behaviors they find unacceptable, such as unfaithfulness, spending a lot of money and time away from the family, and heavy drinking. Aleftina finds it very difficult to stay married because her husband leaves early, comes home late, earns very little money, and only then gives half of what he earns to the family. She cannot understand how he can force her to turn to her own parents for financial support when he is spending money on himself rather than on the family. For now, her husband has convinced her that they should stay together for their son's sake. Still, she finds it hard to avoid feeling like she is destroying herself to stay married: "For Gleb's sake we've been trying to get along. I've working on changing my outlook. It didn't happen overnight. I don't want to say that I changed for the worse, that I just made peace with everything and suppressed myself as a person. No. But I started to behave differently. . . . I stopped feeling hostile about him bringing home a small salary and then only giving half of it to the family. I decided that as long as I can make sure that we have enough, we can go on living."

Married women such as Aleftina recount in painstaking detail how difficult it is for women to ensure that their husbands respect their contributions at home and at work. Aleftina manages to leave work at 3 p.m. every day to spend time with her son and supervise his homework. She constantly reminds her husband that she is contributing the same amount of money to the family that he is—after all, her entire salary equals his half—while also holding up everything else on the home front. In contrast to her husband, she comes home from work and starts her second shift, what she refers to as her *vtoraia smena*. Paradoxically, it is paid work that allows her to respect herself and earns her the respect of others, yet paid work does not appear to be enough to earn her husband's respect; besides, there is still so much unpaid work to be done. Aleftina explains: "I want to feel important. A job gives me more confidence, as a person and as a woman alongside a man."

The lack of societal value given to women's unpaid labor on behalf of their families is well known; it is typical for female caregiving work to be taken for granted.[18] Certainly, Russia is not the only case of the extent to which women's unpaid labor is undervalued. Russia, however, is a glaring, almost extreme case of this persistent phenomenon and the double bind women then so frequently find themselves in. Married women believe the bulk of housework and child care is their inexorable duty as women, but women are acutely aware that this work is not institutionally valued. In society, even more so now under neoliberal market capitalism than in late socialism, women feel they must earn respect as paid workers and not just as housewives. Women discount the unpaid work that they do routinely, typically refusing to count it as work at all, but married mothers do this more frequently, even though married mothers do more of it than single mothers. When I asked Vera, a twenty-two-year-old mother of a two-year-old son, about her typical day, she visibly flushed as she replied: "Oh, right now it's just the day of a housewife. Nothing interesting I'm afraid." Her commitment to work is absolute, she loves to work and yearns to make something of herself, but these days it is hard finding affordable day care for any child under three years old. She is the kind of woman who takes pride in being able to "work all day every day, from 8 in the morning till 8 at night." But because her own mother is still working and intends to remain doing so, she has no other choice but to stay at home a while longer. To engage in unpaid care work means that one is disadvantaged in the struggle for better jobs.

Although married, Vera fervently believes in divorce. She is glad that divorce has become more socially acceptable and that women no longer need to humiliate themselves by staying married to men who abuse them or are alcoholics. Before beginning the interview, I was making what I thought was small talk, asking her how she came to know Lena, the single mother who had suggested Vera as a potential respondent. She replied: "Honestly? I know her because my husband had an affair with her two weeks ago. He lived with her for four days before I decided to let him return home." She explained that were it not for her child, who does seem attached to his father, and her low income at the moment as she tries to sell Oriflame cosmetics and piece together the day care necessary to get her career off the ground, she would have already divorced her husband. Vera is amazed that there are so many single mothers considering that it has become so difficult for mothers to divorce because of their lower incomes and the minimal amount of child support most receive. She exclaimed: "Just imagine if Russian women were earning close to what men can earn! We married mothers would be nearing extinction!"

Although some women remain married for economic reasons primarily, married mothers describe how times have changed since the late Soviet period, with fewer women willing to put up with any kind of behavior just to have a man. Even more so than single mothers, married mothers consider housework "trivial" (melochi) and are willing to do it themselves as it is not difficult for them. But they are angry when husbands are detached from rearing children. Lubov, a forty-four-year-old teacher, explained that her husband does not really seem interested in helping her raise their eleven-year-old son. This detachment makes her unhappy. Although she once considered divorce, she feels that she is a weaker person than the many strong single women choosing to go it alone: "My mom always said to me, 'he's your husband, and no matter what he's yours and you must make the best of it.' But these attitudes are changing. In Soviet times women were supposed to put up with anything from their husbands, considering themselves lucky to have a man. Women don't think this way anymore. But my mother had a big influence on me."

Olga described pressures in the other direction. Chuckling at my question about whether married mothers have social status, she said she has a hard time holding her head up at work because so many of her girlfriends feel she should divorce: "I cannot divorce for material reasons. But in my situation, well even at the factory, my friend Luba and others constantly say, 'how can you live like that, with your husband drinking all the time!' The girls at work ask me about it and actually encourage me to divorce, telling me that things would eventually be easier." Among married mothers, those women who put up with alcoholic husbands are pitied; heavy drinking is considered a justifiable reason to divorce if the drinking cannot be managed to avoid unduly affecting a mother and her children. Reasons such as not getting help at home with housework or with child rearing, or even infidelity, are still considered situations where women should try to wait it out—at least if there is also money coming home.

Married mothers argue that even if most husbands do not help as much as they should, the presence of a husband in the home signifies hope for eventual support, at least at some point in the future. Alyona, for example, stays married to her alcoholic husband despite feeling single: "I'm the main person for Sasha, for in spite of the fact that I'm supposedly married, it's a case of being married yet single at the same time since I'm really raising her on my own." Although her husband remains uninvolved with Sasha and the household in general, Alyona said that because her husband has complied with her central demand—he has not touched the bottle in seven years—she remains with him. Besides, he might become more involved at some point in the future.

Nadia, a forty-one-year-old manager at a state radio company, has given up hope that her husband, also a manager, will ever stop drinking or help out more at home. But she has found a way to get what she can from him and manage his drinking so it does not harm the family. She tried to leave him twice, but he seems to need her when he drinks, for her moral support. She could not follow through. So now when her husband binge drinks, once a month for several days, she sends him to his office, where, according to Nadia, other (male) members of the creative intelligentsia also drink and protect one another from scrutiny. She has learned to live with this arrangement. Her husband knows not to come near her or her daughter when he drinks. But at the same time, it is understandably difficult to feel well supported in this kind of marriage: "Let's just say we have separate budgets. I don't take his money and he doesn't take mine. We have come to an agreement whereby he pays for the apartment utilities and groceries and I cook the food. . . . I don't use his money for buying things for myself and very rarely do I take his money for buying something for our daughter. I try to just buy those things myself." The idea that women use all of their lower salaries for the family's needs, whereas men may contribute just a portion of their income toward the family, has been studied throughout the developing world. More international aid programs are trying to ensure that women are the beneficiaries of development funds considering the extent to which women are ultimately responsible for providing for a family's needs and tend to do so, on average, more responsibly. The assumption that all family members enjoy the benefits of the main breadwinner's salary is clearly based more on an ideal than on reality in many countries of the world, including Russia.

But perhaps learning to live with reduced expectations is a big part of why some marriages last and why a growing number of women will not live this way if they perceive an acceptable alternative. Women's rising expectations of men, alongside the shrinking pool of marriageable men, is part of why women increasingly postpone marriage, even when they do not necessarily postpone having a child.[19] Besides, Russian married mothers who have considered divorce are often coping with issues that require working hard to maintain a sense of their own self-worth: issues that range from chronic infidelity and alcoholism to feeling materially and emotionally abandoned in their families by husbands whose concerns lie elsewhere. Talking to married mothers reveals, gradually, from a different perspective than that of single mothers, a similar baseline for what constitutes a good-enough marriage in Russia: a sober, employed man who does not forget his wife and children. Anything else, whether infidelity, not helping out at home, remaining distant, or even contributing only a limited portion of his earnings toward the family's needs, is a situation women feel they should be able to manage, often in spite of their feelings.

Zoya, for example, had once considered divorce, but she feels that her husband loves the family. Furthermore, she put her rationale for staying married rather bluntly: "I couldn't find anyone better, at least in Russia. He doesn't drink, smoke, or cheat, and he works hard and doesn't forget that he has a family." Still, because Stepan is significantly overweight and ignores Zoya's admonitions that he take better care of his health and exercise, Zoya confided that she needs to prepare herself for eventually winding up as a single mother. Her own mother lives in the capital and is not around as frequently as when Sofia was younger. Zoya knows that should something happen to Stepan, she must be able to make it on her own.

☛ Winning the Lottery

The happily married, too, are shaped by a broader divorce culture. Six of twenty women in my sample had never considered divorce seriously, but half of them spoke explicitly about how lucky they are concerning their husbands, arguing that their situation is quite unusual. Others feel that they are not exactly happy but get enough out of their relationships with husbands to remain married. Tamara, for example, has two hearing-impaired daughters. Because her husband helps her with the girls and is devoted to them, she would never consider divorcing him. Other married mothers explain that their husbands love them, are faithful when so many men are not, and take an interest in the family. But what these mothers say and what remains unsaid reveal much about what women expect of marriage in today's Russia. Lena, a thirty-five-year-old English teacher, feels that she and her husband can overcome their conflicts. She, like Tamara, has always had practical support from her husband in raising their daughter. This means a great deal: "My husband spends time with our daughter whenever he can. She sees him a lot. It's not like he brings home money and leaves. I mean judging from the husbands of a lot of my colleagues, many husbands earn money, in business or whatever, even good money. But they never spend time with their kids, they hardly ever see them. This isn't right, but this is, I am sorry to admit, typical. . . . Many women put up with this because they are getting some material help." Adding that she considers herself lucky to have a good man, she noted that her husband "even reads bedtime stories" to their daughter sometimes, observing that this is unusual for fathers. This kind of involvement is needed, Lena declares, so that her daughter feels like she has a father.

Lusya, a thirty-year-old bank cashier, also feels she has been incredibly lucky with her husband, mainly because he does more than bring home a paycheck. Her husband really cares about the family and is involved in all aspects of raising their daughter. He helps her with cooking and cleaning, and they argue mostly because he constantly puts off making needed repairs in their apartment. As long as husbands are involved with and committed to their families, other issues are trivial, Lusya explains. She feels particularly fortunate because once women reach the age of thirty, it becomes nearly impossible to find a decent man. There may still be a few available men, but generally the men available are not the kind most women want anything to do with. This, at any rate, is the widespread perception.

Some married mothers who have never considered divorce are not necessarily happily married but feel that they have had to compromise considerably on some issues. Aurika, a forty-two-year-old mother of two who works in an auto parts store owned by her husband, accepts infidelity, for instance, as the price for security and an intact family in Russian society. Fortunately, her husband is not openly adulterous, as some men are, but she cannot, she confided, call herself "happily married." She feels that every marriage has its problems, and she has chosen to remain committed to her husband because although he has many faults, he still cares about his family. When the subject of divorce arose, Aurika abruptly replied: "All men cheat. The main thing is that it doesn't affect the family and the woman doesn't know anything about it." She implies that women who expect otherwise should simply lower their expectations to save their marriages. Other women, too, share this negative view of weak men who invariably cheat, noting that this can be hurtful to women and difficult to bear temporarily, but "it's not the worst thing that can happen."

In spite of this dominant mood of resignation concerning the nature of men and what can be reasonably expected from marriages, there were a few memorable exceptions. Masha, a thirty-five-year-old mother of two, beamed as she introduced me to her husband, who was helping the kids with homework in the living room when we met. She spoke about how "most Russian men have many problems," before going on to describe how wonderful her husband was with her and the children, praising the uniqueness of her marriage. She radiated happiness, even though she was reluctant to probe too deeply as to why her marriage was so unique, apart from the fact that even though she had felt lukewarm when marrying him she loved him more over time. She said, "Unfortunately it may be somewhat boring to talk to me. You know the famous saying of Leo Tolstoy: 'Happy families are all alike; every unhappy family is unhappy in its own way.' Probably single mothers have more problems, but many also lead much more interesting lives!"[20]

Masha enjoyed talking about her marriage and her family because normally she keeps her happiness in check somewhat, aware that most others face a very different kind of family life. Because so many mothers are forced to make do without reliable men, she explained, she refrains from talking too much about her husband with other women at work; she does not want to make them unnecessarily envious. Unfortunately, she added, and this is a serious problem in Russia, her marriage is not the norm. She feels *kak za kamennoi stenoi*, "as if behind a stone wall," a phrase women use to describe feeling protected and cared for by a completely reliable and strong loving man. Behind this wall, a woman can forget about her worries and trust in her husband. Mostly, women use this phrase in reference to a cultural ideal, with Masha fully aware of how exceptional her marriage is. In spite of her good fortune, Masha feels that there is no longer any social status in being married. Instead, she is convinced that every woman wants a good man so that her soul can be at peace.

But life for Russian women, Masha declared, is "not what it should be." Her own situation should be the norm, but instead she feels set apart from others because of the unusually tranquil state of her family life. Like many Russian women, Masha accepts rather traditional ideals of gender roles and described how hard it was to have to learn how to cook when she had first gotten married, but in practice, notably, she feels supported in all aspects of her daily life: "Whoever gets home first cooks dinner. My husband has never thought that cooking is somehow not a masculine job or anything silly like that." She trusts him completely, and he is the biggest source of support in her life.

Besides her husband, Masha admires her friend Olya, a single mother of two teenage girls left by her husband after he became involved with a younger woman. In spite of Olya's disappointment, and her sadness at the ending of her marriage, Masha notes that Olya is strong. Unlike others in Olya's predicament, she has never lost her joy for life. Nor has Olya given up on life in any way. Women with superhuman reserves of strength, who maintain the positive front required by practical realism, are admired by all kinds of ordinary Russians, including married mothers. Russian women, regardless of the marital-status distinction dividing them, find the situation of Russia's critical mass of "weak, unreliable men" and plethora of strong women a far cry from what should be considered normal in any society. But, many women argue, reality remains.

✒ Raising a Monument to Single Mothers

Whether or not they consider divorce seriously, married mothers think about single motherhood. Because married mothers also subscribe to the negative discourse on men, if not in reference to their own husbands, then in reference to most Russian men, they rarely judge single mothers. Many women, like Masha, refer to the negative discourse on men to justify why so many Russian women become single mothers. Sighing, Masha explained: "We have many unfortunate men. They are egotistical, many are drinkers, many don't care about their families, and many women feel that they are better off alone than with such men. But all of those women who can preserve their families, trust me—they find a way to preserve them. The rest are right to divorce." Similarly, Lena clarified that when Russian women divorce, "Mothers are not at fault. Because you have to understand that our women will put up with all kinds of things until the very end. If a woman divorces, then it was all over."

Alla, a crane operator who almost divorced her husband because of his drinking early in their marriage, could not imagine that anyone in Russia would have the nerve to judge single mothers: "I really like single mothers and relate to them superbly. I think we almost need a monument to them, for they set such an example for us. . . . I respect them. Because of their independence, and, well . . . I'm not a very independent person. I respect them for taking the step they did for it's very difficult to raise a child alone these days. Especially with our small salaries, there's never enough money, and if they took the step they did, then they are very independent women. . . . In most cases, they are right to go it alone." While Alla's praise of single mothers is more effusive than most, other mothers explain that single mothers who can provide for their families materially are admired, while those who show signs of struggling may be more harshly judged. Furthermore, no one expects mothers to put up with alcoholic or abusive husbands, but many married women tell cautionary tales about mothers who divorce for less weighty reasons, such as occasional infidelity. Masha described a woman at work who divorced her philandering husband: "She divorced him and now she's all alone. He easily found himself another woman and he now has kids by this woman. But my husband's father, who tormented my mother-in-law with his infidelity for years, well, since his wife has fallen ill, he has been taking care of her every day, devoting himself to her care." In general terms, married mothers respect single mothers, but some imply that single mothers must demonstrate that they did everything possible to save their marriages, or someone else will take that same guy and make a man out of him. Married mothers may admire single mothers, or at least their confidence and independence, but they do so from afar. Few want to trade places with them. Instead, married mothers fear the possibility of themselves becoming, and remaining, single.

☛ There's No Man Like Babushka

Although married mothers project less confidence and optimism overall than many single mothers, suggesting that differences do coalesce around the blurred boundaries dividing married and single mothers, other aspects of their lives share much in common with those of single mothers. Most married mothers describe their own mothers, their children's babushki, as the main source of practical support in their lives. Yet, although babushki do help their married daughters, married mothers, as a rule, seem to benefit a bit less overall (though still significantly) from the kind of ongoing, daily support that many single mothers enjoy. Fewer married mothers live with their own mothers,[21] but this is only part of the story given that support between mothers and adult daughters often takes place even when the two generations of women live separately. Babushki may help their single-mother daughters more than married daughters because they perceive that single-mother daughters have no one else to rely on; husbands are still viewed as sources of some tangible, or at least potential, support.

Some married mothers argue that if they had the support of their mothers, or someone else similar to a babushka, they might have already divorced their husbands. Varvara, married to the philandering businessman husband, explained that if her mother had not died shortly after the birth of her first son, she might have been able to summon the courage to divorce. For Oksana, the major event of 1991 was not the collapse of the Soviet Union; it was the death of her mother.

Like Oksana, some married mothers without much babushka support envy what they perceive that single mothers enjoy. For instance, Irina glossed over her lack of babushka support during the interview, as if it were not a big deal, and it did not seem that this lack of support encouraged her to stay married to a man away for half the year. Yet there were hints of babushka envy while we were having tea after the interview. Once our conversation touched on a mutual single-mother acquaintance, Irina cautioned: "Don't forget, of course things are easy for a woman like Natasha! I mean she may work all day, but her kids are with her babushka and she can come home and have a home-cooked meal prepared by her mom. She doesn't have to worry about shopping and cooking and all the rest of the everyday stuff."

Of course, just as single mothers long for a good man instead of a babushka (even if many also appreciate having a supportive babushka nearby), most married mothers do not feel that having a babushka's support replaces what they hope their husbands might still provide. However, the support of a babushka makes the lack of support from one's husband all the more glaring in some ways, causing women to feel like they are not married and quite alone. It may be that babushki step in to provide support for their daughters out of necessity, but once they consistently provide such support there is even less of a chance that a woman's husband will become more involved in his family. Instead, he may find reason to become even more detached. Although Katya does not know what her husband does for a living, or even if he is actually working while he is gone all day, Katya travels to her mother's town an hour and a half away every summer to work selling clothing at the market, traveling to Moscow each weekend to buy more clothing. Her mother looks after Katya's daughter during this time. And during the rest of the year, Katya travels to Moscow once each week to get more clothing, and her mother travels from her town to Kaluga to watch her granddaughter for the day. This mother–daughter institution of support and care for the next generation (see chapter 4) functions in the absence of men but may end up keeping men—many of whom are not necessarily eager to be more involved in the first place—on the margins of family life.

For Katerina, a thirty-six-year-old teacher, it is her mother, not her husband, who has supported her in all ways, even financially. Until her son, Volodya, now thirteen, was four years old, her mother watched him while Aleftina worked, and after he started going to preschool her mom picked him up every day. Her mother was always available to help, and she currently helps Katerina by paying for Volodya's English lessons, buying clothing, and giving the family large sums of money as holiday gifts. Because Katerina is using all of her salary to pay for the household's needs, and her mother and in-laws are helping out financially, Katerina has had an extremely difficult time accepting her husband's lesser contribution to the household. Just as single mothers must make ends meet on their own, so many married mothers do the same.

For some married women, given a choice between their own mother and their husband, they would take their mother's side. Marina, a forty-five-year-old mother of two working as an in-home caregiver for the elderly, presented herself as a very traditional woman. She believes divorce is justified but really only in cases where the husband drinks heavily or beats his wife. However, she went on to admit that she once considered divorcing her husband, who works as a taxi driver in Moscow. She thought of divorcing him only after her mother got sick and moved in with them, and her husband wanted his mother-in-law to live elsewhere: "I didn't want her to live alone. Even though my mother never said anything, I didn't want this. So I took her and helped her move into our two-room apartment. . . . I couldn't leave my mom and he was faced with a choice: leaving me, or keeping me and my mother. I had spent twenty-two years living with my mom and just seven years with him! I decided I could not leave my mom. We didn't divorce but we did separate for five months."

Marina, who used to work as the director of human resources at a state-owned factory, explained that she had little trouble balancing work and motherhood, mainly because of the support she received from her own mother: "My mom was at home while I worked at the factory, and she took responsibility for most domestic, everyday concerns. . . . When I got home from work, dinner was already ready. My mom did the laundry during the week, and the major washing was left till the weekend, when I tried to do it myself, because she was already getting older. I did the general cleaning on the weekends. I tried to do everything on Saturday and to rest on Sundays. . . . But still, she did most of the everyday housework. This was a great support."

Clearly, the support of grandmothers is not particular to single-mother families, even if there are differences of degree that require further study. Nadia, who raises her daughter with the limited help of her alcoholic husband, also turns to her parents (while using examples of her mother's support) in times of need: "I support my daughter with the help of my mom. My mom takes on a lot of responsibilities for my child. . . . And both of my parents buy her major things that she needs." The difference a babushka makes in the lives of their adult daughters is huge, however understudied. Babushka support shapes the dynamics of marriage, both within intact marriages and after marital dissolution.

Married mothers differ from single mothers in some ways. They may feel less confident or ambitious because they have not gone through the transformative experience of divorce or breakup with their children's fathers. The experience of going from married or partnered to single changes mothers' perspectives in some ways and requires wielding cultural resources to craft a life with new purpose and direction. However, many of the differences between the two groups of women are differences of degree rather than of kind.

It is not uncommon for married mothers to consider divorce as one of their options or to prepare themselves to make it alone in the New Russia. These mothers also share the negative cultural discourse on men so pervasive in Russia, whether they use it to condemn or absolve their own husbands. Finally, considering the extent to which extended mothering practices flourish in Russia, in spite of a divorce culture, varying levels of babushka support lie behind many of the differences between married and single mothers. Married mothers may have somewhat less babushka support on average, and several feel much more single than those well-supported single mothers.

Marital status does have cultural meaning in the Russian context. Generally, it is considered better to have been married than not, and doing all that one can to preserve one's marriage is expected of Russian mothers. Nevertheless, not only do married mothers express admiration for single mothers, but many also identify with experiences of having to "rely on themselves alone." Assuming that married mothers receive income, support, or psychological well-being from their marriages may be assuming too much, depending on the contours of an individual marriage, at least during Russia's unfolding quiet revolution in family life. The boundaries separating mothers of varied marital statuses are blurred. Perhaps they have always been blurred, but distinctions of marital status today mean much less than they did before, when the state helped all mothers more and marriage itself had a more definitive social status.

Considering that Russian families, single or married, still tend to function as matrifocally in the absence of men, how do Russian men feel about it? Do Russian men want to be more involved in family life but cannot since women collectively keep them out? Or are men relatively satisfied, or accepting of, the status quo concerning Russian family life? The next chapter answers these questions and more, analyzing the perspectives of nonresident fathers in the New Russia.

↵ CHAPTER 6

Marginalized Men
Settling for the Status Quo

As I got off the trolleybus at Kaluga's Victory Square and walked toward the shop where Oleg made keys and locks, I was a bit apprehensive. I knew from a friend who worked in an adjoining shop that Oleg, a thirty-three-year-old separated father, was nervous about being interviewed. He had already canceled twice before because of illness. Discussing fatherhood, after all, is not likely to be a comfortable prospect for nonresident fathers living apart from their children. Most men consider these conditions of fatherhood already, by definition, far from optimal. Yet men's perspectives on the meaning and challenges of fatherhood while living apart from children after a divorce or breakup are a critical part of understanding Russia's quiet revolution in family life.

For the most part, I was immersed in a world of mothers, grandmothers, and children, a world of getting to work on time via crowded public transport, grocery shopping during lunch hours, helping with schoolwork, making dinner while also preparing soup for the following day's meal, and saving up for Boris's private judo and English lessons. I had also spent countless hours listening to single mothers and grandmothers describe most men as husbands and fathers in a less than flattering light. Most mothers point out exceptions to the general rule, but men as fathers are described routinely in terms of irresponsibility, heavy drinking, infidelity, weakness of character, or lack of commitment to children and family life. Indeed, many women speak of men—those who do not directly make women miserable by drinking, cheating, or engaging in abusive behavior—as if they are wallpaper.[1] Women might want men to be strong or at least useful around the house, but they are routinely disappointed. Even the growth of single motherhood itself typically is seen as a problem caused by men retreating from family commitments, leaving women with few real choices.

Apart from occasional visitors, men are rather marginal to single mothers' worlds, except for the few cases where fathers provide substantial material support. These cases are lauded by women themselves as exceptional. Even though women believe that there should be a good husband and father at their side, after divorce or breakup most men are either absent or provide limited, sporadic financial support and visits with children.

Some fathers, I anticipated, would flatly deny women's descriptions of most men as fathers. They might be defensive and intent on setting the record straight, arguing that men have it much harder than women ever bother to acknowledge. Others might be hostile, accusing women of misrepresenting their child support payments or bearing grudges that dissuade fathers from regularly visiting their own children. Of course, some men, alternatively, might admit to being much happier with their lives after a divorce or breakup (as many women themselves are, though on different grounds), freed from the daily grind of caring for children and instead enjoying the freedoms of unattached men. In any case, surely men would have their own distinct stories to tell.

Yet what I found in this regard surprised me. There were some nuanced differences, in tone and in emphasis, between men's and women's accounts, but most fathers agree with the basic contours of what women say about most men. Men agree that they are at best not much more than "appendages" to single-mother families. Rather than being angry about it, most nonresident fathers just accept it, minimizing the importance of men as fathers and accentuating the significance of mothers.

After we found a place to talk over a couple of beers, Oleg described at length how taxing family life had been for him, as it probably is for many men, he added. For instance, his former wife always wanted him to come home directly after work, and he could no longer just hang out with his friends without her nagging every time he was more than twenty minutes late. He still wanted to see his old girlfriend, however, as she had qualities distinct from his wife. ("If you could somehow merge the two women into one, there you go! You'd have the perfect woman," Oleg clarified.) To top it off, his wife (who worked, but it was "just a secretary job," according to Oleg) resented cooking all the time. His own mother, in contrast, hardly ever leaves the kitchen and never grumbles about it. Oleg continued, reflecting on his fathering: "I'm a so-so father. An appendage of the family. I hardly see my son so I cannot influence his upbringing or world view. And what difference does it make whether I give my son money or some other guy tosses him the same amount? Of course he calls me 'papa' and is glad to see me, but that's very little in terms of all he needs. Although on the other hand, what can a father really give? A good mother, however, is fundamental."

Despite revealing an awareness of newer discourses of involved fatherhood, most men accept the negative discourse on men as fathers and as partners. Many reproduce elements of this same discourse themselves. Oleg, like most of the nonresident fathers I interviewed, expresses varying degrees of ambivalence and negativity about fatherhood and family life. Fatherhood is seldom at the center of men's lives in the way that motherhood is for women. In the interview, Oleg shows that he is aware of new ideals of involved fatherhood and admits that his son needs more from him ("he calls me 'papa' and is glad to see me, but that's very little in terms of all he needs"), and rather than getting defensive, he admits, without hesitation, that he is only a "so-so father." Yet at the same time he dismisses the value of fathers ("on the other hand, what can a father really give?") compared with that of mothers. While mothers are essential for children, he argues, a father's main contribution, providing money, is easily replaceable. Single mothers in Russia see many men, at least those who are not committed to being good fathers and responsible men, as superfluous. What is surprising is that many nonresident fathers agree.

In recent years, ideals of involved fatherhood have been growing in Russia, but no one is surprised by disengaged fatherhood, particularly after divorce.[2] Nor is it shameful to be only minimally involved with one's own children; it remains so commonplace. Oleg pays some child support informally, noting that his wife could never get much by officially filing for support since his earnings on paper are lower than what he actually brings home. When asked about what he does as a father, he replied, evading the question: "Let's just say that his grandmas and grandpas really spoil him." He went on to explain that of course he spanks his son's bottom and tries to enforce discipline whenever he sees him. He calls himself a Sunday papa (*Voskresen'ye papa*), emphasizing that although he only sees his son some weekends, he is nevertheless much better than most Russian fathers. Most guys, in Oleg's view, forget their kids entirely or drink so much that they cannot hold down a real job. According to Oleg, anyone who is a decent guy—a man who works, keeps his drinking and any other vices under control, and who does not completely forget about his child—is already a decent father.

Oleg mumbled toward the beginning of our interview: "There are these blunders that we later call children." Besides keeping the bar low for fatherhood, Oleg's comments confirm much of what women describe in terms of men who have little interest in living in a family or contributing to family life. Oleg had gotten married "unexpectedly," letting it happen rather than actively seeking to tie the knot, primarily because his girlfriend was pregnant. Because he was thirty years old at the time, he decided that it was time to give settling down and starting a family a try even though he did not really love his wife and married officially only as a result of parental pressure. He continued seeing another longtime girlfriend, and when his baby son was just two months old, his wife found out about his repeated incidents of cheating and promptly kicked him out of her apartment. In total, he lived together with his wife for five months. Although his unfaithfulness was the main reason why she kicked him out ("Everyone cheats these days," he added, "it's just that some women know about it, some don't, and some smarter ones know but choose to ignore it"), he said that another one-third of their conflicts had to do with his lack of help at home.

Currently Oleg lives with his mother and father. He helps them at their dacha two days each month, but nothing is required of him at home, where he lives rent-free. The fridge is always full of homemade food, including at least one first course (soup) and several second courses. All of this is thanks to his mother, a woman of peasant stock accustomed to working hard her entire life. His wife had tried to cook, but she was a far cry from the kind of housewife his mother is. This irked him. Oleg knows his wife would like to live like a normal family, but he prefers a freer lifestyle than family life offers, and he does not want the daily nagging about returning home a half hour late from work. He added, however, that if his wife could be the kind of housewife that his mother is, well, perhaps he could learn to love her more. Currently his wife's own mother is helping her out, and she ("oh, that woman!" Oleg exclaimed, rolling his eyes) cannot stand the sight of him.

Of course, Russian nonresident fathers differ in terms of how ambivalent they are about fatherhood and family life—several fathers present themselves as more committed to family life than Oleg. Variations are plentiful, even among this group of nonresident fathers, who by their own definition are already subpar given that they are fathers living apart from their families. But even those more sympathetic than Oleg to newer ideals of a father's involvement in family life still end up accepting a low bar for men as fathers and as husbands.

In this chapter, I show that in spite of differences among men vis-à-vis children and the idea of family life, most fathers tend to accept the broader negative discourse on men. Doing so allows them to feel better about their situation and to forsake responsibility. If the bar for fatherhood is kept low, then fathers can still conceive of themselves as decent, if not ideal, fathers. In addition, I argue that fathers' beliefs about the powerlessness and deficiencies of nonresident fatherhood, compounded by the increased pressures and loosened constraints surrounding fatherhood in post-Soviet Russia, push men toward settling for detached fatherhood and minimalist standards of involvement in family life. Despite sympathies for newer ideals, the prevailing cultural and socioeconomic context in Russia likewise encourages fathers to revert to the status quo of detached fatherhood. By detached fatherhood, I mean the opposite of involved fatherhood; detached fathers show low levels of engagement, accessibility, and responsibility.[3] The old, narrow standards of a fatherhood limited to economic provision are no longer as dominant in Russia as they once were. But these limited standards still resonate with Oleg and many other men.

✎ Men Marginalized as Fathers

Oleg sees fathers as peripheral in many families, but his views reflect decades of men being relegated to the margins of family life. Official and public discourse in Russia has long excluded fatherhood, compounded by a dearth of research on fathers. The meager existing research from the Soviet period focuses on "histories of laws concerning paternal rights and obligations, and time-use studies on gender-typed domestic activities."[4] Some newer research examines the effects of the marginalization of fathers and how the transition to capitalism is affecting fathers' involvement in family life.

The legacy of the Soviet period lingers on, in terms of societal attitudes toward men as fathers. In the Soviet period, the state protected motherhood rather than parenthood in general. Official policies promoted a cult of maternity aimed at increasing falling birthrates and portrayed motherhood as being of intrinsically greater worth than fatherhood. The terms "parenthood" and "fatherhood" entered the scientific lexicon only in the late 1980s. Even today commissions still have the Soviet-era phrase "for the affairs of families, women, and children" in their names, without mention of fathers. Ideas about fatherhood are contested and vague. There are highly developed discourses about what mothers should be, but "the notion of what a father is or should be is far more hazy, sometimes, effectively, to the point of nonexistence."[5] Although there is an idea that each child should have a man in his or her life to provide material necessities, the relational bond between fathers and children is rarely acknowledged.

In addition to fatherhood's negative popular image and its absence from official discourse, the real absence of men has long characterized fatherhood. As discussed in previous chapters, several generations of men and women grew up without fathers after the Second World War devastated the male population. The Soviet legacy of matrifocal families, in which family life relies on cross-generational assistance and caregiving among women, may also estrange husbands as parents.[6] Though ideals of involved fatherhood are nascent in the post-Soviet era, Russia has a dominant institutional and historical legacy, too, whereby strong, self-sacrificial women are partnered with infantile, irresponsible men. This discourse of strong women and weak men dates back to nineteenth-century Russian literature and was reinforced during the Soviet era.[7]

Furthermore, since the collapse of the Soviet Union, Russia has been experiencing profound changes in family life, including fatherhood. Two major developments have affected families profoundly: the withdrawal of state supports and the loosening of ties binding men to families. As the post-Soviet state has cut back its support for families, especially for women and children, it has essentially "reneged on its paternal role as the protector of mother and child." Women are looking to men to become more involved fathers during a time when there is both increased pressure on men to be good providers, and it is much harder to provide well for families.[8] New ideals of fatherhood valorizing a more engaged father–child relationship are growing, but for some men providing for their family may require working multiple jobs or doing temporary work for higher pay in Moscow, leaving less time and fewer opportunities for involved fatherhood.

Along with the increased pressures on men as primary breadwinners, men's ties to families have been loosened relative to the late Soviet era. Nonmarital births have increased since 1992, marriage is no longer required to advance in one's career, and cohabitation and multiple divorces are more accepted. Most important, the legal enforcement of child support has decreased. In the Soviet era, everyone worked for the state, so child support was automatically deducted from a worker's paycheck. Today the situation is more complicated. Child support is now calculated, in practice, on official income alone, even if a man earns significantly more money than his official salary suggests. Geographic and occupational mobility along with a lack of effective sanctions have also increased the nonpayment of child support.[9]

According to Russian legislation, mothers and fathers have identical rights and duties concerning children after divorce. But in everyday life this almost never occurs. The vast majority of mothers have custody of their children after divorce, with equal parental responsibility existing mainly on paper. The general Soviet pattern of men losing contact with their children after divorce continues in the post-Soviet period, with divorce usually meaning the divorce of children from their father.

Besides an entrenched negative discourse on men, fatherhood's marginal status relative to motherhood, and the lack of child support payment, even prior to divorce men are weakly integrated into Russian households, living precariously at the margins of family life. Some scholars observe that in Russia "husbands do not consider the possibility of sharing the caretaking domain of women nor being a parent emotionally as well as figuratively."[10] Ashwin and Lytkina argue that women may unwittingly contribute to men's disengagement from the household.[11]

Yet although the puzzle of why men are marginalized in Russian families requires analysis from multiple angles, many men also accept and actively participate in their disengagement from families. Men use widespread cultural discourses to justify a limited, voluntary notion of paternal duty, even though other, newer discourses on fatherhood are also available. The well-documented problem of men in crisis in Russia—men are drinking more and dying earlier than ever before—is linked inextricably to a related crisis of Russian fatherhood. Men's marginalization is not only, or even mainly, the fault of women; many women are eager for a more involved, engaged fatherhood and yearn for men who might offer more practical support in their lives. Many men acquiesce in their own marginalization. Moreover, without discounting the unique history and state policies that have shaped fatherhood indelibly, this Russian case of detached nonresident fatherhood is hardly exceptional. The detached form of nonresident fatherhood is, unfortunately, still quite common elsewhere in the world—even as other fathers are becoming more involved with children than ever before.

In contrast to the scant research on Russian fathers, present or absent, we know much more about nonresident fathers in other contexts, including the United States. This Russian case magnifies the phenomenon of detached fatherhood elsewhere, especially in the United States, where it is also widespread but poorly understood. In both countries, fatherhood is a contested identity—that is, what it means to be a father is in flux, with several ideals competing for dominance. But whereas deeply negative views of men as fathers are confined to subgroups in the United States, in Russia the penchant for disparaging men as fathers is common society-wide.[12] New ideas about fatherhood are emerging in post-Soviet Russia, but they remain embryonic.

If there is a general theme surrounding fatherhood worldwide, it is likely the diversity of fathering practices and circumstances. However, the assumption that fatherhood is somehow more voluntary than motherhood, more of a choice, remains pervasive. Scholars have documented broad variation in how much U.S. nonresident fathers care for their children. There are involved fathers and "deadbeat dads," and both tendencies are increasing simultaneously.[13] Even though involved fatherhood has begun to take hold, disengagement after divorce is common, and wives mediate men's relationships with children. Fathers who see their involvement in their children's daily routines as more intermittent and supplementary than a mother's constant and essential care are more apt to neglect paternal responsibilities after divorce. Divorced fathers sometimes feel like victims of injustice and express dissatisfaction over relationships with nonresident children, but many consider absence a viable option.[14]

Separate studies of low-income, mostly never-married fathers have produced contradictory findings. Some research suggests that low-income African American men may not aspire toward involved fatherhood if they are having difficulty providing adequately for their families. Fathers who want to provide for their children may not if they lack supportive structures or if a culture of distrust strengthens negative views of women as mothers.[15] Other research emphasizes that ideals of involved fatherhood are growing in poorer communities, with the breadwinner model receding as fathers begin to view economic support as necessary but insufficient for good fathering. A recent study found that no ethnic or racial group stands out for being higher or lower in terms of nonresident father involvement.[16]

Even as ideals of involved fatherhood become more widespread, the persistence of disengaged fatherhood remains puzzling. After a union dissolves, many fathers partially withdraw from parenting; they retain symbolic rights as fathers but relinquish most of their concrete responsibilities. In practice the role of the nonresident father is voluntary; most have little contact with their children and rarely assist them apart from buying gifts and paying some child support.[17] Fathers overstate their contributions, and three-quarters of all nonresident fathers in the United States pay no child support. Many pay sporadically, less than the required amount, or contribute informally.[18] Scholars agree that involved fatherhood is on the rise, but we do not yet fully understand why disengaged nonresident fatherhood remains so pervasive.

✒ "Of Course," Men Are Fathers

AUTHOR: Do you have children?

ILYA: Of course! . . . You know, there's a famous scene from a World War II film, where one soldier asks another, "Do you have children?"

The second soldier replies, gesturing towards the vast steppe: "Of course! Russia is a great, enormous country. Somewhere, probably, I have children!"

Ilya, a thirty-nine-year-old divorced father and welder, insists that most Russian men are fathers. Men are fathers regardless of whether they live with their children, visit them, pay child support, or even acknowledge paternity. Although he spoke in vivid detail about work, politics, and people in general, Ilya was also typical in that he spoke in vague generalities about his children (and money), sharing few memorable details even when probed. Considering that even resident fathers can be poor sources of information about the details of their children's lives when they feel involved or express an awareness that they should be involved, this reticence is not surprising.[19]

But the circumstances surrounding my interview with Ilya also reflect the challenges of studying nonresident fathers. After completing an interview with Vladimir in a dark, smoky billiards hall, he introduced me to Ilya, whom I met a few more times before he agreed to an interview. After several last-minute cancellations, Vladimir called me on my cell phone to say that Ilya had some time that afternoon. I cleared my schedule, and Vladimir picked me up within the hour and dropped me off at Ilya's office building, where Ilya greeted me at the front door. Echoing the observations of other women interviewing men, I had much less control over the place, time, and process when interviewing nonresident fathers than I did with single mothers.[20]

Initially I hoped to speak to the former husbands and partners of mothers interviewed. But this is a sensitive issue given the ongoing and contentious nature of many relationships after divorce or breakup, and doing so proved impossible except in one case. Mothers generally asked me to refrain from contacting former husbands and boyfriends. Some were reluctant to ask former partners to grant me an interview because they felt men would view this as needing a favor or as trying to get more information on them. But in most cases former partners had moved to distant cities, lost contact with mothers entirely, or declined to meet with me. Instead I located fathers through drawing on other friends and acquaintances. I tried to use a snowball sampling method as I had done with single mothers, but only three men were willing to introduce me to other potential respondents. Others said that they knew only men who lived with their children, did not know which of their friends had nonresident children, or could not bring themselves to introduce me to men whom they did not respect or trust. Some men said they did not want to waste my time by having me meet with useless men or with men whom they felt would try to take advantage of me in some way, emphasizing the tropes of male mischief and dangerousness.[21] Indeed, the distrust men had in relation to most other men was striking. Several tried to dissuade me from bothering to talk to men at all. "Why do you want to interview men when single motherhood is your focus? These guys won't have much to say," Alexei, an unemployed railroad worker, declared. Later he added, "Sure, some men are involved. But look at my stepdaughter, a single mother living with her parents and the kid's father is a nobody, completely out of the picture. One day several months ago he came by to 'see his son,' and delivered a birthday gift. But he's never around."

Given this distrust of other men, arranging interviews with nonresident fathers was much more difficult than with single mothers. Most of my networks were with Russian women, and many Russian men find living apart from their children and the whole predicament of nonresident fatherhood uncomfortable, awkward, or painful. Though there were a few exceptions, most clearly preferred to discuss work, politics, life in the United States, or almost anything else besides fatherhood. To maximize potential sources of data, I chose to triangulate using a combination of three methods: formal interviewing, opportunity interviews and observation, and observation in households. Fathers seemed a bit more candid during informal interviews, but I did not find significant differences in the results between formal and informal interviews and observations. In any case, the advantages of using multiple methods outweighed any disadvantages, especially given the dearth of research on Russian fathers and the difficulties of gaining access to nonresident fathers and observing families in their households.[22]

First, I conducted in-depth, recorded interviews with twenty-one nonresident fathers. Fathers ranged in age from twenty-two to forty-seven, and the average father was thirty-five years old with one or two children. No father was excluded from the study as long as he had at least one nonresident child under the age of eighteen. Ten fathers were divorced at the time of interview, three were still officially married, seven had remarried, and one had never married. Even though just one father had never been married, four men had fathered children without being married to the mothers, either in between marriages or while still officially married. Several men lived with wives or girlfriends or with relatives, but the more fluid nature of men's living arrangements (relative to women's) became apparent over time; some men alternated between living alone and with a wife or girlfriend, while others lived alone yet next door to a girlfriend's apartment or alone while regularly eating at their mother's place nearby. Fathers who had remarried also reproduced the dominant gender discourse and accepted narrow ideals of fatherhood, but those who had new resident children evaluated their fathering the second time around more positively. I interviewed fathers with extremely wide-ranging income, education, age, marital status, and employment characteristics. Seven men had no higher education and about half earned less than $400 a month, with earnings ranging from zero (while unemployed) to several thousand dollars a month. I purposefully sought a diverse sample to illuminate the similarities among fathers of different class backgrounds. Like other qualitative studies of low-income and middle-class fathers, my sample probably overrepresented fathers who paid child support and had some contact with nonresident children.

Second, I supplemented formal interview material by conducting opportunity interviews and observations. While living in Russia, I met men who were nonresident fathers in a wide range of contexts, including streetcars, bars, trains, and cafés. Though the exchanges were informal, I spoke with ten additional nonresident fathers about their experiences as fathers before and after divorce, taking detailed notes.

Third, I conducted participant observation in several households and in some cases witnessed how interview data corresponded to actual behavior. While living with a single mother and her daughter, for example, I was present during several of the twice-monthly visits of her former husband. During extended visits with single-mother friends, I observed interactions between mothers and their children's fathers stopping by with cash, gifts, or for visits, as well as conversations over the phone. I also met men (many of whom were also nonresident fathers, I subsequently learned) who were guests and occasional companions of single mothers. I participated in children's birthday gatherings with single mothers' former husbands and boyfriends; accompanied a father on an all-day outing with his nonresident teenage daughter; and spoke with fathers informally at several social gatherings.

➴ Accepting a Negative Discourse on Men

Nonresident fathers and single mothers typically tell different stories,[23] but Russia's fathers are surprisingly negative concerning the state of men in Russia, disparaging men as fathers. Few fathers criticize the mothers of their children as mothers or describe restricted access to children. The dominant gender discourse on Russian men has many aspects, but most women emphasize that men behave irresponsibly and immaturely, lack an interest in and commitment to family life, abuse alcohol, and are prone to infidelity, depression, and violence. After a divorce or breakup, mothers argue that fathers pay infrequent child support, visiting children sporadically, if at all. Surprisingly, most nonresident fathers agree with some of these complaints, whether in reference to themselves, to their own fathers, or to other Russian men. Other fathers affirm the negative discourse indirectly, through speaking candidly about their own infidelity or detachment from child rearing.

☛ Drinking: The Scourge of Russia

Just as men argue that (nearly) all men are fathers, they affirm that most men drink. Male drinking is ordinary and considered hegemonically masculine in everyday life.[24] Although the subject of drinking alcohol may not typically be foregrounded in relation to good fatherhood, in the Russian context both women and men consider it fundamental. As discussed in previous chapters, Russia is the world's hardest-drinking nation, with a primarily male alcohol culture and a long tradition of binge drinking. Apart from the problem of binge drinking, fathers talk about drinking as an integral part of men's daily lives.[25] Most fathers focus on drinking in terms of other Russian men, either condemning binge drinking as "the scourge of Russian society" (as several men put it) or accepting the ordinariness of Russian drinking by noting that "all men drink." Slava mentioned drinking in reference to his own absent father: "I assume my father drank as all men do. . . . All men drink in Russia! What's the difference between 'getting drunk regularly' or just 'drinking'? There's no real difference. I can drink two liters of vodka without collapsing. But I don't do this. Or if I do, then it's only once a month or so. I don't have time for more than that. But someone can drink every day yet only have half a glass. That person also drinks." Though few men admit to drinking heavily, most men, like Slava, volunteer descriptions of their own drinking habits when discussing fatherhood.

Men openly discuss the pervasiveness of drinking among Russian men and the intensification of drinking during the post-Soviet period. Tendencies to drink heavily have gotten worse, not better, since the collapse of the Soviet Union, apart from a small minority of elite businessmen who carefully manage their drinking. While some refer to male drinking as an incontrovertible fact, for most it is linked to the broader discourse of responsible women and irresponsible men. Alexei, for example, quickly launched into the absence of a drinking habit when asked about what a good father meant to him. "First of all, in terms of alcohol, well, [a good father] shouldn't even glance at a shot glass. . . . And fathers must pay more attention to their kids. . . . I couldn't say that I'm . . . well . . . I'm a lousy father. . . . Well, I could have been better. I guess I'm not a total good-for-nothing, but I'm pretty bad. . . . I mean in terms of raising the kid, I didn't spend enough time, nothing was enough. . . . Sometimes I'd drink and then not go to see my son because I didn't want him to see me in an unattractive light. So drinking got in the way." In Alexei's account, alcohol is one of the many reasons why men behave irresponsibly. In his second marriage, Alexei is much more prudent about drinking, and his estimation of himself as a father has improved as well.

Though fathers decry heavy drinking, they acknowledge that drinking, however lamentable, is a socially acceptable outlet for men's frustrations and celebrations. Mikhail, a well-off married man who owns several rental properties in Kaluga, is providing for his four-year-old son and girlfriend in another city. He feels strongly that heavy and, more importantly, uncontrolled bouts of drinking are a direct response to men's inability to support their families: "Most men earn 200 dollars a month! . . . Therefore, a man doesn't feel like a man since he cannot fulfill his role. . . . Everything is connected to this. He cannot carry out his role, so his wife nags him constantly, so there's no love, so he's lousy in bed, so he's useless with his child. He has not developed like a man should. What does he do? He drinks with his friends, they talk, and everything is kind of normal again. Drunkenness starts there." Mikhail argues, like other men and most single mothers, that men drown their problems in drink mainly because it feels good and because they can. Drinking is still accepted as an alternative outlet for the expression of masculinity, albeit a compensatory form. In a vicious cycle, many men seek refuge from their responsibilities in drink, and drink likewise keeps many men from carrying out responsibilities.

In near unison, men concur that a man's role, his main responsibility as a man and as a father, is to provide for his family materially, to earn money through work. Men expect to earn more than women, and many argue that men can always find temporary work of some kind whereas for women it is harder to get jobs with decent pay. Therefore, most men argue they should be primary breadwinners, given men's ability to command higher salaries. Fathers emphasize the importance of a father's duty to provide for his family but, like mothers, stress that it is more important that fathers sincerely attempt to provide, even if they cannot bring home as much money as others. As long as fathers try to provide, they should not be blamed if they cannot provide as much as they would like. But expectations surrounding successful breadwinning are ambiguous; given the onset of capitalism and increased income inequality, there is always the idea that a man might do something more to earn better money. The question of how much is enough appears to be an open one for many Russians, which puts many pressures on men expected to be providing adequately.

Fathers point out that some women drink as well, and some drink more than they did in the late Soviet period. But all agree that women do not drink like men, justifying this gender difference by falling back into the discourse of responsible women and irresponsible men. Mikhail said: "Women are more responsible since they have children. They have more of a desire to have children than men. So they're more responsible." Other men make the link between drinking and male irresponsibility but place more emphasis on the cultural acceptance of drinking for men. Igor noted, "Men are more irresponsible, or to be precise, they do not let themselves feel responsible for things in the way that women do. Men can allow themselves, through drink or whatever, to become completely degraded, whereas women cannot."

In men's accounts, women are in the driver's seat when it comes to decisions to have children, whereas men may or may not be along for the ride. Whether they attribute the gender difference in drinking to culture or biology or some combination of both, fathers unanimously view children as primarily women's responsibility. In any case, fathers cannot be counted on to accept responsibility for them. Paternal responsibility, unlike maternal responsibility, is assumed to be contingent on a variety of circumstances.

Because male drinking is an unavoidable part of life in Russia, nonresident fathers distinguish between men who can and cannot handle their drinking and between drinking with negative and relatively harmless consequences. Fathers construct arguments about drinking and rate themselves as fathers in similar ways; in both cases, they compare themselves with "most Russian men" (who are typically assumed to be absent fathers and heavy drinkers), casting a more favorable glow over their own actions. Pavel, a land surveyor in Moscow, barely knew his own father growing up but knew enough to roughly compare their drinking habits: "I know that my father drank a lot, and after drinking . . . well, he behaved very badly. . . . He got aggressive. If I drink, then I don't drink a lot. And the most I'd ever do is go somewhere and lay down to sleep. I don't get aggressive."

Without excusing heavy drinking, some fathers argue that a certain amount of drinking, typically related to business, is frequently necessary for men. Women acknowledge this as well, but men emphasize it more. Yuri, a recent convert to Jehovah's Witnesses, explained that his second wife, unlike his first, understands that drinking is a part of male friendship and business. His second wife is also a great improvement because she realizes that he is the man of the family, responsible for the entire family's material well-being, and knows to defer to him in this regard. His car repair work is frequently accompanied by drinking, especially when he needs spare parts from others.

He also drank while doing some side jobs for extra money several years earlier, noting: "I wasn't sitting somewhere in a café like an alcoholic getting his fix. I got drunk, but I solved a problem. It was business." There is a productive kind of drinking that is part of male breadwinning and friendly business relations, so few men condemn all forms of drinking in the way that some women do. Of course, many of these business rituals exclude women, on the grounds that they have family members to care for and have no time for this kind of socializing and networking. Another nonresident father agreed that drinking is part of men's business and work, offering a concrete example: "How do men thank one another? They say, 'Let me pour you a glass, let's drink 50 grams.'"

Fathers, like single mothers, distinguish between various types and amounts of drinking. But fathers agree that men are more likely than women to ruin their lives through drinking, justifying this tendency, once more, by reference to the dominant gender discourse. Igor, a local state official, argued that women are simply more pragmatic than men, making them less likely to drink: "Women manage things better. Quite frequently when men no longer feel needed by society, they lose heart. . . . Two-thirds of the Russian

FIGURE 7. A Russian man proposes a toast, the first of several, before he and several friends enjoy grilled *shashlik* (a Russian shish kebab popular at summer parties), salads, and plenty of vodka at a school class reunion in a secluded Kaluga park. Photograph by the author.

population drink and they are drinking themselves to death. I mean literally ruining themselves. But it seems to me that women are much less likely to do this. Women just have too many responsibilities at home to allow themselves to do this." Other men discuss this in terms of women's "naturally" greater strength and ability to endure hardships. Men, in this sense, are considered weaker in that they are more apt to lose heart. Like single mothers, nonresident fathers condone some drinking, but most still go on to blame many men for seeking solace in the bottle too frequently, emphasizing that male drinking and irresponsibility go hand in hand.

☛ Infidelity: A Male Prerogative

Like drinking, for most Russian women infidelity is another issue that affects how men carry out their fatherhood duties. Women sometimes allow for exceptional cases where men are able to remain committed and responsible to their families despite having lovers, but for most women (especially when women have experienced it personally), infidelity is a major problem. For women, male infidelity is associated with being an immature, subpar father, distracting men from their commitment to their families. Overall, men's comments surrounding infidelity confirm women's accounts, in terms of infidelity serving as a serious reason behind the breakup of marriages, both in contemporary Russia and since Soviet times.[26] Yet while both men and women see heavy drinking as an intractable problem for many men in Russia, men and women view infidelity differently.

Supporting a double standard, Russian fathers argue that infidelity is not a big deal for men; it is a serious problem only when women have affairs or in those cases when liaisons on the side lead men to lose sight of their primary responsibility to their families. Men can have lovers, many men explain, and still remain committed to their families. Infidelity is routine and mainly needs to be managed properly. Women may also be unfaithful, but both men and women speak of male infidelity in relation to broken marriages.[27] Fathers suggest that infidelity is a grievous offense for women (e.g., two men described unfaithful former wives, looking away as they described the humiliation of learning of these affairs), but for men the main issue is that infidelity be managed, so that it does not interfere with men's primary breadwinning responsibilities.

More than half of the nonresident fathers interviewed acknowledged cheating on their wives or girlfriends while living with them. Men draw distinctions among women, in terms of their suitability as sexual partners and as wives or mothers. Sexual fulfillment appears to be a male entitlement, but men give women who are mothers of their children a special status. Many do not want to divorce women who are mothers of their children but at the same time feel entitled to pursue affairs, as normal men. As one father put it: "I had other women. But still, I would not have divorced her had she respected me. She was the mother of my child." For Mikhail, too, cohabitation and marriage have little to do with fidelity: "I constantly had other women while I was living with Nadia. I was always wondering how this one might be as a mother, or how another one might be. But once I decided that Nadia was the one, I knew she would be a great mother, then I decided to get married. . . . The main thing is to never admit to cheating. Sure, she could probably guess that there were others, but I never told her, 'yes, there's someone else besides you.' I said, 'no, no, there's nothing going on.'"

Accounts of infidelity arose spontaneously during several interviews, especially when men were explaining why they divorced or were no longer living with their children. Oleg, the thirty-three-year-old locksmith introduced at the beginning of this chapter, was very matter-of-fact concerning his lack of commitment to family life, as well as his infidelity and failure to contribute to housework during the five months when he lived with his wife: "Let's just say that my wife wasn't pleased—well no one would be pleased I suppose—that I was often out with another woman. . . . Yeah, she found out. I tried to keep it a secret but she found out everything! As they say, the pitcher can only go to the well so many times before it breaks."

Yet other nonresident fathers referred to occasional acts of infidelity more casually, as if very few men ever depart from conforming to the double standard. Infidelity is discussed as an everyday reality rather than as a site of moral outrage. Over time, as men explained why they had divorced, I began to probe as to whether relationships with other women also influenced their breakup:

> ALEXEI: Maybe I stopped doing things to help, starting checking out other women. . . .
> AUTHOR: Were you involved with other women?
> ALEXEI: Of course! What, am I not a man?! All men have lovers these days.

Infidelity is a masculine entitlement normalized among men at least discursively. Some argue that men, unlike women, need lovers. After all, because men argue that they are relatively weak by nature, at least relative to strong women who can endure so much, men are prone to seeking pleasure and comfort wherever they might find it. Other men justify having lovers by noting that since they still "did their duty" in terms of material provision, infidelity should really have been a nonissue. One nonresident father added: "Honestly, it's almost embarrassing these days to only sleep with your wife."

Even the minority of fathers who do not admit to cheating speak of leaving their options open. Boris, an engineer and involved father to his second daughter from a subsequent marriage, explained: "For their child, men have a wife. But for being indulged, men have a lover. . . . No, I don't have a lover yet actually. But I think lovers are sometimes necessary." Nonresident fathers confirm single mothers' general accounts of male infidelity within marriage, either through reports of their own actions or by generalizing from the actions of other men around them. In doing so, they also reinforce aspects of the broader negative discourse on men. Few fathers condemn unfaithfulness outright, although one father (the Jehovah's Witness) did. Unlike those who fervently speak out against male binge drinking (as opposed to managed drinking), men justify having lovers as yet another accepted, optional expression of masculinity. Many men argue that as long as infidelity is properly managed, as drinking could and should be, it need not become a major problem. Some women, too, normalize some infidelity, and many would not leave a man because of isolated incidents of infidelity. But women speak more about chronic infidelity and the humiliation of it. There is clearly a "his" and "hers" to infidelity in Russian marriages.

✒ Voluntary Child Support

Although just two fathers admitted to paying no child support, most fathers described minimal, sporadic, and voluntary child support. Paradoxically, even though fathers wholeheartedly agree that materially providing for one's family is fundamental—the essential core of fatherhood—nonresident fatherhood is held to a different, and consistently lower standard. Fathers' reports of child support were vague and contradictory, with amounts that did not add up and long lapses in payment with minimal explanation. Seven fathers paid child support officially but often just for several months or a couple of years before they left official jobs and worked in the informal sector, where they then paid no child support at all.

Those who do pay child support feel superior to the majority of Russian men. Dmitri, a divorced businessman, was described by one of my closest single-mother informants as a paragon of virtue. "If more men were like Dmitri, Russia would have far fewer problems!" she declared. (Her mom lamented that Dmitri even had a little crush on her daughter in high school,

if only her daughter could have chosen a man more wisely.) Like other fathers, Dmitri warned me about the veracity of men's accounts, especially concerning child support and visitation. He said that getting anything useful out
of Russian men would be nearly impossible:[28]

> Most Russian men only care about their kids as long as they are
> involved with a particular woman. And men will pay attention to a
> woman's kid, play some little game with them or whatever, just to
> appeal to a woman's maternal instincts. It often works for them. But
> they don't really care about kids, they just want the attentions of a par-
> ticular woman and they know this will work. As a matter of fact, most
> men don't even know how many kids they have. Once they are no
> longer involved with a woman they don't think about providing for
> her kids. This is all very unfortunate, and I'm ashamed to tell you all
> of this, but I won't lie. One has to face the facts of life in Russia.

In condemning other men, Dmitri valorizes his own efforts to support his
three children (by two different women) and remain in contact with them.

Yet even Dmitri, likely the most responsible and involved of nonresident
fathers interviewed, feels it is beneath him to pay a fixed amount of child
support. He contradicted himself later in the interview but at first said he
pays "most of his salary" to his kids: "I have never had some fixed amount
withheld from my salary, because I simply help my kids. I'm not prepared to
pay, for example, 25 or 50 or 30 percent. Whatever they need, I will give,
assuming that my earnings allow it. . . . No, it's not that we have a mutual
agreement or I agree to pay what I can, but I pay what's realistic. I know, for
example, what it costs to feed one child normally. . . . If she were to go to
court she'd get several times less. . . . I'm their father, so of course I know
what my kids need!" Fathers like Dmitri are insulted by the idea of having
money withheld from their salaries for child support. They describe trying
to buy what their kids need rather than giving money outright, arguing that
they know what things really cost; yet these same fathers admit that they
have never been responsible for the family budget, shopping, meal preparation, housework, or most child care while living with children. In most
Russian families, managing the household's money is the wife's responsibility and involves ensuring that all of the family members' basic needs are met
and balancing the household budget (not investing in the stock market or
real estate, as the phrase "managing money" may imply in some contexts).[29]
Regardless of their actual earnings, men with above-average earnings feel
that rather than a fixed percentage of their income (as required by law), they

should instead pay a kind of subsistence minimum for the upkeep of their child.

A few men, like Ivan, a thrice-divorced geologist with three children, feel justified in refusing to pay any child support, arguing that it is merely money that ex-wives can "waste on hairpins": "I never gave anyone child support and I don't think that it should ever be paid. . . . Because I have known many women who got support and they became lazy right away. It's as if money from somewhere—boom!—just fell from the sky. It's not earned. And these women prefer to live poorly and do nothing rather than working hard. . . . So I never paid any regular money for my kids." When I asked Ivan how his two former wives who were the mothers of his kids felt about this, and whether they did anything to obligate him to pay, such as taking him to court, he looked puzzled at first. Then he explained that he had simply given them ultimatums: "I said, 'Choose!' Either I relate to you well, help you if possible and so on, and we have good relations, or you can sue me for support, but then we are no longer friends, no longer close people. You'll be my enemy! . . . And as for materially helping them, I never paid anyone regularly, like some definite amount every month—no way! But if they called me and said 'You know, the child needs a new jacket' or he has begun to play an instrument and needs to buy an accordion, then I said, 'fine.'" Although most men were not as vehement as Ivan in their refusal to pay child support, elements of Ivan's description, such as not wanting to waste money on nonnecessities and distrusting where the money paid would go, were echoed by many fathers.

In lieu of Ivan's passion, to my surprise most fathers reported even minimal and sporadic support nonchalantly. Yuri, like several other fathers, no longer counts his nonresident fourteen-year-old son as one of his own children. Although he had agreed to meet with me as a nonresident father, when I asked him how many children he had, he answered "three" in reference to his eight-month-old son and the two stepchildren with whom he now lives, discussing his first son only when directly asked. I had developed a good rapport with Yuri, for I had the pleasure of having dinner with his family prior to meeting on a different occasion for a formal interview (as a "guest from America" for his wife, a former English teacher). But information on child support was not forthcoming:

AUTHOR: Did you pay any child support?
YURI: Early on I think I paid, then I didn't.
AUTHOR: Do you remember how long you paid? Officially or unofficially?

YURI: When I worked they simply withheld some for child support, and then they stopped. It was maybe around eight months, or almost a year.

AUTHOR: How much did they withhold?

YURI: Some percentage, I don't know, I never looked. Some percentage was deducted.

AUTHOR: Did you have an official and unofficial salary?

YURI: Well, yeah, I worked as a taxi driver. The official salary was on paper, a small amount. And then I got paid on top of that, separately.

AUTHOR: Was the child support deducted from your official salary?

YURI: Yes.

In spite of this terse exchange, Yuri was talkative when discussing work, his new wife (his friends were envious of him because so few wives these days respect their husbands as his wife respected him, he added), and fatherhood in general. Nonresident fathers confirm single mothers' accounts that despite a father's duty to materially provide for his family, after a marital breakup the payment of child support is basically voluntary. My questions about how fathers "worked out a mutual agreement" regarding support with former wives or whether women threatened to take them to court met blank or quizzical expressions. Fathers generally appear to tell their wives what they can or will pay, knowing that if wives take them to court they will receive very little because a smaller official salary can be arranged informally through the help of connections. Although I tried probing the issue in several ways, a vague quality permeated any discussion of child support:

AUTHOR: How much did you pay in child support?

ILYA: Whatever I could.

AUTHOR: What was the general amount?

ILYA: I honestly don't remember.

AUTHOR: How often did you pay?

ILYA: Sometimes once every six months, sometimes once a month. It just depended.

Boris, for instance, was very involved with raising his second daughter from a new marriage, even though he had not been involved with a child from his first. He sees supporting or maintaining a relationship with his nonresident daughter as optional. He explained, "I no longer wanted to go to visit some other family again and again, for it wasn't very pleasant for me. I don't think the child understood the situation, why some guy kept coming by." So even though "the child" in question is his daughter, Boris felt like an intruder as a nonresident father and not much like a father at all. Fathers acknowledge that child support calculated on the basis of artificially low official salaries cannot even begin to cover the basic costs of raising a child. Yet because they contribute something (or did at some point) or keep in contact with nonresident children, they still see themselves as better than most fathers who completely disappear.

Through repeatedly referencing the negative discourse on men, where absent, detached fatherhood is normalized, fathers highlight any of their own efforts to remain fathers to nonresident children. Fathers resemble one another in accepting the general contours of the negative discourse on men, but to varying degrees many fathers also sympathize with newer ideals of involved fatherhood. Yet even those who waver between old and new ideals end up acquiescing to narrow ideals of fatherhood. The remainder of this chapter examines how and why fathers settle for the older status quo.

✒ Varieties of Ambivalence: Fathers Accepting a Low Bar

All kinds of nonresident fathers accept a rather low bar for father involvement. Minimal fatherhood requires providing for one's family, at least while living with them. If not living with children after a relationship ends, minimal fatherhood requires not forgetting about them entirely and paying some support. However, if a father ends up with new kids to care for in a subsequent relationship, whether he remains involved with children from a previous relationship is mostly voluntary. But while many fathers end up reverting to the low bar for fatherhood, some fathers embrace a detached provider ideal, whereas other fathers are more sympathetic toward emerging ideals of involved fatherhood.

✒ Embracing a Detached Provider Ideal

Some fathers not only acknowledge the dominance of the father-as-detached-provider ideal but embrace it as the correct standard. These fathers blur distinctions between good men and good fathers. Like any man, a father must simply do his best to provide for his family. He should not be faulted for failing to provide adequately. These fathers minimize or ignore other dimensions of fatherhood (such as loving children or spending time with and being emotionally engaged with them), even though they have some awareness of newer, more expansive conceptions of fatherhood. They discuss fathers, instead, as soldiers, hunters, and protectors, emphasizing fathers' strength and detachment. Ivan proclaimed: "In my view, the main quality of a good father is that his children should be proud of him. . . . As a matter of fact there's nothing that a father really *should* do as long as his children don't feel like orphans. . . . A father is always a hunter, a go-getter. He is not the keeper of the nest. He's always out there, somewhere, hunting or at war. Fathers are out hunting mammoths . . . they are not meant to raise children!"

While Ivan is unusual in comparing the work of fatherhood to mammoth hunting, others, too, normalize paternal absence and absolve fathers of most responsibilities for their children. Ivan was not alone in expressing some hostility toward the idea of family life, intimating at one point that a lover can compensate somewhat for the lack of an official family and does so without the ensuing burdens: "Sometimes I long for the comforts of family. But I've become an egoist. . . . I don't want responsibilities. And I don't want someone trying to manage me, telling me what I should and shouldn't do. But I do have a young lover. And I do for her exactly as much as I can. Not more and not less." After our interview, Ivan reflected on the whole idea of family life a bit more fully. "While love is wonderful and makes you feel alive, love is always fleeting." Scrunching his face in disgust, he added, "And all of that family stuff . . . is just nonsense really."

Ivan keeps the bar for fatherhood so low that as long as a father is not completely absent or indifferent, he still qualifies as a good father. In doing so, he justifies his own disengaged fatherhood. He argues that nothing really changed for his children after his divorces because "they already knew very well that sometimes I lived with the family and sometimes I didn't." Speaking vaguely about the time he spent with his children, noting that he had his work, music, and other hobbies that occupied his time, he concluded: "But even now I'm certain that none of my kids would ever say that they'd been abandoned. . . . And that's the main thing."[30]

Through embracing detached fatherhood, Ivan makes his own casual attitude toward fathering acceptable and even laudable, arguing that he still does more than most fathers. While he says that most men drink, lie on the sofa, and live at the expense of women, he works hard and never abandoned his children.

However, even men like Ivan reference newer ideals of fatherhood; they are aware that there are other options besides detached provider standards. Chatting after our interview, Ivan admitted that he could have done much more than he actually did for his children and perhaps should have been more involved. Clinging to a minimalist conception of fatherhood protects him from general criticism (most men do so little, so at least he does more than most) and provides a culturally accepted way out of a psychological tension. Still, it does not necessarily protect him from his own criticism.

Most fathers embracing narrow discourses of fatherhood emphasize economic provision as a father's sole duty. Slava, a divorced father of a teenage daughter, added to this that fathers have an additional obligation: fathers must ensure that their family has a place to live. (Of course, this is far from a straightforward task given Russia's challenges in creating an affordable housing market.)[31] He spoke of "teaching" his daughter by paying for her education, not by spending time with her. Complaining about the many men who fail to carry out the financial duties of fatherhood after divorce, he admitted that it has become much more difficult to provide for a family in the post-Soviet era: "These days I have begun to rely more on myself. . . . One needs to think more, about how to do what, and where. It's more complicated today." Despite Russians' historic cultural fatalism, since the onset of capitalism there has been a shift toward a self-reliant "mastery orientation" common in the West.[32] Mirroring the rhetoric of many single mothers, Russian men describe relying on themselves, without counting on the state or anyone else. Fathers like Slava conclude that as long as fathers do the hard work of supporting their families economically, they need not be burdened with additional expectations.

The divorced head of a security services company, Valeri also emphasized how difficult providing for a family is today but stressed how people's values have become much more mercenary. Salaries were low but stable in the late-Soviet period, Valeri explained, so previously men did not really have to worry much about meeting their family's basic needs. Now, Valeri lamented, everything is "money, money, money," people have become hard-hearted and indifferent in their relations with others, and men take refuge from the struggle to provide in drink. Although Valeri feels he provided for his wife and daughter in other ways, he has never paid child support but has arranged (through his connections and friends, he implies) for his former wife to get payment from the Swedish government as an unmarried mother. He is estranged from his daughter and saddened about this. The country where his former wife now lives he describes as "a wonderful place for women, children, and old people. But not a place for real men." Because he believes he no longer has a family, he has severed the sense of responsibility he said he used to have for his child.

He regrets what he refers to as the loss of his daughter, whom he has not seen in three years, but at the same time Valeri naturalizes fathers' detachment. He notes that fathers, unlike mothers, do not notice a child's runny nose. In any case, fathers cannot help but raise their children as long as they are not completely absent: "Even if a father comes home only to sleep, and never sees his child, the child knows that father comes home to sleep—and all the same, this is indirectly raising the child. Simply because papa is there!"

Occasionally fathers who embrace narrow conceptions of fatherhood discuss love for one's children or mention spending time with children as laudable. But none of this is required, in their view, for good fatherhood. These men reject any notion of men as nurturers or caregivers; indeed, men seem hardly capable of these activities in their accounts. Fathers forgive other fathers a great deal as long as they are relatively reliable breadwinners. Kostya, a divorced small business owner, explained that his own father had affairs, drank heavily, and left the child rearing and nearly everything else to Kostya's mother. But, quite tellingly, he does not fault him because his father provided for the bulk of the family's material needs. And so many other fathers, Kostya added, fail to take even this basic duty of financial provision seriously.

Similarly, Sergei, a freelance computer repairman, mentioned "love" along with material provision but then went on to conflate them: "First of all, probably, a father needs to support the family materially. And second, he needs to love his child. Because if you love your child, you will look after him. Probably these two things are the same. . . . You don't have to see your child every week. . . . You can go somewhere to work for a year, come back home, and still be a good father." Fathers face considerable pressures to earn as much money as possible for their families in the New Russia; they are not expected only to work a steady 9-to-5 job as they did in the Soviet Union. Fatherhood itself is in a state of anomie, in Durkheimian terms—the norms are ambiguous and unclear, with fathers vacillating between the idea that fathers trying to provide well is enough but at other points contradicting themselves to say that real men must find a way to earn money and support their families at any cost.[33] Yet most fathers still deem as acceptable fathers who are absent, as long as they are putting effort into breadwinning.

Dmitri, the businessman described by others as unusually responsible, highlighted the exceptional nature of his own commitment to supporting his three children financially by disparaging other men. He accepts a narrow conception of fatherhood, mainly because he sees no point in upholding higher standards for men given that most fathers cannot handle even their most basic obligations: "Women approach life's issues more responsibly. It's a woman who most often raises a child, and the man is out there somewhere, maybe. One cannot just assume that he helps. If a family breaks up, as a rule, papa is gone, that's it. He forgets his child, he forgets his first wife, and moves on.

He lives however he wants. Women are more accustomed to making serious decisions. In most cases they hold everything together." Dmitri explained that he was also a detached father while married, noting that spending time with children is less important than providing for their well-being. He replied, "Papa came home to sleep," when asked to describe time spent with his children.

Dmitri feels that the bar for fatherhood is doomed to remain low. Like most fathers, Dmitri rejects the argument that some men cannot manage to support their families. Most Russian fathers concur that providing for a family, although difficult, is nonetheless possible and is much easier for men than for women. Dmitri emphasizes that although men can find work, whatever their qualifications, many choose to behave irresponsibly: "Men prefer to do nothing, earning absolutely nothing, while their wives feed them. There are a lot of these cases. Unfortunately, most Russian men don't want to work. . . . This doesn't occur in any other country in the world! Russian men would rather sit around than work, living at someone else's expense. . . . This is an indisputable fact." He added that he is a better father than most, even though, he admits, he is far from the ideal because he lives apart from his children.

Oleg, too, feels he is a good-enough father in his final estimation, for he sees his son on occasional weekends and pays some support. Besides being convinced that mothers are everything for children, he feels that women, especially Russian women, are just stronger than men and hence better suited to parenthood. Men focus on providing mainly because they earn more, as men: "in terms of their physiology, women are more stable. They are able to endure twice the radiation that men can, bear heavier loads, and so on. You are not the weak sex! Physiologically you are even stronger than men. I mean generally women's minds are more flexible than men's are. You are more cunning. . . . But in terms of the amount of providing . . . all the same it is men who hold the managerial posts and men get paid more for most jobs. . . . It was always this way and it's the same now."

Although life has gotten much harder for the average man since Communism's collapse, it is interesting to note that most Russian men do not think women have it easier than men. Instead, they describe women as being built for endurance. Life is harder for men because men are naturally weaker. But men, regardless of their individual struggles, benefit from an overall advantage on the job and in their pay, simply by virtue of being men. Echoing the words of single mothers, Oleg implies that regardless of women's strength, endurance, and natural aptitudes, men must strive to be the primary breadwinners in their families. This struggle defines men. Without bringing home money, however replaceable this task may be, men are not considered, nor do they consider themselves, as needed in families.

➤ Sympathizing with an Involved Provider Ideal

Other fathers are more sympathetic toward newer ideals of a more involved kind of provider ideal. Fathers are struggling to navigate between the old and the new. Fathers who vacillate between varying views tend to still prioritize economic provision above all else, but some feel that spending time with children, offering moral guidance, and paying attention to their children's needs are also worthy goals. Like those fathers embracing narrow ideals, fathers who shift between older and newer ideals still end up settling for a low bar. I argue that beliefs about the deficiencies of the nonresident form of fatherhood and the socioeconomic context of post-Soviet Russia prevents them from fully embracing a more involved fatherhood. Fathers agree that nonresident fatherhood (a) is deficient by definition, (b) makes them feel powerless and marginalized, and (c) is always more optional than motherhood.

Fathers' views fall along a continuum in terms of how receptive they are toward involved fatherhood, but most fathers view nonresident fatherhood as inherently deficient. This strong belief not only dampens their spirits but discourages them from getting more involved in their children's lives. Andrei, a divorced engineer in his early thirties, believes that a good father must take an active interest in his child's life. He considers himself better than most fathers in that he sees his daughter almost every week, pays some informal support, and values his daughter's place in his life, but he does not consider himself a good father: "If I live in another family, if I divorced, then that already means that I'm not exactly a good father. At least not fully. I have a complex about this. Personally I think I'm not a bad father. Not bad, but far from ideal. . . . I don't live in a full-fledged family with her mother, but I'm not that bad because I am interested in my daughter's life. . . . My own father was a worse father than I am and he lived with us. He liked to drink and he wasn't very interested in what was going on with me." Andrei has a difficult time seeing any nonresident father as a good one, yet at the same time the fact of residence does not necessarily mean a father is any good either. It is as if the best one can do as a nonresident father is to be better than most fathers, whether resident or non-, who check out entirely from their former family commitments.

Men like Andrei are caught between two competing ideals of fatherhood, but they resolve the internal struggle by relying on a culturally accessible low standard. They argue that the newer ideals are difficult to apply given their nonresidential situation. Andrei visits his daughter and takes more of an interest in her than his own father did with him, yet he doubts that any of this matters much. Shared beliefs about nonresident fatherhood encourage fathers to accept a low bar for fatherhood, and once fathers accept a low bar they can still argue that they are at least doing more than most men. Furthermore, because there is no culture of involved fatherhood after divorce, the route toward involved nonresident fatherhood seems arduous.

Convinced that nonresident fatherhood is a subpar experience, many fathers do not fault themselves for their estrangement from their children. Instead, they openly long to be "real fathers" someday—but at a time of their own choosing. Although powerless to change their current experience of fatherhood, they feel, unlike mothers, that they have some choice about when to become the kind of fathers they would like to be. The comments of Mikhail, a successful businessman who is officially married but has an "unofficial wife" (in his words) and four-year-old son in another city, reflect this view. Mikhail visits his son once per month, confiding that he is really driven to visit his girlfriend more than his son. Yet he longs for the experience of full-fledged fatherhood, having missed out on many of fatherhood's joys. For Mikhail and others like him, being a nonresident father is not real fatherhood. But fathers might enjoy becoming real fathers later, under more auspicious circumstances. Mikhail feels he is a father only from an economic point of view and that to be a good father he would have to start over with another child and probably also with another woman: "I would like to be a normal father. To live with my child, to participate in raising him, to see the child everyday. To teach him what I was never taught as a child. . . . Am I pleased with the way I am carrying out my role as a father? No, I'm not. I would like to be the kind of father who would lead his child, raise him in the way that I chose, teach him things that might help him to learn from my mistakes." In Mikhail's case, he cannot bring himself to leave his childless wife, recovering from cancer, in order to live with his "unofficial wife" in another city. So becoming a real father will have to wait.

Fathers feel powerless to change much about their relationships with their nonresident children. Some feel that because they are not real fathers, they no longer need to support or maintain ties with children. Stefan, a divorced doctor of alternative medicine with a twelve-year-old son, visited his son monthly during the first year after his divorce, but his visits dwindled as the years passed and he has not seen his son in three years. He has paid some child support for the past two years, but only after his wife sued him for it. Unlike many other fathers, he feels that a father should be a real presence in his child's life and not merely a "pocketbook." In fact, Stefan no longer considers himself a father: "If only I were a father. Then I could tell you what I like about it. Because I have a son . . . but I have not raised the child. . . . But I think that if I had raised him I would have loved being a father." Gradually fathers convince themselves that there is no longer much of a reason to try being a father. At the same time, many still reserve the option of becoming good fathers someday, but at an unspecified future time, with another child, or with a different woman. Stefan, like most men, feels that he has a choice about when to be a father, and at least for now, he frankly admits that he does not want the responsibility: "The way I now live my life, well, I'm not a family man. I'm probably too much of an egoist. I want to spend my time succeeding at work, working out, and I long to see the world. This is a conscious decision, and maybe it's not right, but it's my own decision. . . . A family takes time. But I'm a lone wolf. . . . It's not that I'm afraid of responsibilities . . . I simply don't want any."[34]

Notably, several nonresident fathers do consider themselves good fathers, but only to new children with whom they reside. Many no longer consider themselves fathers at all to nonresident children. Nonresident fatherhood is entirely optional in everyday life. Ignoring his nonresident son, Yuri claimed to have just three children: two kids from his wife's previous marriage and their joint eight-month-old son. Given his recent conversion to Jehovah's Witnesses, Yuri considers himself a man with enormous responsibilities: ensuring the spiritual development of his family, teaching his children, and providing for the family. Although attracted to newer ideals that valorize fatherhood beyond economic provision, he admits that he is focused on earning money and repairing his cars because he wants to buy his own home more than anything else.

Although Yuri, unlike Stefan, is a family man who accepts his many responsibilities, conversations with him revealed a broader cultural tendency, among men of all kinds, to believe that they have considerable choice in terms of when and under which circumstances to become good fathers. Yuri is untroubled by his failure to support his nonresident child, because child support, whatever the law specifies, is seen as voluntary. When pressed, fathers concede that child support calculated on the basis of artificially low official salaries does not cover the costs of raising a child. But if they pay something or keep in touch with nonresident children in some way, they still see themselves as better than those fathers who completely disappear from children's lives. Besides, Russian women can manage. They always have.

For instance, Leonid, a Moscow land surveyor, vacillated more than most between divergent standards of fatherhood. Sometimes he judged himself according to newer standards of involvement: "My son doesn't have enough contact with me, in my opinion, so I'm not really a good parent. I need to see him more often." Later on in the same interview, he shifted his standards, accepting a lowered bar: "But some would say I'm a good father. I guess it's true because I'm still in contact with my son and . . . well, there are fathers who leave their families and don't appear again for eighteen years. . . . My father never saw me." By accepting lower standards and comparing themselves not with mothers but with previous generations of Russian fathers, Leonid can see himself, whatever his faults, as a decent father.

Men associate becoming a nonresident father with accepting a marginalized, powerless, and deeply unsatisfactory status. It is hardly an enticing prospect. Some further estrange themselves to avoid additional feelings of powerlessness. After all, the mothers of their children could also replace them with other men. Two men described feeling usurped by men who seemed to be better fathers to their children than they themselves had ever been or could ever be now. Sergei, a divorced computer freelancer, wavered between arguing that a good father need only provide for his children, which he sees as synonymous with loving them, and emphasizing that he must also spend time with his children. He does not consider himself a good father because he fails to spend enough time with his daughter. He rarely spends the time because another man is already the better father: "The guy who lives with my wife now, well, unfortunately he's a good father. It's my great misfortune. He has too much influence over my daughter. And there's absolutely nothing I can do about it besides biting the hand that feeds me."

Similarly, Igor, a divorced state official with a ten-year-old nonresident daughter and a two-year-old resident son from a new marriage, feels uncomfortable concerning his relationship with his daughter and powerless to change much about the time he spends with his son. Igor favors a newer ideal of fatherhood in which good fathers put the interests of their children first and remain in constant contact with them. However, he sees these new ideals as impossible to achieve at the present time. He and his daughter live in different worlds, with few interests or activities in common. Despite his belief that a good father should spend time with his children, Igor admits that he spends too little time even with his resident son. For now he prioritizes providing for his new family, while paying some child support. Whatever their sympathies for newer ideals, the intensified pressures on men to become successful breadwinners in the post-Soviet era end up further encouraging men to accept older, detached ideals of fatherhood.

But even when there is no man taking their place, some men choose to remain distant from their children. Even though they feel that they should want to spend time with their children, in reality, spending the time feels burdensome. Involved fathers, unlike mothers, are laudable but still somewhat optional. Roma, a divorced computer programmer with an eleven-year-old son, explained that he left his wife because of her constant nagging that he spent too much time at work and too little with his child. Yet he admits he was focused on work and spent little time at home. Having grown up with a distant father, Roma told me he had come to view detached fathering as normal. He has changed in his outlook. He now refers to newer standards, emphasizing that he should want to spend more time with his son: "I cannot consider myself a good father if only because I willingly abandoned my child. I can sit here and say all kinds of things, that I try to stay in contact with him, that we are in contact, but it is nothing compared to what it should be. Sure, I like talking to my son, sure, I like spending time with him, sure, I try to see him, but at the same time I either don't try hard enough, or I don't want to see him badly enough, because I rarely see him. I don't know what the reason is. So no, I don't consider myself a good father." Despite his former wife's encouragement to spend more time with his son, Roma never based his identity around developing a strong bond with his child. Although not a good father in his own estimation, he argues that he is still better than most because he pays child support.

Although Yuri had warned me about his sister's husband, a man he dismissed as a "worthless alcoholic, the kind of parasite who wants a woman to support him," Alexei and I developed a great rapport. After the first twenty minutes of our conversation, he told me that he had nothing to lose or fear, that he did not care about defending Russia's reputation, and that he would just tell me the way things are and I could let the world know about the reality of family life in Russia.[35] Alexei, a divorced unemployed railroad worker with a teenage nonresident son and two stepchildren from a new marriage, supports newer ideals of involved fatherhood. He now judges himself as a decent father relative to his younger days. However, he still supports a double standard of parenthood. Mothers are essential, whereas fathers are more marginal and optional: "If a man abandons his kids one can quietly indulge him, give him a break. What can you get from a man anyway? A man is a man, but a woman! . . . A woman is everything, she's a mother and a housekeeper and certainly nature gave her more responsibilities than a man. . . . In general, men have fewer responsibilities. They believe they should work, bring home the money, and nothing more. They bring home that money and that's it. . . . They think they've done their duty! [laughter]" The view that a woman is "everything" whereas a man or a father is somewhat superfluous apart from primary breadwinning is repeated frequently in Russia.[36] By citing this popular belief, men justify their own disengagement from family life.

Alexei's sarcastic laughter at men who believe bringing home money means that "they've somehow done their duty" suggests that men are aware of the existence of alternative ideals that are beginning to challenge the dominance of disengaged fatherhood. But acting on these newer ideals is another matter. The discourse of responsible women–irresponsible men (clearly a Russian variant of "boys will be boys") continues to shape ideas and behavior, offering an essentialist justification for male irresponsibility. Even Alexei, who offered the novel (among my respondents) suggestion that men's "natural" irresponsibility might be tamed through engagement with taking on more of "women's work," still embraces the negative discourse on men: "When my wife was in the hospital for three months I had to sit at home with our three-month old baby. Can you imagine what this is like for a man?! It's hard. . . . For men it's very hard. First of all, you don't get enough sleep and then you don't know what's going on, it's a little baby. . . . It is much easier for a woman. A woman can endure a lot of things that men somehow cannot. . . . I will never forget just how hard this was for me, really hard. Now I know how difficult it is for women to be home with babies. How hard it is to raise them." While greater father involvement in child care could eventually chip away at the disengaged fatherhood norm, Alexei and most other fathers continue to rely on a biologically essentialist version of the negative discourse on men. In Alexei's account, men can learn to appreciate the work that women do, but men still seem destined to encounter difficulties in carrying out work that women more easily perform. Even fathers who admire the ideal of involved fatherhood believe that paternal absence is still rarely, if ever, a catastrophe.

✎ Explaining the Persistence of Marginalized Fatherhood

Russia's nonresident fathers may seem extreme, at least in the level to which many accept disengaged, voluntary fatherhood. But the absent or disengaged form of nonresident fatherhood is quite prevalent elsewhere in the world, even if more involved versions compete for dominance. Yet whereas the attitudes of Russian nonresident fathers might characterize subgroups of fathers in the United States, in Russia all sorts of men seem to believe some of the calumnies that women, popular culture, and the state have long cast on them: that they are weak, irresponsible, and of marginal importance to their children beyond a responsibility to provide for their progeny materially. Furthermore, material provision, too, appears to become optional, at least in practice, after divorce. People frequently consider fatherhood to be more of a choice than motherhood, but in Russia this belief has rather striking breadth and depth.

The post-Soviet Russian case of nonresident fatherhood is puzzling: Why are nonresident fathers willing to remain minimally involved with their children at a time when the post-Soviet state has curtailed its involvement in family life? I see four main reasons. First, Russia's entrenched historical legacy of absent or disengaged fatherhood (particularly after divorce) poses a challenge to the broader realization of newer involved fatherhood ideals. Even fathers sympathetic toward newer ideals are familiar with the negative discourse on men and fathers and have likely internalized its components. The negative discourse on men as fathers may wield more influence over nonresident fathers since most are starting from a view of nonresident fatherhood as inferior. When confronted with nonresident fatherhood and its many uncomfortable aspects, fathers end up accepting the secondary, marginal importance of fatherhood. Especially if their children have either a grandmother or a new father figure (i.e., mother's new spouse or boyfriend) closely involved in their upbringing, nonresident fathers come to believe in their own superfluousness.

Second, although the ideal of involved fatherhood is more prevalent in postsocialism, it is still an ideal gradually gaining a stronger foothold rather than a common practice. Regardless of the state's decreased involvement in family life, fathers may sympathize with ideals of involvement while lacking the cultural road map necessary to put ideals into practice. Men have been excluded from what scholars have referred to as the state-mother-child triad for so long that the retreat of the state may have caused women's expectations of men to rise without doing much to change men's behavior.[37] Beyond Russia, too, the culture of fatherhood is changing more rapidly than the conduct. Although describing the United States, Townsend argues that this central paradox of fatherhood is most apparent after divorce: "Very many men say they want to be involved fathers, but frequently they are not involved and remain emotionally distant and unsure of their ability to connect to their children."[38]

Most Russian fathers do want to be good fathers, but they are clearly less defined by their fatherhood status than women are by motherhood. Women are still evaluated more by their performance as mothers than men are as fathers, but the emergence of an involved fatherhood ideal in Russia may gradually shift this norm. Newer ideals of involved fatherhood are growing, however slowly, offering an alternative to the entrenched negative discourse on men. It must be acknowledged that any change concerning ideals of fatherhood is likely to be slower among nonresident fathers given the status of this form of fatherhood. Nonresident fathers, I have argued, whatever their sympathies for involved fatherhood ideals, still end up settling for an older, detached version of fatherhood. According to this older standard of fatherhood, most conclude that while they are not ideal fathers, they are certainly better than most. Drawing on the social psychological literature, it makes sense that nonresident fathers would engage in downward comparisons with fathers they perceive to be doing worse than themselves. In situations where people feel under threat, or in this case where men feel uncomfortable concerning their performance in a less-than-ideal situation, downward comparisons or explicit self-evaluations may help to raise fathers' self-esteem.[39]

Third, being exposed to new ideals of involved fatherhood is unlikely to change men's behavior as long as they face concerns that strike them as more pressing, such as job insecurities, unemployment, and heightened expectations of economic success.[40] Certainly the transition to market capitalism is challenging men with a range of these kinds of pressing concerns. New expectations of paternal involvement may fall by the wayside. Relative to late Soviet Russia, when everyone was guaranteed a state job and there was much less social inequality, today it is harder to provide for a family and more is expected of people at work. Men may be even more apt to defer or even decline involved fatherhood at this historical juncture.

Finally, although there are new moral incentives for fathers to become more involved in their children's lives, fathers today are also freer to opt out of this involvement: social mores have changed since 1992, and nonmarital births, cohabitation, and multiple divorces are more common; the legal enforcement of child support has decreased and there are more opportunities to earn money in unofficial capacities; and along with increased geographic and occupational mobility, there are many more consumer items and ways to spend money. Goode argued that, even when the state did play an active role in family life, "in response to continued government repression, more people eventually sought their own interest, rather than that of their families."[41] Today fathers face fewer legal and social sanctions for failing to support their families. Of course, rather than forming two disparate groups, men may embrace or flee fatherhood at various points in their lives, moving from one category to the other. Some fathers become more involved with resident children in their new families, at a later time in their lives, even when they remain detached from nonresident children.

Beliefs about nonresident fatherhood and the socioeconomic context (i.e., increased pressures on men as primary breadwinners, loosened ties binding men to families) powerfully shape men's preferred discourses and practices of fatherhood. Existing research on nonresident fatherhood highlights the barriers fathers face to becoming more involved in their children's lives, including conflict with residential mothers, geographic distance from children, ambiguity regarding the father role, and competing parenting responsibilities for both resident and nonresident children.[42] Besides these critical barriers, we need to know much more about how all kinds of men experience and attempt to navigate the unenviable situation of nonresident fatherhood.

In Russia, the idea of involved fatherhood is relatively recent. The conversation about fatherhood and what makes a good father has begun, but fathers, like most Russians, swing between old and new ideals. There are deep, unresolved conflicts between the pressures of economic provision and spending time with children in many capitalist societies, which may explain why some men express a desire to become involved fathers while remaining uninvolved.[43] Furthermore, in many diverse cultural contexts, scholars of family life, such as Gerson have argued that "Fatherhood as an economic, social, and emotional institution is increasingly based on what men want and find meaningful rather than on what they are constrained—by women and social regulations—to do."[44] In addition to a more favorable socioeconomic context that supports involved fatherhood, the culture surrounding fatherhood in Russia must continue to change. We know that along with a changed culture, when men know that women have the power to pursue child support, for example, the failure to take paternal responsibility carries real consequences, eventually changing behavior.[45]

What is perhaps most troubling is that so many Russian men question their importance as fathers, all while normalizing the idea of mothers' greater importance. Women, the media, and government may eventually play more of a role in promoting fatherhood and pressuring men to become more involved fathers, but the main advocates of the new, involved version of fatherhood throughout history have been men themselves.[46] In Russia, too, real change will take place only once fathers become convinced of the importance, as well as the desirability, of a more engaged fatherhood.

Conclusion
Normalized Gender Crisis

Toward the end of my fieldwork in Russia, a prominent billboard in Moscow caught my attention with its bold proclamation: "The Balzac Age, or All Men Are Bast----" (*Bal'zakovskii vozrast, ili vse muzhiki svo----*).[1] Taking its name from a popular expression about women getting on in years and portraying four distinctive, fashionably dressed thirty-something women, the billboard advertised a Russian television program, a clear spinoff of HBO's *Sex and the City* series about single and sassy career women looking to find good men.[2] Although themes in the Russian series overlap somewhat with the American version, in the Russian version families, particularly women's own mothers, feature much more prominently. There is also less romanticism among the Russian heroines and a rather pessimistic slant concerning the possibility of finding a good man.[3] Whereas the series elaborates familiar themes, the story—given the legacy of a negative discourse on men and of women turning to other women for practical support—is in some ways uniquely Russian.

This book, too, tells a story about Russia's quiet revolution in family life, exploring the cultural meaning of single motherhood in the historically unique transition from state socialism to neoliberal capitalism. Yet at the same time, many aspects of this Russian case of family transformation are hardly unique, given the growth of single motherhood in many industrialized countries. The Russian case offers a critical comparative dimension to our understanding of the growth of single motherhood worldwide, challenging many assumptions embedded in the sociological literature on the subject. In privileging the experiences of single mothers in a country where most families have long functioned matrifocally, I sought to bring the margins to the center of our analysis. After all, as in Russia, single motherhood is hardly marginal in countries like the United States, with many patterns of family life once found most commonly among the poor now expanding to middle America. Single motherhood is an increasingly common phase in a woman's life course, and perhaps we should no longer treat distinctions of marital status as paramount in dividing women.

In addition to expanding our knowledge of the many changes in Russian family life in recent years, I have argued for using the Russian case to interrogate some themes and to problematize categories and assumptions embedded into our theories of family, gender, and social change over time. Single mothers are trying to survive and succeed in post-Soviet, Putin-era Russia, joining forces with their own mothers and doing fairly well for themselves and their families in spite of the odds stacked against them. The Russian case shows us, in particular, how discourses and practices still commonly pathologized and treated as aberrational "minority" phenomena in the United States are normalized and treated as taken-for-granted aspects of family life in the New Russia.

The move toward neoliberal discourses of self-reliance among women disappointed in both men and state, attitudes of profound gender distrust, and heavy reliance on extended family members rather than marriage for support in life—all are well studied and documented, especially among the working poor in the United States. In Russia these themes are inflected with the historical and cultural nuances of Russian life, but they are hardly unique to the post-Socialist transition. Framing changes as unique sometimes means missing opportunities for continued productive comparisons.

In the United States, the postindustrial economy is marked by a "privatization of risk," whereby social policies do much less to protect individuals and families than they did previously, and citizens are increasingly saddled with navigating insecure workplaces and other institutions on their own.[4] Patterns previously documented among poor African American or immigrant communities are becoming more widespread and are likely to shape the middle classes as well in the years to come. When instability and insecurity are the norm at work and in society, trust in intimate relationships will prove difficult, whether this distrust is most endemic among inner-city African Americans, low-income single mothers in Philadelphia, or working-class young Americans more generally.[5] Marriage might be more precarious

FIGURE 8.   A single mother and her mom laugh together over tea, fruit, and cookies after showing the author some family photos. Photograph by the author.

among the working classes and families more fragile, but insecurities also plague middle-class Americans in workplaces and intimate relationships. In a divorce culture, the possibility of divorce, for instance, looms over even the happiest of marriages.[6]

While Russian families may at first blush seem unusually reliant on extended kin support, typically grandmothers, new research shows that multigenerational bonds are increasingly important for all kinds of Americans as well, not only for particular subgroups of immigrants or racial-ethnic minorities. Middle-class families are turning to extended families for support more frequently, in spite of the image of middle-class self-reliance. Hansen argues that our families are not so nuclear and that "white middle-class families are restructuring kin relationships, following the path of African Americans, immigrants, and members of the working class."[7] Other scholars point out how an aging population as well as the decreased stability of modern marriages converge and are likely to make extended kin relationships in families only more important over time.[8]

In stark contrast to the U.S. case, Russian society does not generally consider the growth of single motherhood a problem. When people do recognize it as problematic, they argue that it reflects broader problems with weak men and the weak state in contemporary Russia. Can women really be blamed for eventually giving up on a bad marriage when there is little or no income, child care, or other forms of assistance offered by children's fathers? Or when women have to protect their children from a father's drinking, violence, or serial affairs, all while providing for children as best they can through their own paid work? Although this may not be the only story of single mother-hood, I heard narratives like these repeatedly in Russia, forming a consistent pattern over time. Marriage has less social status than it once did, with many single mothers now holding their heads up high as long as they manage to provide for their children's needs. Women's standards for what they can ex-pect from marriage have gotten higher than in Soviet times, but for the most part Russian women do not exit marriages frivolously. Mothers strive to do all they can to save marriages, as long as men are being useful to the family rather than becoming unnecessarily burdensome.

In spite of the formidable economic challenges inherent in supporting families on a single income (with women getting by on a single income typi-cally earning less than men in many countries), single motherhood makes sense for some women, especially in situations where matrifocal families pre-dominate and women cannot really count on men or the state. Whether or not outsiders consider the turn to single motherhood "rational," given mea-ger supports and material challenges, women perceive it as a reasonable op-tion. Few consider single motherhood ideal, but it has become an alternate path for a dignified life for themselves and their children. Women will con-tinue to turn to single motherhood in spite of their preference for two-parent families as long as they see more benefits to going it alone than they do for staying in troubled or abusive relationships.

Writing about the unfinished gender revolution in the very different con-text of the United States, Gerson observes: "All things being equal, it is surely better to grow up with two parents who remain strongly committed to each other. Yet all things are rarely equal."[9] If things are rarely equal in the United States, these inequalities, I argue, are exacerbated in contemporary Russia. With its lack of grassroots feminism, societal hostility toward feminism, and the rise of neo-traditionalist ideologies concerning gender relations at work and at home (supported by political, economic, and religious institutions), Russia is a glaring example of how inequalities in gender relations shape fam-ily change. The Russian context is, of course, critical to any understanding of how the turn to single motherhood is experienced quite frequently as a relief compared with the demands of married life under patriarchal capitalism.

Many women gain an increased sense of control, peace, and well-being once they become single mothers, and these gains should be taken seriously by scholarship and policy.

Although this book tells the story of relatively successful single motherhood in the face of incredible odds, it is a story of ironic success. Many Russian single mothers are not especially poor and unfortunate, or at least not more so than other Russian mothers, and many are managing relatively well despite cutbacks in the state's symbolic and material supports for families. But let me be clear: certainly these relatively successful Russian single mothers are not strong matriarchs happily living out a feminist utopian dream. The circumstances within which women become single mothers are not circumstances of their own choosing. Single mothers would prefer to have a good man shouldering some of their many responsibilities instead of having to rely on their own mothers. Most, though not all, would prefer to be part of an intact, full-fledged family rather than making do as single mothers with occasional male companionship. They work hard to transform themselves into the kind of single mothers who can make it in the New Russia, who can (and must, apart from relying on their own mothers) rely on themselves alone, yet most would much prefer to have a partner to reliably assist them, along with some symbolic and material supports and protections from the state, which have diminished since the collapse of state socialism.

Yet Russian single mothers are surprisingly supportive of new neoliberal capitalist ideologies of independence and self-reliance. The idea that you are responsible for your own destiny has become popular among women who see few alternatives emanating from men or the state. But while trying hard to put their faith in themselves alone and in the promise of the capitalist marketplace, women still feel unprotected in a "man's world" where they cannot even count on getting paid regular child support and where they practically expect to be discriminated against as women and as mothers by private employers. Single mothers feel wistful about the loss of a social order that, whatever its faults, provided some basic guarantees in terms of housing, health, education, employment, and a kind of baseline security for its citizens. But feeling wistful is different from believing that the protections and guarantees Soviet mothers enjoyed can be their own. In the neoliberal context of disappointment in men and the state, the idea of being in charge of their own destinies resonates with single mothers. Most make a virtue out of the necessity to conform to the dominant cultural code of practical realism. After all, who can better rely on themselves than mothers who have decided to divorce or have a child on their own under far from idyllic circumstances? Even those mothers who had the decision of divorce or breakup made for them still experience life as going it alone. Regardless of what women really feel, practical realism demands that single mothers present themselves as autonomous and competent—for the sake of their own dignity.

However ironic, the surprising success of many Russian single-mother families is real. Yet even their success is hardly a triumphant one. Russian single mothers are managing as best they can despite confronting some of the worst elements of neoliberal market fundamentalism and patriarchy combined. Many of the regulations and institutions that moderate the effects of capitalism in other contexts are still absent or relatively undeveloped in Russia. Some single mothers have faith in the new opportunities presented by market capitalism and strive to remake themselves into practical realists who can succeed in Russia. Others feel constrained by this code of practical realism and hope they will see more opportunities, given effort enough and time. But at the same time, single mothers cannot trust that the legal mechanisms for ensuring child support regulations work well, they expect to be discriminated against as women in workplaces, and they do not feel protected by the state as workers or as mothers.

In terms of Russia's many male-dominated institutions and practices, some Russian mothers would willingly take on some extra burdens at home in exchange for more material and moral support from a decent, sober, reliable man. But given what they see in most Russian families, single mothers do not trust that their extra work at home would be rewarded by adequate material and moral support from men. Support from men, after all, is traditional compensation for submitting to private domination at home, but the patriarchal bargain has changed. So instead single mothers make do by trying to be as successful as possible for themselves and their children.

It is a shaky success, indeed.

Russian single mothers do not conform to dominant stereotypes. (Of course, neither do most single mothers conform to pervasive societal stereotypes.)[10] They are not desperate to find men, nor have most sworn off men entirely. They cannot rely on state support and have long worked outside the home, and though they struggle to make ends meet they consider material difficulties routine and not the main story of their lives. Single mothers would like to find a good man, and they would like more support from the state, but they are counting on motherhood instead, in three ways. First, as scholars have observed in other contexts, Russian single mothers believe that only by having a child can a woman be completely fulfilled. Motherhood, even though in Russia this most often means having just one child, is compulsory in terms of "doing gender" properly in a way in which having a man at one's side simply is not. Mothers' commitment to their children's futures, to a large extent, inspires them to survive and to succeed. Getting married is still important to many women, but the main status-related issue is only whether one has been married for a while. Given Russia's divorce culture, most women know that many marriages, in spite of high hopes, do not last. Alongside marriage, cohabitation is an increasingly acceptable, and sometimes preferable, option. In any case, marriage is not considered nearly as important to a woman's identity as having a child. Second, single mothers are counting on themselves as mothers, to transform themselves into savvy practical realists who can make it in the New Russia. If they attempt to be otherwise, they are not demonstrating their competence in front of others, and they may be reprimanded for their naïveté in addition to feeling isolated from a critical mass of "successful" single mothers. Whatever dreams they may have had for a two-parent family life, most women are expected to attempt to "get a hold of themselves," change their outlook, and make do for their families by themselves. Third, in most cases single mothers are counting on their own mothers, their children's babushki, to help them create families in which children have many (if not more) of the advantages of two-parent families. In many cases, these single mother–grandmother families work remarkably well, functioning in a similar manner to the strongest of two-parent heterosexual families. Certainly many of these two-woman partnerships offer more stability (even if many may have less income) than some two-parent heterosexual families.

Besides counting on motherhood in these different ways, single mothers are increasingly counting on the market. Because the Russian state has pulled back the support it offered families in the late Soviet period, and because the Russian state and society generally ignore growing numbers of single mothers, single mothers no longer realistically expect much from the state or from most men and, consequently, are resigned to taking what they can get from both. Many single mothers are increasingly focused on making money in the capitalist marketplace. Some single mothers, especially those with significant backstage babushka support allowing them to approximate unencumbered male workers (and nondrinking ones at that), believe that they can do fairly well. Because single mothers feel as though they are going it alone, relying only on themselves (even if they are also relying heavily on babushki), a new ideology of independence and self-reliant success has accompanied Russian capitalism that resonates with single mothers' experiences and provides them with dignity.

In some ways, single mothers, much more so than married mothers, are prototypical capitalist workers. Disillusioned with grand narratives of social change (whether socialism or feminism), single mothers have little support apart from their own mothers as they strive to make it in post-Soviet society. With this lack of feasible alternatives, many come to believe in the promise of capitalism. Even single mothers who continue to work in the low-paid state sector are not stuck in the Socialist past or separated from market opportunities; instead these women take on side jobs, private tutoring, and other creative ways to improve their families' standard of living. Other women live relatively poorly but argue that at least they have time with their children under a more flexible system of work than their own mothers experienced in the period of state socialism, when working full-time during the week was mandatory for all. Single mothers' beliefs, however, must be considered in context. Many single mothers believe in the capitalist system, not out of fervor, but because they have a hard time believing in the state or most men. This kind of belief is akin to "the choice of the necessary," in Pierre Bourdieu's terms. Although Bourdieu was writing about taste and how it varies by class, elements of his observations can be applied to Russian single mothers "making do" with family lives that differ from their ideals: "Necessity imposes a taste for necessity which implies a form of adaptation to and consequently acceptance of the necessary, a resignation to the inevitable."[11] Single mothers adopt particular cultural styles, in terms of "making do" by transforming themselves into practical realists and turning to their mothers for support, because these attitudes and strategies make sense in solving the dilemmas they face. But the way in which single mothers take on social problems of patriarchal capitalism and gender inequality in labor markets and focus on their own attitudes and selves in order to make their lives better has serious consequences. Doing so ultimately comes at great personal and societal cost.

The meaning of single motherhood is always dependent on the wider social and cultural context. Russian women are not only becoming single mothers in response to marital or relationship problems, but they are doing so in a broader context of neoliberal market capitalist ideologies and policies as well as a resurgence of patriarchal ideas, or what has been called by some scholars "gender neotraditionalism."[12] Given the context of discriminatory labor markets, the normalization of male heavy drinking in society, the retrenchment of the state, and the rise of self-reliance as a life strategy for individuals, single motherhood is an increasingly common response to family life. There is a yawning gap between women's ideals of family life based on complete two-parent, supportive nuclear families, on the one hand, and local realities, in which families are matrifocal and women turn to other women for support in the perceived absence of reliable men and the state, on the other.

All kinds of single mothers face the common dilemma of making do with lives that depart from dominant two-parent family ideals; practical realism provides the unifying framework for sometimes contradictory discourses and practices among women. Single mothers focused on "doing it all" today and conforming to the tenets of practical realism share a great deal in common with Soviet superwomen of the past; nevertheless, the bar for today's Russian superwomen has been set even higher, with more dire consequences for falling short. New ideologies of successful self-reliance accompanying neoliberal market capitalism allow for even less weakness or complaint among women. Women must be even stronger as they cannot count on the state or most men for support. Life was not idyllic in Soviet times either, but back then there were more basic securities for families, especially for women and children, and the state enforced, at least to some degree, men's responsibility to provide for their families, whether in the form of a paycheck or child support.

❦ Beyond Exceptionalism

Challenging assumptions about single motherhood and grappling with family change requires that we move beyond exceptionalism of both the Russian and American varieties. Scholars see post-Soviet Russia as exceptional because of the unique aspects of postsocialism and the legacies of feudalism and state socialism. Similarly, scholars see U.S. single motherhood as exceptional because of low rates of marriage, dependence on female kin networks, and gender distrust, at least where rates of single motherhood are highest. Internationally comparative studies typically exclude Russia.

Yet narratives emphasizing matrifocal families, gender mistrust, and economic breakdown are widespread among all kinds of Russian mothers and are reminiscent of similar narratives found in the literature on African American families in inner cities. In ethnographies of low-income communities in the United States, men are often absent or relatively marginal in relation to female-based support networks.[13] Of course, one should not minimize the differences between countries as vast and diverse as Russia and the United States. But neither should differing historical circumstances lead us to ignore striking parallels in common, especially parallels with theory-generating potential. When Elijah Anderson describes grandmothers and adult daughters bonding and relying on each other in U.S. inner cities because they agree that alcoholism, violence, and irresponsibility are problems of men, he might also be describing grandmothers and single-mother daughters in Russia. When

Kathryn Edin and Maria Kefalas describe low-income women who value motherhood over marriage not because they reject the institution of marriage but because decent, trustworthy men are in short supply, they might also be describing many of Russia's single mothers.[14] Yet in spite of some intriguing parallels, scholars of Russia have noted only in passing the commonalities between Russian families and families in U.S. inner cities.[15]

The Russian case makes several important contributions to what we know about single motherhood more generally. A close analysis of Russian single motherhood forces us to interrogate many purported differences between types of single motherhood, all while challenging assumptions that marriage is a solution to single motherhood, and that material difficulties are the most critical component of single mothers' lives. First, the Russian case transcends many of the divisions present in the Western literature, especially those of race, but also differences of marital status, work status, and class (e.g., welfare- versus work-reliant). Most U.S. research reinforces a broader binary division between the low-income, unmarried variety of single motherhood more prevalent among women of color and the middle-income, divorced single motherhood more prevalent among white women.[16] It is the former, rather than the latter, that is frequently (though erroneously) viewed as a problem that marriage could solve.

Practices of women relying on their children's grandmothers and expressing distrust in men as partners, at least when it occurs in African American communities, have long been pathologized in the United States. Most controversially, the Moynihan report argued that the "Negro family" was "highly unstable" and approaching breakdown, even citing a "tangle of pathology" in many urban areas.[17] Although later criticized by Carol Stack and others as dismissive of a different kind of order and organization, the idea of the nuclear family as the normative cultural ideal continues to hold sway.[18] Of course, these divisions in the broader literature may at times make sense. In the United States, unmarried childbearing is three times more common among the poor, and especially among African Americans, than it is among the affluent.

But even though whites are more likely to marry and subsequently divorce, and blacks are more likely to never marry at all, "half of all children living in single-parent households are in that situation because their parents divorced, not because they failed to marry."[19] The latest studies indicate that this proportion is growing in the United States, with fewer than half of today's single mothers unmarried. Divisions have become too entrenched in scholarship, preventing us from understanding a much more fluid and rapidly shifting reality. More mothers than any official statistics suggest experience a period of time when they are, either officially or unofficially, single.

A snapshot picture of single motherhood based on cross-sectional data grossly underestimates the number of children who have spent or will spend time in a single-mother family, while also exaggerating racial differences as a contributor to the likelihood of participating in this family type.[20]

Nuclear families are culturally dominant in spite of recent evidence that marriage, regardless of its merits, is also a "greedy institution" that "separates men and women from other social connections and therefore detracts from ties to extended families and broader communities."[21] Given what we know about the marriage markets that lower-income women in the United States face, where drug abuse, domestic violence, infidelity, poor employment prospects, and other problems are common, the fact that marriage remains so highly valued might be seen instead as rather surprising.

This book has moved beyond the binaries dividing various kinds of single mothers to highlight questions of cultural meaning while seeking out diversity in terms of route to single motherhood, income, and the inclusion of nonresident fathers' perspectives. As Margaret Nelson (2005) has noted, conservative scholars of single motherhood have tended to emphasize the differences in outcomes between single mothers who acted according to the "right values" versus those presumed to be morally deficient, whereas liberal scholars have tended to assume that material constraints make discussions of choices and values among single mothers irrelevant. Looking at single mothers as groups of women living in either extreme poverty or reliant on welfare also tends to fix single mothers as if they are always in one situation, assuming that the routes to single motherhood determine the issues mothers face. In a review of three prominent books on U.S. single motherhood, Cameron Macdonald was struck most by how much women "from very different social locations" share in common, noting that while women of all kinds find motherhood "mandatory," romantic partnerships are more optional, seen as "both risky and rare."[22]

Indeed, there are many similarities in terms of the issues that concern single mothers on a daily basis. Though there are some important differences among Russian women who become single mothers in various ways, the differences are still emergent while the similarities are more striking. Single mothers confront similar cultural dilemmas even when their material circumstances differ; these similarities also require analysis as we come to grips with Russia's quiet revolution in family life.[23] Culture both enables and constrains Russian single mothers, shaping, alongside state policies, women's perceptions of material difficulties and the circumstances of their lives. We need to move beyond old ideas of culture as a system of meaning opposed to structure and recognize more fully that culture is constitutive of the structures in people's lives. Women draw on a tool kit of cultural resources, of habits, skills, and styles as they implement strategies of action, adapting both to neoliberal capitalism and to life as a single mother.[24]

Looking at single motherhood from a global perspective, we see that what has been pathologized as exceptional in the United States is normalized as the status quo in Russia. Understanding why Russian single motherhood is so normalized in spite of nuclear family ideals has required that we interrogate the dominant discourse about the weakness and unreliability of men in Russia and the related discourse on the weak, apathetic state. Heterosexual relationships are frailer in Russia than the stronger bonds of kin. Many women in Russia depend on their mothers' support in raising their child at least as much as, and frequently more than, they depend on their children's fathers. Since men are marginal in Russian families and women talk of relying more on their mothers than on the state or on any man, what then is "normal" family life anyway?

Second, besides challenging many differences frequently assumed between groups of single mothers, unlike in the United States marriage in Russia is not seen as a solution for single mothers. Americans value marriage highly (with around 90% projected to marry in their lifetimes), and the United States spends $150 million annually on promoting marriage through the Healthy Marriage Initiative.[25] Russians, too, value marriage highly. Marriage is less sacralized in Russia, and although marriage rates have declined since the late Soviet period, Russia still has one of the higher marriage rates among industrialized countries. Just as Americans value marriage highly but are prone to changing their partnership status quickly and frequently, stepping on and off "the carousel of intimate relationships,"[26] Russians, too, tend to marry early and divorce quickly. However, because the Russian state is concerned primarily with replenishing the population, most recently by offering women incentives or "baby bonuses" for bearing a second or third child, there is minimal concern for the precise form of motherhood (as long as women continue to do the work of bearing and raising children). The Soviet state once supported two-parent families and made marriage essential for getting ahead. Today there is no such commitment on the part of the state. Rather than using marriage promotion as an antipoverty program, the state is preoccupied with solving a perceived demographic crisis and giving women incentives to bear more than one child. Like most Russians, the state accepts the normalized gender crisis as the status quo, rendering single mothers, and the grandmothers supporting single-mother families, invisible.

Third, this book decenters material difficulties as the main narrative in single mothers' lives. Many would have expected a book about single mothers, particularly one focused on Russia, to foreground hardship and misery. Yet while many of Russia's single mothers do face material challenges, they deny that material difficulties are the main facet of their lives. In fact, many single mothers argue that they endure less domestic drudgery than married mothers, especially if they have their own mother supporting them at home. Research on single motherhood in other settings has noted some of its more positive aspects. For example, avoidance of violence and an increased sense of control over their lives are noted by many mothers. However, these findings have not yet dented the dominant narrative in the literature that emphasizes hardship.

Single mothers never have it easy. But the Russian case sensitizes us to the fact that in spite of single motherhood's challenges, and the moral hand-wringing that still surrounds it, more women continue to turn to it as an alternative when partnerships turn toxic. However much two-parent families are valued, mothers are becoming single in spite of the considerable challenges, accepting hardship in the pursuit of freedom. Understanding the full contours of women's lives helps to explain why single motherhood is increasingly an acceptable, and even admirable, option for all kinds of mothers.

✐ Implications of Russian Single Motherhood

This in-depth analysis of Russian single motherhood has important implications for the sociology of families more generally and for the study of Russia and East Europe in particular. Two major themes in this book—the unreliability of men and the importance of female kin networks—echo studies of low-income, urban, single motherhood in the United States, especially among African American single mothers. But the Russian case should not be seen as a mere extension of these themes, nor is the Russia case simply akin to the "ghetto" writ large. Instead, Russian women, most of them mothers, have long been expected to be society's social workers, to nurture men, and perhaps even to nurture a traumatized patriarchy, back to health. More and more women now refuse to do so, while still wishing that men, and the state, were otherwise: reliable, strong, sober, supportive.

Lessons from the Russian case should be used to build our theories and inspire future studies focusing on how growing numbers of women manage, and do relatively well, even in the most difficult of circumstances. The normalization of these themes in Russia, among all kinds of women who remain strong supporters of traditional, two-parent, nuclear families, suggests that families are not changing because of deficient values. Rather, families are changing regardless of the values individual women may hold. Women are increasingly becoming single mothers because they cannot count on the state and do not trust that they can really count on most men. But some women, and a fairly large number of women in Russia, still believe they can count on motherhood. That is, women count primarily on themselves, their children, and oftentimes their own mothers. All of this is instructive in the U.S. case, where some scholarship continues to imply that if only single mothers would realize that two-parent families are better for their kids, trends would begin to change. Of course, some scholars do acknowledge that "returning to substantially lower rates of divorce and nonmarital childbearing, although a worthwhile goal, is not realistic, at least in the short term."[27] Rather than condemning the rise of single motherhood or, worse still, blaming single mothers themselves, we learn from the Russian case that the growth of single motherhood is taking place under circumstances largely beyond women's direct control. Moreover, single mothers are seeking to do right by their children and by themselves.

In addition, the Russian case demonstrates that the idea of marriage as a panacea for single mothers, or as a "solution" for poverty, is misplaced, misguided, and indeed harmful. The dominant debate in the United States, about why poor single mothers do not marry even though marriage might improve their well-being and the well-being of their families, would be meaningless in Russia. Women marry in Russia and then divorce later, or they give birth as a single mother after a cohabiting relationship goes sour or in a variety of other circumstances. But women's daily lives, especially in Russia where divorced mothers face severe obstacles to receiving adequate child support, do not differ significantly from one another on the basis of the individual's route to single motherhood. And the idea of marriage as a guarantee of anything in Russia is almost laughable.

The lives of single and married mothers differ, but not nearly to the extent that the literature dividing women according to differences of marital status suggests. The differences between black and white mothers, or between unwed and divorced mothers, which figure so prominently in the United States in creating distinctions among mothers, do not play a prominent role in the case of Russian single motherhood. The Russian case foregrounds the ambiguities obscured in the distinctions scholars often assume in writing about single and married women. Distinctions based on race and class among single mothers are not inevitable, and there may be more similarities among diverse women based on the everyday dilemmas they have in common.

Finally, the Russian case shows the importance of weighing culture and the state more heavily in the study of single motherhood. I mean "culture" not in the sense of whether women have the presumed "right" values but in terms of how women wield particular styles and strategies to solve problems in their daily lives. Bringing culture in, as recent studies have begun to do, allows for a fuller and more accurate picture of single motherhood.[28] After all, single motherhood rarely makes sense from a material point of view considering how difficult it is to get by on one salary instead of two; but that has not stopped the growth of single motherhood in contexts where it seems to make the least material sense. In addition, the Russian case illuminates just how much the state matters in shaping the character of women's lives and the meaning of marital status. Because the Russian state is currently more concerned with encouraging women, regardless of marital status, to have a second or third child (given that most Russian women will have one child anyway), the state is de-emphasizing marital status. With the retrenchment of state protections for mothers and children, the state encourages women to make motherhood a choice and to focus on developing their own self-reliance as they navigate new workplaces and social institutions.

Moreover, this study suggests that ordinary Russians, despite the poverty and hardships that have affected so many in the New Russia, are doing much more than surviving. In many ways, single mothers are succeeding, perhaps not compared with the standards of success that men hold for themselves (but we have seen that women seldom compare themselves to men in Russia), but according to the standard of providing as best one can for one's family. Considering the cards they have been dealt, single mothers are relatively successful, or at least they believe success is within reach. In order to understand single mothers' belief in success, we must look beyond their struggles for material survival. While important, culture also shapes the very meaning of survival in Russia, with many women dismissing the centrality of material difficulties as the main story of their lives. Understanding these cultural meanings of what it means not only to survive but to succeed as a single mother might also help to illuminate, for example, people's support for Putin-era policies associated with stability or neoliberal capitalist ideologies promising increased opportunity for those willing to work hard.

Still, considering the talents and capacities of Russian single mothers, their relative success comes at great cost. Single mothers are left unsupported by the state, and by most men, and are succeeding and working on becoming optimistic, practical realists in a society lacking in protections from the market and from abusive or alcoholic men. In such a context, a great deal depends purely on women's individual pluck and luck. Pluck and luck are hardly factors that provide a secure foundation for raising children. Although the Russian state is preoccupied with increasing the birthrate, it would do well to pay more attention to the struggles of single mothers, of all kinds, including many bereft of their mother's support, as they make their way as best they can in an indifferent world. Putin's speeches have paid some attention to women's struggles as workers and as mothers, and some have even argued that "few other politicians of this level, anywhere in the world, have so strongly endorsed women's economic independence."[29] Yet single motherhood is so normalized that single mothers and their struggles remain relatively invisible. Moreover, fathers and men are glaringly absent from political speeches and in Russian society, and no attention is paid to the grandmothers who shore up Russia's fragile families, at great cost to their own health and leisure as they grow older.

Although one might easily blame the Russian state for marginalizing men as fathers in families, what else might one conclude from this case study concerning Russian men as fathers and as potential partners to women? After all, Russian women are without men in more ways than the literal phrase suggests. Single mothers do not have men they can reliably count on in most cases, but even married men, fathers, and other ordinary Russians are apt to describe Russian men in less than flattering terms. Russian men, they argue, are weak, drink too much, are too indifferent to their families, and are less likely to adapt successfully to the demands of market capitalism than women are. Listening to the complaints about Russian men, one might momentarily forget that it is men who are nevertheless solidly in charge of dominant political and economic institutions in the New Russia. Yet in the realm of family life the negative cultural discourse on men creates a self-fulfilling prophecy. Although there are a few signs of shifting cultural attitudes, men remain for the most part unconvinced of their importance to their children or to families in general. Nonresident fathers are especially apt to argue that women are naturally stronger in Russia, better able to endure, to work and raise children, to get by no matter what the circumstances.

Even though patriarchy is intact in Russian society, perhaps it is traumatized. Whether men's patterns of infidelity and marginalization in family life date back to the tragedy of the Second World War and policies legislating women's responsibility for family, with the help of grandmothers, or whether it has a deeper cause yet to be fully explored, the matrifocal aspects of Russian family life, and the situation of many men on the margins of families, require more attention. Russian men are objectively freer to opt out of family involvement than ever before, and some are satisfied with being on the margins of family life given all that it takes to be breadwinners under market capitalism. Single motherhood, however liberating it may sometimes feel to some women, only exaggerates the differences between women's and men's lives. With growing single motherhood, fewer men participate in family life and more women bear the social burden of single-handedly raising children and holding families together. Ideally, according to Russian women and most scholarship, both parents should be involved in helping to raise the next generation.

In Russia, women have long been expected to do whatever it takes to hold their families together, to become superwomen able to endure and move forward at all costs. But while Russian men have been marginalized in Russian family life over time, a growing number of women are refusing to live in intact families for the sake of what others might think or even for the sake of a normative ideal. Instead, single motherhood is a reasonable response to what can be seen as a normalized gender crisis. Even though few single mothers consider their lives ideal, most are proud of their efforts, holding their heads high. Many are doing relatively well for their children, themselves, and their extended families, and while they may hope for a brighter future with a strong, supportive government and men who are reliable, relatively sober, and helpful partners, they are not really counting on these developments in the near future. Practical realism offers an alternative route to success, based on relying on oneself and improving one's chances in the marketplace, with help from other women along the way.

Life as a single mother offers dignity, in spite of the challenges of trying to succeed with minimal supports in what many women experience as a man's world of market capitalism. With few other options, most single mothers are counting mainly on motherhood—on themselves, their own mothers, and the promise of their own children in the years to come.

◆ Notes

Introduction. A Quiet Revolution

1. Ellwood and Jencks, "Spread of Single-Parent Families."

2. For instance, the number of single-parent families across the thirty-four member countries of the Organisation for Economic Co-operation and Development (OECD) is projected to increase over the next couple of decades (by as much as 22 to 29 percent overall), with single-parent families comprising an even greater proportion of all households with children. OECD, "The Future of Families to 2030," 8, 10–11, 13.

In Russia, growing single motherhood is a trend, in that by 2010, 24.1 percent of the total number of families were composed of single-parent households headed by women. See Sobolevskaya, "Fragmented Families." However, according to Russian demographer Sergei Zakharov, "The most significant thing about this trend is that we don't know enough about it. We don't know who these women are." Russia keeps few statistics on single mothers. Megan Twohey, "1 in 3 Babies Born to Unmarried Moms," *Moscow Times*, November 29, 2001, http://www.russialist.org/archives/5571-3.php.

3. Casey and Maldonado, "Worst Off"; Rampell, "Single Parents." I use "single mothers" in lieu of the gender-neutral "single parents" to emphasize that single parenthood is overwhelmingly a gendered phenomenon, and all the more so in Russia.

4. Mathur, Fu, and Hansen, "Alarming Rise of Single Parenthood."

5. U.S. nonmarital birth rates increased from 32 percent in the mid-1990s to 41 percent in 2011, but most single mothers are separated, divorced, or widowed. Casey and Maldonado, "Worst Off."

6. Shattuck and Kreider, "Characteristics of Currently Unmarried Women."

7. Mathur, Fu, and Hansen, "Alarming Rise of Single Parenthood."

8. Brooks, "Opportunity Gap."

9. Lemmon, "America's Silent Crisis."

10. Murphy and Kroll, "Santorum: Single Moms Are 'Breeding More Criminals'"; Marcotte, "Romney Blames Single Parents"; Appelbaum, "Study of Men's Falling Income Cites Single Parents." Recent survey data suggest that seven in ten Americans consider increasing single motherhood "bad for society," with 61 percent agreeing that a child needs both a mother and father to grow up happily. A large percentage of Americans still disapprove of single motherhood, according to survey data published by the Pew Research Center on January 6, 2011. See http://www.pewresearch.org/daily-number/disapprove-of-single-mothers/.

11. Mayor, "Single Mom Stigma." As cited by Mayor, LeBlanc argues that the left sees single mothers as "victims of failed social policy," whereas for the right they are a "symptom of moral failure."

12. Since 2007, the Russian government has begun incentivizing second and third births for women, with money paid out after a child turns three years old. These "capitals" amount to the world's largest bonus payments relative to income for child-bearing. See Zavisca, *Housing the New Russia*; Rivkin-Fish, "Pronatalism."

13. Poizner, "Sorrows of Mother Russia."

14. Stanley, "Russian Mothers." Emphasis is mine.

15. Although "patriarchy" has been a contested and controversial term in recent years, several scholars acknowledge that it still may be useful as a description of male dominance, even though it is not an explanation (see Pollert, "Gender and Class Revisited"). I generally find theories of gender relations and intersectionality more useful for illuminating aspects of how gender systems work, but perhaps we still need a descriptive term for structures of male domination, even if such structures are always in interaction with other sources of domination (see Einspahr, "Structural Domination"). Particularly in Russia, the term has continuing relevance, considering male dominance of church and state. Given the tendency to declare looming "matriarchy" in recent years, perhaps we should be more cautious before moving "beyond patriarchy" in feminist scholarship.

16. The term "matrifocal family" was first coined by Raymond T. Smith in 1973 (*The Matrifocal Family*, reprinted in 1996). Just as men dominate West Indian society while being marginal as husbands and fathers, so in Russia men are marginal as fathers compared with the social significance and practical and emotional responsibilities given to mothers.

17. Russia has the world's largest CDR (crude divorce rate) of five divorces per thousand people, according to figures published in the *Demographic Yearbook of Russia* (Goskomstat, 2012). However, measuring divorce is complicated, and the TDR (total divorce rate) is a more specific measure because it takes age and marital status of the population into account. Unfortunately, Russia has incomplete divorce statistics, and since 1997 the TDR has not been available in Russia. Both CDR and TDR show similar dynamics in Russia; see Jasilioniene, "Premarital Conception and Divorce Risk in Russia," 4.

18. Eberstadt and Shah, "Russia's Demographic Disaster"; Moskoff, "Divorce in the USSR"; Zakharov, "Russian Federation."

19. Zabel, "Patterns of Partnership Formation." The Russian pattern of nonmarital childbearing seems to have more in common with the U.S. pattern of lower rates of marriage among disadvantaged women; Russian women with higher education are more likely to marry after an unexpected pregnancy. See Perelli-Harris and Gerber, "Nonmarital Childbearing in Russia."

20. Motivans, "Family Formation in Russia," 35.

21. Shevchenko, *Crisis and the Everyday*.

22. Pascall and Manning, "Gender and Social Policy"; Kanji, "The Route Matters."

23. Edin and Kefalas, *Promises I Can Keep*.

24. Because the dramatic rise in cohabitation is relatively new in Russia, I excluded those women living with a male partner. However, I learned that even this choice is somewhat arbitrary given that women cohabiting with a man do not

necessarily have additional financial support or practical help with raising children. I met women who referred to their cohabiting partners as "husband," but when I talked to their male partners individually, several referred to their partners as "girlfriend." A few noted that they "had other women as well." It is highly unlikely that cohabitation in Russia implies the kind of stability that it does in countries like Sweden or Norway; it is likely just as unstable and temporary as it is in the United States.

25. I borrow this phrase from Sidel, *Unsung Heroines*.

26. Pesmen, *Russia and Soul*, 46–51.

27. I also interviewed another fifteen grandmothers informally, taking notes rather than recording them, following interviews with single-mother daughters.

28. Duneier, "On the Legacy of Elliott Liebow and Carol Stack."

29. Macdonald, "Life without Father," 93. In a review essay featuring three landmark books on single motherhood, Macdonald asks, "What about the family members who are silent in these narratives? What about the men? Why are they so absent from their children's lives?"

30. Ledeneva, *Russia's Economy of Favours*.

31. Goskomstat, *Demographic Yearbook, 2002*. According to census data, a Russian woman today has, on average, 1.3 children.

32. Mirroring Russia's most recent statistics, nearly one-third of mothers sampled had experienced a nonmarital birth at some point during their lives.

33. Mazzei and O'Brien, "You've Got It." At times I was forced to negotiate scripts very carefully, especially when nodes in social networks intersected. One married mother told me her husband had cheated on her two weeks earlier with one of my single-mother informants. A few weeks after a different interview with a single mother, I was able to interview her former husband, allowing me to get differing perspectives on the same life events. Most single mothers asked me to refrain from contacting their children's fathers, fearing repercussions in terms of an already fragile, and often thoroughly broken, relationship. Nodes intersected most frequently when interviewing single mothers and their own mothers.

34. Hackstaff, *Marriage in a Culture of Divorce*.

Chapter 1. From State Protections to Post-Socialist "Freedoms"

1. *Santa Barbara* was a very popular television program in Russia after the collapse of the Soviet Union. The name "Santa Barbara" has come to metonymically represent soap operas in general and any stories about love filled with divorce and intrigue.

2. *Byt* has a negative connotation, referring to the petty and mundane concerns of everyday life. See the introduction.

3. Avdeyeva, "Policy Experiment in Russia," 369.

4. Ashwin, *Gender, State and Society*, 11.

5. Stephenson, review of *Single Parents and Child Welfare in the New Russia*, 1174.

6. Although the war ended in 1945, I date the beginning of the postwar period from 1944. The Family Law passed in July 1944 created the category of "single mothers" and marked a new, distinct era in family policies concerning marriage, divorce, and single motherhood.

7. Nakachi, "N. S. Khrushchev and the 1944 Soviet Family Law"; Parsons, *Dying Unneeded*.

8. Lunyakova, "O sovremennom urovne zhizni semei odinokikh materei."

9. Nakachi, "N. S. Khrushchev and the 1944 Soviet Family Law," 41.

10. Bucher, "Struggling to Survive."

11. Nakachi, "N. S. Khrushchev and the 1944 Soviet Family Law," 47. See also Bucher, "Struggling to Survive"; McKinney, "Lone Mothers in Russia"; Lapidus, *Women in Soviet Society*.

12. Randall, "'Abortion Will Deprive You of Happiness!,'" 25.

13. Lapidus, *Women in Soviet Society*.

14. See Nakachi, "N. S. Khrushchev and the 1944 Soviet Family Law," for an insightful analysis of the disastrous effects of the law.

15. Central Statistical Bureau data for 1945–1955 show 8.7 million illegitimate births; see Nakachi, "N. S. Khrushchev and the 1944 Soviet Family Law," 64.

16. McKinney, "Lone Mothers in Russia." These rates are similar to contemporary rates of nonmarital births.

17. Bucher, "Struggling to Survive"; McKinney, "Lone Mothers in Russia."

18. Kanji, "The Route Matters," 208.

19. Carlbäck, "Lone Mothers and Fatherless Children," 92.

20. Randall, "'Abortion Will Deprive You of Happiness!'"

21. Scholars disagree about whether the Soviet state approached goals of gender equality in the wrong way (McAuley, *Women's Work*), or whether equality was ever truly a top priority since the Soviet state was more concerned with mobilizing women into the workforce (Lapidus, *Women in Soviet Society*).

22. To put this in perspective, McKinney, "Lone Mothers in Russia," 43, notes that "In 1980, lone mothers still received only 5 rubles per month for one child, 7.5 rubles for two, and 10 rubles a month for three, exactly the same amounts they were entitled to in the late 1940s and only a fraction of the official monthly poverty line of 66.6 rubles per capita."

23. Kiblitskaya, *Ispovedi odinokikh materei*; Lapidus, *Women in Soviet Society*.

24. Randall, "'Abortion Will Deprive You of Happiness!,'" 30–31.

25. Ibid.

26. Yurchak, *Everything Was Forever*.

27. McKinney, "Lone Mothers in Russia."

28. Lapidus, *Women in Soviet Society*.

29. Moskoff, "Divorce in the USSR."

30. Kiblitskaya, *Ispovedi odinokikh materei*.

31. Bucher, "Struggling to Survive"; Rotkirch, *Man Question*; Nakachi, "N. S. Khrushchev and the 1944 Soviet Family Law."

32. Lapidus, *Women in Soviet Society*; Gray, "*Soviet Women: Walking the Tightrope*."

33. Kelly, *Children's World*, 396.

34. Lapidus, *Women in Soviet Society*; McAuley, *Women's Work*. Studies that use archival data, autobiographies, or interviews to analyze Soviet single motherhood tend to focus on the postwar rather than the late Soviet period (e.g., Bucher, "Struggling to Survive"; Rotkirch, *Man Question*; Nakachi, "N. S. Khrushchev and the 1944 Soviet Family Law"). Although the press relentlessly portrayed the ideal Soviet

woman as a Stakhanovite (a Soviet worker who overachieved on the job) at work and at home, according to Bucher's research on women in postwar Moscow, women were in reality more practical about what they could accomplish.

35. One Soviet single mother had four children. She explained that she had an abortion when she was very young and had decided then to never again have an abortion. Although she does not regret having a large family, her comments reveal much about the lack of available contraception in the USSR; in her view, she faced two choices: having a large family or having abortions to prevent subsequent children. Abortions during this period were often provided in "assembly-line fashion and without anesthetic" (Randall, "'Abortion Will Deprive You of Happiness!,'" 31).

36. Draitser, *Making War, Not Love*, 62.

37. Gray, *Soviet Women*.

38. MacFadyen, "*Moscow Does Not Believe in Tears*."

39. Gillespie, "Soviet and Russian Blockbuster Films," 480.

40. Gray, *Soviet Women*, 55.

41. Lapidus, *Women in Soviet Society*.

42. Motivans, "Family Formation." See also Cartwright, "Shotgun Weddings."

43. Cartwright, "Shotgun Weddings." See Gray, *Soviet Women*, on the state's support of the rush to marriage.

44. Cartwright, "Shotgun Weddings," 6.

45. More than 80 percent of Soviet women underwent at least one abortion by the end of their childbearing years and often between two and four abortions per woman. Contraception was hard to come by and of poor quality. See Kotkin, *Steeltown, USSR*.

46. Bondarskaia and Darskiy, "Brachnoe-sostoianie i rozhdaemost'"; Cartwright, "Shotgun Weddings." See also Motivans, "Family Formation," on fear of abortion.

47. Russians, including both Soviet and post-Soviet single mothers, use the phrase *grazhdanskii brak* in reference to people living together without being officially registered as married. The term literally means "civil marriage" and is used to describe a marriage in a civil registry office as opposed to a marriage taking place in a church. But in colloquial speech people routinely use *grazhdanskii brak* to refer to the practice of cohabiting or living together without registering the union. This colloquial usage is confusing since technically all official marriages were civil marriages in the Soviet Union.

48. Although her inquiry discomfited me, she asked whether I was married, brusquely responding: "Well, I assumed a woman like you would be married." Clearly some of the status differences women felt in the Soviet period have not completely disappeared in spite of post-Soviet freedoms.

49. Kiblitskaya, *Ispovedi odinokikh materei*.

50. Rotkirch, *Man Question*, 111–112.

51. Gray, "Reflections (Soviet Women)," 76.

52. Officially Soviet courts also cited a third major reason meant to encompass all reasons for divorce other than alcoholism and infidelity: "incompatibility of character" (in the United States the closest reason might be "irreconcilable differences"). See Lapidus, *Women in Soviet Society*.

53. Kukhterin, "Fathers and Patriarchs," 88.

54. Kiblitskaya, *Ispovedi odinokikh materei*; Klugman and Motivans, *Single Parents and Child Welfare in the New Russia*; McAuley, *Economic Welfare in the Soviet Union*.

55. Lokshin, Harris, and Popkin, "Single Mothers in Russia," 2184.

56. Ledeneva, *Russia's Economy of Favours*, 1.

57. Gurko, *Roditel'stvo*.

58. Ledeneva, *Russia's Economy of Favours*, 120.

59. Gray, *Soviet Women*; Rotkirch, *Man Question*.

60. Kukhterin, "Fathers and Patriarchs," 82.

61. McKinney, "Lone Mothers in Russia," 41. See also Lapidus, *Women in Soviet Society*, 272–273.

62. Cubbins and Vannoy, "Division of Household Labor"; Pridemore, "Heavy Drinking and Suicide in Russia"; White, *Russia Goes Dry*.

63. Pridemore and Kim, "Research Note"; Richardson and Ivanov, "Little Water of Life."

64. See Mackey, "Tackling 'the Russian God.'"

65. White, *Russia Goes Dry*.

66. Parsons, *Dying Unneeded*. During fieldwork, I most commonly drank tea with women. Alcoholic drinks were featured at weekend gatherings with friends or holidays but were seldom part of any routine among women.

67. Bobak et al., "Contribution of Drinking Patterns."

68. World Health Organization (WHO), *Global Status Report on Alcohol and Health*, 27.

69. Hinote and Webber, "Drinking toward Manhood," 299, 306.

70. Ashwin, *Gender, State and Society*; Ashwin and Lytkina, "Men in Crisis"; Kay, *Men in Contemporary Russia*.

71. Zdravomyslova and Chikadze, "Scripts of Men's Heavy Drinking," 49.

72. See Höjdestrand, *Needed by Nobody*; Parsons, *Dying Unneeded*.

73. Parsons, *Dying Unneeded*.

74. Bobrova et al., "Gender Differences in Drinking Practices."

75. Zhenochka is a diminutive form of the name Evgenia, used here affectionately. Evgenia is the closest equivalent to the name Jennifer in Russian. I had known this family for several months and was welcomed frequently into their home.

76. Johnson, *Gender Violence in Russia*, 24.

77. Cubbins and Vannoy, "Division of Household Labor."

78. Johnson, *Gender Violence in Russia*, 32.

Chapter 2. Diminishing Material Difficulties

1. Hertz, *Single by Chance*.

2. Ries, *Russian Talk*, 127.

3. Gal and Kligman, *Politics of Gender*; Gray, *Soviet Women: Walking the Tightrope*; Ispa-Landa, "Persistence of the 'Strong Woman/Infantile Man' Discourse"; Kukhterin, "Fathers and Patriarchs"; Ries, *Russian Talk*; Rotkirch, *Man Question*.

4. McLanahan and Sandefur, *Growing up with a Single Parent*.

5. Kanji, "The Route Matters."

6. Kiblitskaya, *Ispovedi odinokikh materei.*

7. My observation is supported by recent Russian census data in which the number of women claiming to be married is much higher than that of married men. In 2002, 65,000 women claimed to be married to men who did not seem to exist, compared with 28,000 in 1989. See Ivashko, "Average Russian Is a Middle-Aged, English-Speaking Woman." Recent studies have found that women of some cultural backgrounds are more likely to consider themselves married even if only cohabiting. In Edin and Kefalas's *Promises I Can Keep,* one in five Puerto Rican women considered themselves married while cohabiting, though few African American and white women made this claim.

8. Rotkirch, Temkina, and Zdravomyslova, "Who Helps the Degraded Housewife?," point out that although Putin, in his 2006 speech on the demographic crisis in Russia, could have used the opportunity to deplore the rising numbers of unwed parents and single mothers, he did not. Instead, he affirmed the economic independence of women and outlined new policies for encouraging women to bear a second child. In general, the Russian state makes little, if any, distinction between single- and two-parent families or between unmarried, divorced, or widowed mothers. See Klugman and Motivans, *Single Parents and Child Welfare.*

9. According to Russian census data, although 65 percent of adults were married in 1989, only 57 percent were in 2002, and of the 57 percent, more than 5 percent are actually in unregistered marriages. The number of adults who have never been married also increased between 1989 and 2002, from 16 percent to 21 percent. The number of divorced adults increased from 7 percent to 9 percent. Goskomstat, 2002.

10. Klugman and Motivans, *Single Parents and Child Welfare.*

11. Ibid., 2.

12. Garfinkel and McLanahan, *Single Mothers and Their Children.*

13. Issoupova, "From Duty to Pleasure."

14. Kiblitskaya, "Once We Were Kings," 67.

15. Kanji, "The Route Matters"; Klugman and McAuley, "Social Policy for Single-Parent Families"; Klugman and Motivans, *Single Parents and Child Welfare.*

16. Klugman and McAuley, "Social Policy for Single-Parent Families."

17. Klugman and Motivans, *Single Parents and Child Welfare*; Prokofieva, "Feminization of Poverty."

18. There may still be some judgment, however, surrounding mothers of many children in Russia, who are defined as mothers with three or more children. There were only three mothers in my sample with three children (one with twins), and generally the situation is fairly uncommon. Only 7 percent of all mothers have three or more children in Russia and only 5 percent in the Kaluga region. See Goskomstat 2002. Among single mothers, the percentage is probably much smaller.

19. Garfinkel and McLanahan, *Single Mothers and Their Children.*

20. Hochschild, *Second Shift,* 251.

21. *Perestroika* refers to the process of restructuring the Soviet political and economic system, begun under Gorbachev's leadership in the 1980s.

22. Shevchenko, *Crisis and the Everyday.*

23. Three women were still officially married but had not lived with their husbands for a long time. They considered themselves divorced, and two had recently

filed for an official divorce, while one woman saw no point in making the divorce official.

24. Abdullaev, "Russians Are Quickest to Marry and Divorce."

25. Although I interviewed many more mothers in Kaluga (seventy) than in Moscow (twenty), I found some differences between the two groups of urban women. In Moscow, women were somewhat more likely to describe falling out of love with one's husband or meeting another man as reasons for divorce, and this was usually among women who had divorced multiple times or who were earning significant money themselves. Women in Kaluga were less likely to offer these reasons. Some single mothers in Kaluga earned above-average incomes, but these incomes were still nowhere near what some professional women earn in Moscow.

26. Edin and Kefalas, *Promises I Can Keep*, 215, note that U.S. women initiate marital breakups two-thirds of the time.

27. Ibid., 81. Similarly, in Edin and Kefalas's study (*Promises I Can Keep*), two-thirds of the mothers argued that their romantic relationships had ended because of a partner's drug or alcohol addiction, crime or imprisonment, abuse, or unfaithfulness.

28. Just 10 percent of families use mortgage loans in Russia, and only 3 percent did in 2002, so the number was miniscule at the time of my research, especially in a provincial city. ITAR-TASS, "Just 10 Percent of Families Use Mortgage Loans in Russia."

29. Kay, *Men in Contemporary Russia*, 172.

30. Rotkirch, *Man Question*, 13.

31. Edin and Kefalas, *Promises I Can Keep*, 75.

32. DeVault, *Feeding the Family*, 129.

33. For example, see Ashwin, "'A Woman is Everything'"; Gray, *Soviet Women: Walking the Tightrope*; Hochschild, *Second Shift*; Lapidus, *Women in Soviet Society*.

34. Rands, "Division of Market and Household Labor," as described in Cubbins and Vannoy, "Division of Household Labor."

35. In *The Second Shift*, Hochschild also describes briefly the extra burdens Soviet women bore on the second shift. Citing the landmark research of Alexander Szalai conducted in the mid-1960s, she notes that Soviet women also worked an extra month per year.

36. Cubbins and Vannoy, "Division of Household Labor," 184.

37. This dramatic increase in the number of nonmarital births is fairly recent: in 1989 only 15 percent of all births were nonmarital. See Ivashko, "Average Russian Is a Middle-Aged, English-Speaking Woman"; also, Goskomstat, *Demographic Yearbook*.

38. Hertz, *Single by Chance*.

39. Shevchenko, *Crisis and the Everyday*.

40. Caldwell, *Not by Bread Alone*, 204.

41. Burawoy, Krotov, and Lytkina, "Involution and Destitution"; Clarke, *Making Ends Meet*; Semenova and Thompson, "Family Models and Transgenerational Influences."

42. DeVault, *Feeding the Family*, 105.

43. Jencks, Foreword to *Making Ends Meet*, xxv.

Chapter 3. "Where the Women Are Strong"

1. Hochschild, *Second Shift*, 26.

2. Hochschild, *Managed Heart.*

3. *Neoliberalism* is used in myriad ways, and there may be neoliberalisms rather than just one model. I use it to describe an ideological system with an intellectual, bureaucratic, and political face. Neoliberalism is unique as a system of ideological thought in that all three faces at their core elevate the market as a sacred "non-political, non-cultural, machine-like entity." See Mudge, "What Is Neo-Liberalism?," 705.

4. Zigon, "*HIV Is God's Blessing*," 13–14, 11; also Yurchak, *Everything Was Forever*, 73.

5. Zigon, "*HIV Is God's Blessing*," 14.

6. Patico, "Kinship and Crisis."

7. While in Moscow, I met Western men several times who generalized about Russian women on the basis of very limited experiences with women in nightclubs and bars catering to an expatriate male clientele. One man, an American chef, told me the main version of this narrative rather bluntly: "You might not see it, but one doesn't need to be a researcher to know a lot about Russian women. They are all for sale." Of course, this narrative tells us much more about some Western men, the women of an imagined Russia, and gendered power than it does about the everyday lives of most women.

8. Collier, DeHart, and Hoffman, "Notes on the Anthropology of Neoliberalism." Also see Swidler, "Culture in Action," on the idea that culture is more visible during "unsettled" periods.

9. Shevchenko, *Crisis and the Everyday*, 169.

10. Williams, *Unbending Gender;* Blair-Loy, *Competing Devotions.*

11. Although a market-based system demands a new kind of habitus from people, I find the concept of a dominant cultural code of single motherhood ultimately more useful here. Bourdieu's concept of *habitus* (See Bourdieu, *Distinction*) helps us to see how objective social realities, especially of class, are experienced subjectively and embodied in taken-for-granted ways of being in the world. However, habitus does a better job of explaining social reproduction than social change.

12. Swidler, *Talk of Love*, 67.

13. Foucault, *History of Sexuality.*

14. Collier, *From Duty to Desire.*

15. Selling Amway, Mary Kay, Oriflame, or Avon cosmetics are popular side jobs among single mothers. Amway engages in direct sales or "multilevel marketing" and is known for its "evangelical approach to inculcating the philosophy, practices and persona of the company." Wilson, "Empire of Direct Sales," 406.

16. Many women mention cleanliness as an important quality for a man. Apart from the main thoroughfare in Kaluga, the side streets are rather muddy, and Russians always remove their shoes at the door. Shoes or boots must be cleaned daily. Women dislike men who simply wear dirty boots and shoes without cleaning them, as one sign of a broader neglect of basic grooming and hygiene.

17. Rosa attended a specialized school for the hearing impaired in Kaluga. Although Russia ratified the Convention on the Rights of People with Disabilities in

May 2012, in general people with disabilities in Russia still face prejudice and significant obstacles to full participation in society. "Russia: Reform Domestic Laws
on Disability Rights," Human Rights Watch, May 4, 2012, http://www.hrw.org
/news/2012/05/04/russia-reform-domestic-laws-disability-rights.

18. Hochschild, *Managed Heart*.

19. Ispa-Landa, "Persistence of the 'Strong Woman/Infantile Man' Discourse."

20. *Ia i loshchad ia i byk, ia i baba, i muzhik.*

21. Höjdestrand, *Needed by Nobody*, offers an original analysis of Russian homelessness, portraying the homeless as negotiating their identities to retain "humanness" in spite of being dismissed frequently, by themselves and by others, as "needed
by nobody." Practical realism, too, can be seen as a gendered strategy for maximizing dignity in a society where material success is becoming more valued as the key
factor determining individuals' self-worth.

22. In the 1990s especially, job advertisements were blatantly sexist, advertising
for secretaries with long legs and "without complexes" (i.e., those open to intimate
relations beyond the job). These have diminished, but gender inequalities persist at
the level of hiring, pay, and promotion.

23. *Mat* is the Russian word for obscene language or swearing, but it comprises
much more than a handful of curse words. It is an extraordinarily fertile, complex
system of generating obscenities that functions as a shadow language of standard Russian. See Smith, "Social Meanings of Swearing."

24. Hochschild, *Second Shift*, 195–196.

25. Shevchenko, *Crisis and the Everyday*, 75.

26. Ibid., 86.

27. Issoupova, "From Duty to Pleasure."

28. Patico, "Kinship and Crisis," 27.

29. Issoupova, "From Duty to Pleasure," 50.

30. Ries, *Russian Talk*, 110.

31. A "New Russian" (*Novyi Russkii*) is a member of the newly superrich class
in post-Socialist Russia, as opposed to ordinary Russians. New Russians are perceived
to have gotten their wealth through semilegal means and are stereotyped as arrogant,
crass, conspicuous consumers.

32. Risman, "Gender as a Social Structure."

33. Gray, *Soviet Women: Walking the Tightrope*, 93.

34. Ashwin and Lytkina, "Men in Crisis."

35. *The Economist*, "So Where Are All the Men?"

36. Kanji, "The Route Matters"; Klugman and Motivans, *Single Parents and Child
Welfare*.

37. Kanji, "The Route Matters."

38. Bourdieu, *Distinction*.

39. Salmenniemi, Karhunen, and Kosonen, "Between Business and *Byt*."

40. In Ashwin's (2002) survey research, 80 percent of women said they would
continue to work even if they had the financial means to discontinue work, compared with 72 percent of men.

41. Rotkirch, Temkina, and Zdravomyslova, "Who Helps the Degraded Housewife?"

42. Gerber and Mayorova, "Dynamic Gender Differences."

43. World Bank, "Country Briefs," 2004 and 2008. Annual income per capita in the region went from $5,807 in 1998 to $8,398 in 2004, and real gross domestic product growth averaged at around 6.5 percent annually between 2000 and 2007. Official statistics report that the number of people living below the subsistence level decreased from 29 percent in 2000 to 20.4 percent in 2003 and to below 14 percent in 2007.

44. In the Soviet Union, marital status was marked by a stamp in one's internal passport.

45. Sewell, "Concept(s) of Culture."

46. Swidler, *Talk of Love*, 75.

47. The ideas of feminism and equality became quite tainted during the late Soviet period. Equality was illusory and mainly a slogan, meaning that women had the right to work like men all day in addition to continuing women's traditional domestic work at home in terms of shopping, cooking, cleaning, and child care, with little or no assistance and with the added burdens of shortages and a lack of amenities. The state did little to encourage men to participate actively in domestic work beyond bringing their paychecks home.

48. Lissyutkina, "Emancipation without Feminism," 185.

49. Hochschild, *Second Shift*.

50. Rotkirch, "'Coming to Stand on Firm Ground,'" 166. Similarly, Hackstaff argues that in American marriages individualism may mean something different for women and for men. Given the history of male-dominated marriages, "For women, putting the self first is a way to counter male dominance in marriage." Hackstaff, *Marriage in a Culture of Divorce*, 3.

51. Pollitt, "Ann Romney, Working Woman?"

Chapter 4. It Takes a *Babushka*

1. *Pirozhki* are baked or fried buns, stuffed with a variety of meat and vegetable fillings, such as stewed cabbage.

2. Höjdestrand, *Needed by Nobody*, 121. See Höjdestrand's study of homelessness in Russia for insightful analysis of close family ties and social networks from the perspective of homeless people estranged from these networks. See also Caldwell, *Not by Bread Alone*.

3. See Shevchenko, *Crisis and the Everyday*, for an important ethnographic analysis of how much one's identity as a post-Socialist subject has to do with demonstrating autonomy and competence as well as managing crisis.

4. Hochschild, *Second Shift*.

5. *Babushki* is the plural form of the Russian word for grandmothers; *babushka* is the singular form of grandmother. Russians address any woman perceived to be of a grandmotherly age as *babushka*, a term of endearment and respect. I refer to grandmothers, babushki, and the mothers of adult daughters interchangeably.

6. For more on the intersectionality of age and gender power relations, see Utrata, *Youth Privilege*.

7. Zdravomyslova, "Working Mothers and Nannies."

8. Tartakovskaya, "Changing Representation of Gender Roles," 128.

9. Clarke, *Making Ends Meet*, 207–208; Shevchenko, *Crisis and the Everyday*, 93.

10. Caldwell, *Not by Bread Alone*, 86.

11. Afontsev et al., "Urban Household"; Gurko, *Roditel'stvo*; Rotkirch, *Man Question*; Teplova, "Welfare State Transformation."

12. Hays, *Cultural Contradictions of Motherhood*.

13. Lesnoff-Caravaglia, "Black 'Granny' and Soviet 'Babushka'"; Rotkirch, *Man Question*.

14. Rotkirch, *Man Question*, 160.

15. Lesnoff-Caravaglia, "Black 'Granny' and Soviet 'Babushka,'" 111.

16. Gray, *Soviet Women: Walking the Tightrope*, 111–112.

17. Sternheimer, "Vanishing Babushka," 328.

18. Zdravomyslova, "Working Mothers and Nannies," 204.

19. Burawoy, Krotov, and Lytkina, "Involution and Destitution"; Clarke, *Making Ends Meet*; Semenova and Thompson, "Family Models."

20. Changes in post-Soviet family leave laws, later incorporated into article 256 of the 2001 Russian Labor Code, do give some recognition to grandmothers' provision of child care since a father, grandmother, grandfather, or other relative may request to be given the child-rearing leave in full or partially. Rotkirch, Temkina, and Zdravomyslova, "Who Helps the Degraded Housewife?"

21. Kanji, "Labor Force Participation"; Lokshin, Harris, and Popkin, "Single Mothers in Russia."

22. Clarke, *Making Ends Meet*; Kanji, "Age Group Conflict"; Tchernina and Tchernin, "Older People"; Teplova, "Welfare State Transformation."

23. For more on how primary breadwinning is entrenched as masculine, see Ashwin and Lytkina, "Men in Crisis." On grandmothers in the new economy, see Zdravomyslova, "Working Mothers and Nannies." Maternal grandmothers seem to help more with grandchildren, perhaps because of the strength of the mother–daughter bond in Russia or because there is little culture of consistent paternal involvement after divorce.

24. Tchernina and Tchernin, "Older People."

25. Höjdestrand, *Needed by Nobody*, 125. See also Utrata, "Keeping the Bar Low," for more on fatherhood after divorce.

26. Höjdestrand, *Needed by Nobody*, 124.

27. I enjoyed spending time with grandmothers, though it is possible that my presence as a researcher, one closer in age to single-mother daughters, shaped grandmothers' perceptions of their experiences with their own daughters. Once in a while, this became explicit. One woman asked me: "Zhenya, why can't my own daughter listen to me as you do?" In these cases, I often explained that I had come to Russia after receiving some funding to gather stories and listen to ordinary people. Their single-mother daughters juggled many more, often competing, responsibilities.

28. Fifteen of these interviews were with Soviet-era single mothers who were grandmothers themselves at the time of interview. I interviewed an additional fifteen grandmothers following interviews with single-mother daughters, although these were not recorded. I rely most heavily on data from fifteen grandmother–adult daughter intergenerational dyads, where I was able to interview both women in the same family.

29. Marina told me she could not remember the last time she had tasted one of these chocolates and said she could never splurge on such an extravagance. At the time of interview, a box of these nicer chocolates was about $6.

30. Although the Russian word *samorealizatsiia* can be translated as *self-realization* or *self-fulfillment*, in Russian it has a connotation from the Soviet era, meaning "the integration of paid employment and raising a family." Turbine and Riach, "The Right to Choose," 178.

31. Ibid.

32. Feifer, "Iron Ceiling." In Russia, sexism is even more blatant than in the West, especially in advertising and the media. See also Edwards, "In Russia, Advertising Is Often Very Sexist." In addition to women's predominance in the lower-paid state sector (health care, education, culture, etc.), women often occupy "front stage" positions in stores, restaurants, and private firms, where a youthful, trim, "emphasized femininity" (Connell and Messerschmidt, "Hegemonic Masculinity") is valued by employers. Even among women under forty, women spoke of employers rejecting them for jobs because their legs were not long enough or they were not sexy enough in appearance.

33. McMullin and Berger, "Gendered Ageism"; Teplova, "Welfare State Transformation."

34. Kanji, "Age Group Conflict."

35. Williams, *Unbending Gender*.

36. Kanji, "Age Group Conflict."

37. Shevchenko, *Crisis and the Everyday*.

38. DeVault, *Feeding the Family*, 105.

39. Hochschild, *Second Shift*.

40. Calasanti, "Theorizing Age Relations," 213.

41. Gal and Kligman, *Politics of Gender*.

42. Zdravomyslova, "Working Mothers and Nannies."

43. Another 25 percent of mothers in my sample lacked babushka support at the time of interview but had enjoyed significant babushka support previously. I distinguish between (a) women who never had babushka support and (b) women who have had in the past, or continue to have, some level of babushka support.

44. Macdonald, *Shadow Mothers*, 4. Like Macdonald, by *micropolitics* I mean the everyday practices of social life, which are infused with power relations—in other words, "small wars" occurring at the interactional level as people "jockey for position."

45. Shevchenko, *Crisis and the Everyday*.

46. See Hochschild, *Second Shift*, for more on how discourses are changing faster than practices, especially when it involves unpaid, and often devalued, care work. See Hackstaff's analysis in *Marriage in a Culture of Divorce*.

47. Shevchenko, *Crisis and the Everyday*.

48. Rotkirch, Temkina, and Zdravomyslova, "Who Helps the Degraded Housewife?"

Chapter 5. Blurred Boundaries

1. Kanji, "The Route Matters," 207.

2. Hackstaff, *Marriage in a Culture of Divorce*.

3. Nelson, *Social Economy of Single Motherhood*, argues that the terms "lone mother" and "single mother" each "give rise to common misconceptions" (3). While "lone

mother" focuses our attention on a woman's solitude or even isolation, the latter term emphasizes a woman's marital status. Nelson's study of single motherhood in rural America interrogates the social construction of, and assumptions about, single motherhood in a powerful way, which pushed my own thinking forward about the Russian case.

4. Cherlin, *Marriage-Go-Round*, argues that people may value marriage, as Americans do, but this does not mean that they are any good at it. Cherlin argues that Americans get married more and have more live-in partners than people in other Western countries, but they also get divorced more often. Nearly 90 percent of Americans are expected to marry in their lifetimes, but half of these marriages will end in divorce. Russia is another compelling case of a continued commitment to marriage alongside high divorce rates.

5. Other scholars concur. For instance, Nelson, *Social Economy of Single Motherhood*, argues that we need more studies comparing single-parent households with married-couple households (and households with gay partners, though these are still rare in Russia) "with respect to the *full* range of activities that enable a household to get by. . . . The practices of studying single mothers separately from other kinds of domestic units and of drawing comparisons within a sample of single mothers . . . highlight some problems but conceal others" (28).

6. Hochschild, *Second Shift*. See also England, "Gender Revolution," for one influential assessment of the uneven and stalled gender revolution in the United States.

7. The average age of the married mothers in my sample was thirty-seven, just one year older than the average single mother interviewed. Nine out of twenty women had a higher education degree.

8. See, for example, Ashwin and Lytkina, "Men in Crisis"; Cubbins and Vannoy, "Division of Household Labor"; Rands, "Division of Market and Household Labor."

9. This married mother's heavy reliance on her own mother and the marginal involvement of her husband in child care is exemplified in one memorable week. Before leaving on a one-week business trip, Zoya, busily cooking meals for her husband, Stepan, to last the entire week of her absence, arranged for her retired mother to return to Kaluga from her job in Moscow to watch their daughter, Sofia, leaving her husband alone in the apartment. Two nights later, Stepan and his friend stayed up till 5 a.m. drinking in the kitchen. The next day Sofia returned home from school to get a change of clothing, only to find her father conked out on the couch, having missed work. Sofia, after tearfully obeying her father's orders to clean up the kitchen's fish bones and take the twenty or so beer bottles down four flights of stairs outside to the garbage, came into my room crying, afraid that her father would continue drinking, lose his job, and even die if her mother did not come home soon to prevent it. After comforting her as best I could, Sofia ran downstairs to meet her grandmother. Despite Sofia's own father being at home, the mother and grandmother were primarily responsible for the child's care.

10. Heineman, *What Difference Does a Husband Make?*

11. Zavisca, *Housing the New Russia*, 69. Zavisca points out that housing is the favored application of this fund.

12. Ibid., 70. Zavisca cites a speech of Putin's, where he describes coining the term upon observing that women bear the main burdens of raising children. See also Rivkin-Fish, "Pronatalism."

13. See Caldwell, *Not by Bread Alone*, 158; also Ledeneva, *Russia's Economy of Favours*, on the continuing importance of social networks in shaping Russians' lives.

14. Kanji, "The Route Matters," 207.

15. Ibid., 211. Using survey data, Kanji points out that in Russia "the proportion of children living in woman-maintained households (3.8 percent) is as high as the proportion of children who live in lone-mother households in which the woman is cohabiting with a man (3.8 percent) and higher than the proportion of never-married lone-mother households (3.6 percent)."

16. Burawoy, Krotov, and Lytkina, "Involution and Destitution"; Clarke, *Making Ends Meet*.

17. Clarke, *Making Ends Meet*, 256.

18. See Crittenden, *Price of Motherhood*; England, "Gender Revolution."

19. Edin and Kefalas, *Promises I Can Keep*.

20. Masha quotes the famous opening lines of Leo Tolstoy's novel *Anna Karenina*: *Vse schastlivye sem'i pokhozhi drug na druga, kazhdaia neschastlivaia sem'ia neschastliva po-svoemu.*

21. Kanji, "The Route Matters," found that 27 percent of the children from single-mother households live with one or two grandparents, compared with 17 percent of children in two-parent households.

Chapter 6. Marginalized Men

1. Gray described Soviet women in the perestroika era as having "an often derisive view of men which might make the most committed American feminist uncomfortable." Gray, *Soviet Women: Walking the Tightrope*, 47.

2. Gurko, *Roditel'stvo*; See Utrata, "Keeping the Bar Low," for more on Russian fatherhood as a more extreme case of the disengagement that is still common among subgroups of men elsewhere.

3. Lamb, "Introduction."

4. Utrata, Ispa, and Ispa-Landa, "Men on the Margins," 283.

5. Kay, *Men in Contemporary Russia*, 127. See also Gurko, "Fenomen sovremennogo ottsovstva" and *Roditel'stvo*.

6. Rotkirch, *Man Question*, 112.

7. Dunham, "Strong-Woman Motif"; Ispa-Landa, "Persistence of the 'Strong Woman/Infantile Man' Discourse"; Kukhterin, "Fathers and Patriarchs"; Lissyutkina, "Emancipation without Feminism"; Ries, *Russian Talk*.

8. Ashwin, "A Woman is Everything,'" 120.

9. Klugman and Motivans, *Single Parents and Child Welfare*; Prokofieva, "Feminization of Poverty."

10. Vannoy et al., *Marriages in Russia*, 61.

11. Ashwin and Lytkina, "Men in Crisis."

12. See Arendell, "Social Self as Gendered" and *Fathers and Divorce*; Furstenberg and Nord, "Parenting Apart"; Teachman, "Contributions to Children." For more on fatherhood as a contested identity, see Kay, *Men in Contemporary Russia*; Townsend, *Package Deal*; Utrata, "Keeping the Bar Low."

13. Furstenberg, "Fathering in the Inner City"; Gerson, *No Man's Land*; Waller, *My Baby's Father*.

14. See Lareau, "My Wife Can Tell Me Who I Know," and Townsend, *Package Deal*, for more on how wives often mediate fathers' relationships with children. See Arendell, *Fathers and Divorce*, for more on how absence is still considered an option for divorced fathers.

15. See Anderson, *Code of the Street*, and Liebow, *Tally's Corner*, for more on how economic difficulties may inhibit more involved fatherhood; see Furstenberg, "Fathering in the Inner City," for more on the culture of distrust.

16. King, Harris, and Heard, "Racial and Ethnic Diversity." See Waller, *My Baby's Father*, for more on how involved fatherhood ideals are growing in lower-income communities.

17. Furstenberg and Nord, "Parenting Apart"; Leite and McKenry, "Aspects of Father Status"; Teachman, "Contributions to Children."

18. Edin and Lein, *Making Ends Meet*; Nelson, "Reciprocity and Romance."

19. Lareau, "My Wife Can Tell Me Who I Know."

20. Arendell, "Reflections on the Researcher-Researched Relationship."

21. Ries discusses the idea of a deep mischief, often coded as male, that is shaping post-Soviet subjectivities, in terms of drinking, sexual carousing, gambling, and the mafia's criminality. Ries also discusses a trope of male dangerousness embraced so frequently by Russian men, who advised her to refrain from speaking with Russian men alone, for her own safety, in the perestroika era. Ries, *Russian Talk*, 77.

22. LaRossa, "Renewing Our Faith."

23. Arendell, "Social Self as Gendered" and *Fathers and Divorce*; Seltzer and Brandreth, "What Fathers Say."

24. Connell and Messerschmidt, "Hegemonic Masculinity."

25. Cubbins and Vannoy, "Socioeconomic Resources"; Pridemore, "Heavy Drinking"; White, *Russia Goes Dry*.

26. Moskoff, "Divorce in the USSR."

27. Kay, *Men in Contemporary Russia*.

28. At first I thought that men might be less willing to speak with a female, American interviewer. However, when I asked several fathers about this in informal settings, they brusquely corrected me. Several said they agreed to meet with me only because I was a woman and they wanted to help me out as an American woman doing research in Russia. Several went on to say that they would have been much less likely to meet with a male interviewer.

29. Cubbins and Vannoy, "Division of Household Labor."

30. I know Ivan did not completely abandon all of his children, for I met his twenty-two-year-old son when visiting Moscow with two of my closer single-mother informants. Ivan and his friends had invited us over one rainy afternoon before the three of us planned to go to the opera. We spent some time drinking (a little, just to be polite, since it was straight vodka with only stale bread offered as a chaser and we had not eaten much) with a very inebriated group of men—Ivan, four friends, and his son—complete with singing, guitar playing, and lots of cigarette smoke. This afternoon was memorable because it differed so much from how most women I knew, whether twenty-two or fifty-two, spent their time. Because of the amount of sexual joking and drinking (Ivan was insulted we were abandoning them for some stuffy cultural outing—what were we women trying to prove?), I was rather anxious to

leave. After an hour, we inhaled the smell of fresh rain and made our way to the Bolshoi by metro. I asked Natasha and Inna whether they had had a good time. Natasha replied, "Those guys are not bad people. Our men work during the week and then feel entitled to a day off like that, with lots of drinking, smoking, and goofing off. But an hour is enough, isn't it? You see, most men here are simply like that, egoistic and self-indulgent. Women don't let themselves go like that. We can't."

31. Zavisca, *Housing the New Russia.*

32. Ries, *Russian Talk.*

33. Durkheim, *Suicide.*

34. The only other person to use the phrase "lone wolf" among my respondents was Zoya, a single mother discussed in chapter 3. Unlike Stefan, who is a lone wolf, in his own words, because he is an egoist who does not *want* responsibility, Zoya feels she is "going it alone" as a single-mother lone wolf because she does not *need* anyone's pity. She is making a virtue out of necessity, romanticizing the fact that she must face all of her responsibilities with just her child at her side. The idea of a mother not facing her responsibilities (although such women do exist) is rather unthinkable, and certainly unmentionable, in the Russian cultural context. For fathers, admitting that one does not need or want to live in a family with its attendant responsibilities appears to be tolerated and even accepted.

35. He had been concerned as to whether I really would ensure total confidentiality, which I assured him of repeatedly, but he did spend some time questioning me about my Russian language skills, my ethnic background, and my marital and family status before he decided that I was trustworthy.

36. Ashwin, "'A Woman Is Everything'"; Lissyutkina, "Emancipation without Feminism."

37. Issoupova, "From Duty to Pleasure," 31.

38. LaRossa, "Fatherhood and Social Change"; Townsend, *Package Deal*, 16.

39. Taylor and Lobel, "Social Comparison Activity," 573.

40. LaRossa and Reitzes, "Continuity and Change."

41. Goode, *World Changes in Divorce Patterns*, 111.

42. Leite and McKenry, "Aspects of Fathers Status"; Manning, Stewart, and Smock, "Complexities of Fathers' Parenting Responsibilities."

43. Townsend, *Package Deal*; Utrata, Ispa-Landa, and Ispa-Landa, "Men on the Margins."

44. Gerson, *No Man's Land*, 273.

45. Edin and Kefalas, *Promises I Can Keep*; Waller, *My Baby's Father.*

46. Pleck, "Two Dimensions of Fatherhood."

Conclusion. Normalized Gender Crisis

1. The billboard omitted spelling out the entire word *svolochi*, the Russian word for "bastards."

2. The "Balzac Age" refers rather ambiguously to a woman who is getting on in years. It is supposed to be a polite way of implying that a woman is getting older, but it is nevertheless sexist, suggesting that women have a kind of freshness date in imminent danger of expiration. Most Russian women are not fans of this connotation,

but they remain keenly aware of their perceived decreasing value in marriage markets over time in Russia. The expression "a lady of the Balzac age" (*zhenshchina balzakovskogo vozrasta*) is from the 1844 novel by Honoré de Balzac, *A Woman of Thirty*.

3. Malpas, "Singled Out."

4. Hacker, "Privatizing Risk."

5. For distrust among African Americans in the inner city, see Anderson, *Code of the Street*. A lack of trust pervades the discourses of the low-income single mothers in Edin and Kefalas, *Promises I Can Keep*. Distrust may be a bit more pervasive among working-class Americans (Silva, "Constructing Adulthood"), but even among the children of the unfinished gender revolution, there is some distrust in institutions like marriage, with many women focusing on strategies of self-reliance. See Gerson, *Unfinished Revolution*.

6. Hackstaff, *Marriage in a Culture of Divorce*.

7. Hansen, *Not-So-Nuclear Families*, 4.

8. Bengtson, "Beyond the Nuclear Family"; Sarkisian and Gerstel, *Nuclear Family Values*.

9. Gerson, *Unfinished Revolution*, 26.

10. Sidel, *Unsung Heroines*.

11. Bourdieu, *Distinction*, 372.

12. Johnson, *Gender Violence in Russia*.

13. See Anderson, *Code of the Street*; Burton, "Teenage Childbearing"; Edin and Kefalas, *Promises I Can Keep*; Liebow, *Tally's Corner*; Stack, *All Our Kin*.

14. Anderson, *Code of the Street*; Edin and Kefalas, *Promises I Can Keep*.

15. For exceptions, see Burawoy, Krotov, and Lytkina, "Involution and Destitution"; Gurko, *Roditel'stvo*; Lesnoff-Caravaglia, "Black 'Granny' and Soviet 'Babushka.'" These authors, however, do not highlight the comparison between single-mother families in Russia and the United States.

16. For research on low-income U.S. single motherhood, see Blum and Deussen, "Negotiating Independent Motherhood"; Edin and Lein, *Making Ends Meet*; Edin and Kefalas, *Promises I Can Keep*; Harris, "Life after Welfare"; Lichter, Graefe, and Brown, "Is Marriage a Panacea?"; Stack, *All Our Kin*; Wilson, *Truly Disadvantaged*. For research on divorced, middle-class single motherhood, see Arendell, *Mothers and Divorce*; Hackstaff, *Marriage in a Culture of Divorce*; Newman, *Falling from Grace*; Peterson, "A Re-Evaluation"; Wallerstein and Blakeslee, *Second Chances*. Although some recent studies concentrate instead on rural single mothers (Nelson, *Social Economy of Single Motherhood*) or single mothers by choice (Hertz, *Single by Chance*), on the whole the broader binary division in the literature between low-income, unmarried single motherhood and middle-income, divorced single motherhood persists.

17. Moynihan, *The Negro Family*, 1965. What is typically referred to now as the "Moynihan Report" was published by Senator Daniel Patrick Moynihan under the title: "The Negro Family: The Case For National Action." While the Report has been widely influential, it is also controversial for the way in which it tended to pathologize African-American families.

18. Stack, *All Our Kin*.

19. Edin and Kefalas, *Promises I Can Keep*, 215. See also Casey and Maldonado, "Worst Off."

20. The more dynamic picture that focuses on lifetime prevalence is a much better indicator of how common single motherhood is becoming as a stage in women's lives. See Garfinkel and McLanahan, *Single Mothers and Their Children*.

21. Sarkisian and Gerstel, *Nuclear Family Values*, xi.

22. Macdonald, "Life without Father," 93. These three groundbreaking books on varieties of single motherhood in the United States include Edin and Kefalas, *Promises I Can Keep*; Hertz, *Single by Chance*; and Nelson, *Social Economy of Single Motherhood*.

23. Nelson, *Social Economy of Single Motherhood*, 27.

24. Sewell, "Concept(s) of Culture"; Swidler, "Culture in Action."

25. http://acf.gov/healthymarriage/about/factsheets_hm_matters.html.

26. http://thesocietypages.org/citings/2009/04/15/andrew-cherlin-on-the-marriage-go-round/

27. Amato, "Impact of Family Formation Change," 90.

28. Edin and Kefalas, *Promises I Can Keep*; Nelson, *Social Economy of Single Motherhood*.

29. Rotkirch, Temkina, and Zdravomyslova, "Who Helps the Degraded Housewife?," 353.

✒ BIBLIOGRAPHY

Abdullaev, Nabi. "Russians Are Quickest to Marry and Divorce." *Moscow Times*, December 8, 2004.

Afontsev, Sergey, Gijs Kessler, Andrei Markevich, Victoria Tyazhelnikova, and Timur Valetov. "The Urban Household in Russia and the Soviet Union, 1900–2000." *History of the Family* 13 (2004): 178–194.

Amato, Paul R. "The Impact of Family Formation Change on the Cognitive, Social, and Emotional Well-Being of the Next Generation." *Future of Children* 15 (2005): 75–96. http://futureofchildren.org/publications /journals/article/index.xml?journalid=37&articleid=107&sectionid=694.

Anderson, Elijah. *Code of the Street: Decency, Violence, and the Moral Life of the Inner City*. New York: W. W. Norton, 1999.

Appelbaum, Binyamin. "Study of Men's Falling Income Cites Single Parents." *New York Times*, March 20, 2013.

Arendell, Terry. *Fathers and Divorce*. Thousand Oaks, CA: Sage, 1995.

——. *Mothers and Divorce: Legal, Economic, and Social Dilemmas*. Berkeley: University of California Press, 1986.

——. "Reflections on the Researcher-Researched Relationship: A Woman Interviewing Men." *Qualitative Sociology* 20 (1997): 341–368.

——. "The Social Self as Gendered: A Masculinist Discourse of Divorce. *Symbolic Interaction* 15 (1992): 151–181.

Ashwin, Sarah, ed. *Gender, State and Society in Soviet and Post-Soviet Russia*. London: Routledge, 2000.

Ashwin, Sarah. " 'A Woman Is Everything': The Reproduction of Soviet Ideals of Womanhood in Post-Communist Russia." In *Work, Employment, and Transition: Restructuring Livelihoods in Post-Communism*, edited by A. Rainnie, A. Smith, and A. Swain, 117–133. London: Routledge, 2002.

Ashwin, Sarah, and Tatyana Lytkina. "Men in Crisis in Russia: The Role of Domestic Marginalization." *Gender & Society* 18 (2004): 189–206.

Avdeyeva, Olga A. "Policy Experiment in Russia: Cash-for-Babies and Fertility Change." *Social Politics* 18 (2011): 361–386.

Baranskaia, Natalia. *Nedelia kak Nedelia*. [*A Week Like Any Other*]. Copenhagen: Rosenkilde and Bagger, 1969.

Bengtson, Vern L. "Beyond the Nuclear Family: The Increasing Importance of Multigenerational Bonds." *Journal of Marriage and Family* 63 (2001): 1–16.

Blair-Loy, Mary. *Competing Devotions: Career and Family among Women Executives*. Cambridge, MA: Harvard University Press, 2003.

Blum, Linda M., and Theresa Deussen. "Negotiating Independent Motherhood: Working-Class African American Women Talk about Marriage and Motherhood." *Gender & Society* 10 (1996): 199–211.

Bobak, M., R. Room, H. Pikhart, R. Kubinova, S. Malyutina, A. Pajak, S. Kurilovitch, R. Topor, Y. Nikitin, and M. Marmot. "Contribution of Drinking Patterns to Differences in Rates of Alcohol Related Problems between Three Urban Populations." *Journal of Epidemiology and Community Health* 58 (2004): 238–242.

Bobrova, N., R. West, D. Malyutina, S. Malyutina, and M. Bobak. "Gender Differences in Drinking Practices in Middle Aged and Older Russians." *Alcohol and Alcoholism* 45 (2010): 573–580.

Bondarskaia, Galina, and Leonid Darskiy. "Brachnoe-sostoianie i rozhdaemost'." In *Demograficheskie protessy v SSSR*, edited by A. G. Volkov, 28–57. Moscow: Nauka, 1990.

Bourdieu, Pierre. *Distinction: A Social Critique of the Judgement of Taste.* Translated by Richard Nice. Cambridge, MA: Harvard University Press, 1984.

Brooks, David. "The Opportunity Gap." *New York Times*, July 9, 2012. http://www.nytimes.com/2012/07/10/opinion/brooks-the-opportunity-gap.html?_r=0.

Bucher, Greta. "Struggling to Survive: Soviet Women in the Postwar Years." *Journal of Women's History* 12 (2000): 137–159.

Burawoy, Michael, Pavel Krotov, and Tatyana Lytkina. "Involution and Destitution in Capitalist Russia: Russia's Gendered Transition to Capitalism." *Ethnography* 1 (2000): 43–65.

Burton, Linda. "Teenage Childbearing as an Alternative Life Course Strategy in Multigeneration Black Families." *Human Nature* 1 (1990): 123–143.

Calasanti, Toni. "Theorizing Age Relations." In *The Need for Theory: Critical Approaches to Social Gerontology*, edited by S. Biggs, A. Lowenstein, and J. Hendricks, 199–218. Amityville, NY: Baywood, 2003.

Caldwell, Melissa. *Not by Bread Alone: Social Support in the New Russia.* Berkeley: University of California Press, 2004.

Carlbäck, Helene. "Lone Mothers and Fatherless Children: Public Discourse on Marriage and Family Law." In *Soviet State and Society under Nikita Khrushchev*, edited by Melanie Ilic and Jeremy Smith, 86–103. New York: Routledge, 2009.

Cartwright, Kimberly D. "Shotgun Weddings and the Meaning of Marriage in Russia: An Event History Analysis." *History of the Family* 5 (2000): 1–22.

Casey, Timothy, and Laurie Maldonado. "Worst Off—Single-Parent Families in the United States: A Cross National Comparison of Single Parenthood in the U.S. and Sixteen Other High-Income Countries." *Legal Momentum*, December 2012.

Cherlin, Andrew J. *The Marriage-Go-Round: The State of Marriage and the Family in America Today.* New York: Knopf, 2009.

Clarke, Simon. *Making Ends Meet in Contemporary Russia: Secondary Employment, Subsidiary Agriculture and Social Networks.* Cheltenham, United Kingdom: Edward Elgar, 2002.

Collier, Jane Fishburne. *From Duty to Desire: Remaking Families in a Spanish Village.* Princeton: Princeton University Press, 1997.

Collier, Stephen J., Monica Dehart, and Lisa Hoffman. "Notes on the Anthropology of Neoliberalism." *Anthropology News* 47 (2006): 9–10.

Connell, Raewyn, and James Messerschmidt. "Hegemonic Masculinity: Rethinking the Concept." *Gender & Society* 19 (2005): 829–859.

Crittenden, Ann. *The Price of Motherhood: Why the Most Important Job in the World Is Still the Least Valued.* New York: Henry Holt, 2001.

Cubbins, Lisa A., and Dana Vannoy. "Division of Household Labor as a Source of Contention for Married and Cohabiting Couples in Metropolitan Moscow." *Journal of Family Issues* 25 (2004): 182–215.

——. "Socioeconomic Resources, Gender Traditionalism, and Wife Abuse in Urban Russian Couples." *Journal of Marriage and Family* 67 (2005): 37–52.

Demographic Yearbook of Russia. Goskomstat. Moscow: Information and Publishing Centre, Statistics of Russia. 2002.

——.Goskomstat. Moscow: Information and Publishing Centre, Statistics of Russia. 2012.

DeVault, Marjorie L. *Feeding the Family: The Social Organization of Caring as Gendered Work.* Chicago: University of Chicago Press, 1991.

Draitser, Emil. *Making War, Not Love: Gender and Sexuality in Russian Humor.* New York: St. Martin's Press, 1999.

Duneier, Mitchell. "On the Legacy of Elliott Liebow and Carol Stack: Context-Driven Fieldwork and the Need for Continuous Ethnography." *Focus* 25 (Spring–Summer 2007): 33–38.

Dunham, Vera S. "The Strong-Woman Motif." In *The Transformation of Russian Society: Aspects of Social Change Since 1861,* edited by C. E. Black, 459–483. Cambridge, MA: Harvard University Press, 1967.Durkheim, Emile. Suicide. [1897] 1951 New York: Free Press.

The Economist, "So Where Are All the Men? Making Children Is Easy, Making a Good Father is Not." Aug. 1, 2002. http://www.economist.com/node/1259838.

Eberstadt, Nicholas, and Apoorva Shah. "Russia's Demographic Disaster." American Enterprise Institute for Public Policy Research, May 2009.

Edin, Kathryn, and Maria Kefalas. *Promises I Can Keep: Why Poor Women Put Motherhood before Marriage.* Berkeley: University of California Press, 2005.

Edin, Kathryn, and Laura Lein. *Making Ends Meet: How Single Mothers Survive Welfare and Low-Wage Work.* New York: Russell Sage Foundation, 1997.

Edwards, Jim. "In Russia, Advertising Is Often Very Sexist—And Very Weird." *Business Insider,* Nov. 17, 2012. http://www.businessinsider.com/sexist-russian-advertising-examples-2012-11?op=1.

Einspahr, Jennifer. "Structural Domination and Structural Freedom: A Feminist Perspective." *Feminist Review* 94 (2010): 1–19. doi:10.1057/fr.2009.40.

Ellwood, David T., and Christopher Jencks. "The Spread of Single-Parent Families in the United States since 1960." KSG Working Paper No. RWP04-008, 2004. http://dx.doi.org/10.2139/ssrn.517662.

England, Paula. "The Gender Revolution: Uneven and Stalled." *Gender & Society* 24 (2010): 149–166.

Feifer, Gregory. "The Iron Ceiling: Sexism Still Strong in Russia." RFE/RL Sept. 19, 2010.

Furstenberg, Frank F., Jr. "Fathering in the Inner City: Paternal Participation and Public Policy." In *Fatherhood: Contemporary Theory, Research, and Social Policy*, edited by W. Marsiglio, 119–147. Thousand Oaks, CA: Sage, 1995.

Furstenberg, Frank F., Jr., and Christine Winquist Nord. "Parenting Apart: Patterns of Childrearing after Marital Disruption." *Journal of Marriage and the Family* 47 (1985): 893–904.

Foucault, Michel. *The History of Sexuality.* Vol. 1, *An Introduction.* New York: Vintage Books, 1990 [1978].

Gal, Susan, and Gail Kligman. *The Politics of Gender after Socialism: A Comparative-Historical Essay.* Princeton: Princeton University Press, 2000.

Garfinkel, Irwin, and Sara S. McLanahan. *Single Mothers and Their Children: A New American Dilemma.* Washington, DC: Urban Institute Press, 1986.

Gerber, Theodore P., and Olga Mayorova. "Dynamic Gender Differences in a Post-Socialist Labor Market: Russia, 1991–1997." *Social Forces* 84 (2006): 2047–2075.

Gerson, Kathleen. *No Man's Land: Men's Changing Commitments to Family and Work.* New York: Basic Books, 1993.

——. *The Unfinished Revolution: Coming of Age in a New Era of Gender, Work, and Family.* New York: Oxford University Press, 2010.

Gillespie, David C. "Soviet and Russian Blockbuster Films: The Sounds of Music: Soundtrack and Song in Soviet Film." *Slavic Review* 62 (2003): 473–490.

Goode, William J. *World Changes in Divorce Patterns.* New Haven: Yale University Press, 1993.

Gray, Francine du Plessix. "Reflections (Soviet Women)." *New Yorker*, Feb. 19, 1990: 48–80.

——. *Soviet Women: Walking the Tightrope.* New York: Doubleday, 1989.

Gurko, Tatiana Alexandrovna. "Fenomen sovremennogo ottsovstva" [The phenomenon of contemporary fatherhood]. In *Muzhchina i zhenshchina v sovremennom mire: Meniaiushchiesia roli i obrazy* [Men and women in the contemporary world: Changing roles and ways of life], edited by I. M. Semashko and A. N. Sedlovskaia, 216–222. Moscow: Rossiiskaia Akademiia Nauk Institut Etnologii i Antropologii, 1999.

——. *Roditel'stvo: Sotsiologicheskie aspekty* [Parenthood: Sociological aspects]. Moscow: Tsentr obshchechelovecheskikh tsennostei, 2003.

Hacker, Jacob S. "Privatizing Risk without Privatizing the Welfare State: The Hidden Politics of Social Policy Retrenchment in the United States." *American Political Science Review* 98 (2004): 243–260.

Hackstaff, Karla B. *Marriage in a Culture of Divorce.* Philadelphia: Temple University Press, 1999.

Hansen, Karen V. *Not-So-Nuclear Families: Class, Gender, and Networks of Care.* New Brunswick, NJ: Rutgers University Press, 2005.

Harris, Kathleen Mullan. "Life after Welfare: Women, Work, and Repeat Dependency." *American Sociological Review* 61 (1996): 407–426.

Hays, Sharon. *The Cultural Contradictions of Motherhood*. New Haven: Yale University Press, 1996.

Heineman, Elizabeth D. *What Difference Does a Husband Make? Women and Marital Status in Nazi and Postwar Germany*. Berkeley: University of California Press, 1999.

Hertz, Rosanna. *Single by Chance, Mothers by Choice: How Women Are Choosing Parenthood without Marriage and Creating the New American Family*. Oxford: Oxford University Press, 2006.

Hinote, Brian P., and Gretchen R. Webber. "Drinking toward Manhood: Masculinity and Alcohol in the Former USSR." *Men and Masculinities* 15 (2012): 292–310.

Hochschild, Arlie Russell. *The Managed Heart: Commercialization of Human Feeling*. Berkeley: University of California Press, 2003 [1983].

——. *The Second Shift*. With Anne Machung. New York: Avon, 1989.

Höjdestrand, Tova. *Needed by Nobody: Homelessness and Humanness in Post-Socialist Russia*. Ithaca, NY: Cornell University Press, 2009.

Human Rights Watch. "Russia: Reform Domestic Laws on Disability Rights." May 4, 2012. http://www.hrw.org/news/2012/05/04/russia-reform-domestic-laws-disability-rights

Ispa-Landa, Simone. "The Persistence of the 'Strong Woman/Infantile Man' Discourse in Post-Soviet Russia." Unpublished manuscript, 2006.

Issoupova, Olga. "From Duty to Pleasure: Motherhood in Soviet and Post-Soviet Russia." In *Gender, State and Society in Soviet and Post-Soviet Russia*, edited by S. Ashwin, 30–54. London: Routledge, 2000.

ITAR-TASS (Information Telegraph Agency of Russia). "Just 10 Percent of Families Use Mortgage Loans in Russia." April 3, 2007.

Ivashko, Sergei. "Average Russian Is a Middle-Aged, English-Speaking Woman." From gazeta.ru, 13 February 2007. http://www.gazeta.ru/2004/02/13/oa_111987.shtmlJasilioniene, Aiva. "Premarital Conception and Divorce Risk in Russia in Light of the GGS Data." MPIDR Working Paper No. WP-2007-025, 2007, Max Planck Institute for Demographic Research, Rostock, Germany.

Jencks, Christopher. Foreword to *Making Ends Meet: How Single Mothers Survive Welfare and Low-Wage Work*, by Kathryn Edin and Laura Lein, ix–xxvii. New York: Russell Sage Foundation, 1997.

Johnson, Janet Elise. *Gender Violence in Russia: The Politics of Feminist Intervention*. Bloomington: Indiana University Press, 2009.

Kanji, Shireen. "Age Group Conflict or Cooperation? Children and Pensioners in Russia in Crisis." *International Journal of Sociology and Social Policy* 29 (2009): 372–387.

——. "Labor Force Participation, Regional Location, and Economic Well-Being of Single Mothers in Russia." *Journal of Family and Economic Issues* 32 (2011): 62–72.

——. "The Route Matters: Poverty and Inequality among Lone-Mother Households in Russia." *Feminist Economics* 10 (2004): 207–225.

Kay, Rebecca. *Men in Contemporary Russia: The Fallen Heroes of Post-Soviet Change?* Burlington, VT: Ashgate, 2006.

Kelly, Catriona. *Children's World: Growing up in Russia, 1890–1991*. New Haven: Yale University Press, 2007.

Kiblitskaya, Marina. *Ispovedi odinokikh materei* [Confessions of single mothers]. Moscow: Institut Sravnitel'nykh Issledovanii Trudovykh Otnoshenii, 1999.

——. "Once We Were Kings: Male Experiences of Loss of Status at Work in Post-Communist Russia." In *Gender, State and Society in Soviet and Post-Soviet Russia*, edited by S. Ashwin, 90–104. London: Routledge, 2000.

King, Valarie, Kathleen Mullan Harris, and Holly E. Heard. "Racial and Ethnic Diversity in Nonresident Father Involvement." *Journal of Marriage and Family* 66 (2004): 1–21.

Klugman, Jeni, and Alastair McAuley. "Social Policy for Single-Parent Families: Russia in Transition." In *Single Parents and Child Welfare in the New Russia*, edited by J. Klugman and A. Motivans, 121–150. New York: Palgrave, 2001.

Klugman, Jeni, and Albert Motivans. *Single Parents and Child Welfare in the New Russia*. New York: Palgrave, 2001.

Kotkin, Stephen. *Steeltown, USSR: Soviet Society in the Gorbachev Era*. Berkeley: University of California Press, 1991.

Kukhterin, Sergei. "Fathers and Patriarchs in Communist and Post-Communist Russia." In *Gender, State and Society in Soviet and Post-Soviet Russia*, edited by S. Ashwin, 71–89. London: Routledge, 2000.

Lamb, Michael E. "Introduction: The Emergent American Father." In *The Father's Role: Cross-Cultural Perspectives*, edited by M. E. Lamb, 3–25. Hillsdale, NJ: Erlbaum, 1987.

Lapidus, Gail Warshofsky. *Women in Soviet Society: Equality, Development, and Social Change*. Berkeley: University of California Press, 1978.

Lareau, Annette. "My Wife Can Tell Me Who I Know: Methodological and Conceptual Problems in Studying Fathers." *Qualitative Sociology* 24 (2000): 407–433.

LaRossa, Ralph. "Fatherhood and Social Change." *Family Relations* 37 (1988): 451–457.

——. "Renewing Our Faith in Qualitative Family Research." *Journal of Contemporary Ethnography* 17 (1988): 243–260.

LaRossa, Ralph, and Donald C. Reitzes. "Continuity and Change in Middle Class Fatherhood, 1925–1939: The Culture-Conduct Connection." *Journal of Marriage and the Family* 55 (1993): 455–468.

Ledeneva, Alena V. *Russia's Economy of Favours: Blat, Networking and Informal Exchange*. Cambridge: Cambridge University Press, 1998.

Leite, Randall W., and Patrick C. McKenry. "Aspects of Father Status and Postdivorce Father Involvement with Children." *Journal of Family Issues* 23 (2002): 601–623.

Lemmon, Gayle Tzemach. "America's Silent Crisis: The Plight of the Single (Working!) Mother." *Atlantic*, July 17, 2012. http://www.theatlantic.com /business/archive/2012/07/americas-silent-crisis-the-plight-of-the-single -working-mother/259935/.

Lesnoff-Caravaglia, Gari. "The Black 'Granny' and the Soviet 'Babushka': Commonalities and Contrasts." In *Minority Aging: Sociological and Social*

Psychological Issues, edited by R. C. Manuel, 109–114. Westport, CT: Greenwood Press, 1982.

Lichter, Daniel T., Deborah Roempke Graefe, and J. Brian Brown. "Is Marriage a Panacea? Union Formation among Economically Disadvantaged Unwed Mothers." *Social Problems* 50 (2003): 60–86.

Liebow, Elliot. *Tally's Corner: A Study of Negro Streetcorner Men*. Boston: Little, Brown, 1967.

Lissyutkina, Larissa. "Emancipation without Feminism: The Historical and Socio-Cultural Context of the Women's Movement in Russia." In *Women and Political Change: Perspectives from East-Central Europe*, edited by S. Bridger, 168–187. New York: St. Martin's Press, 1999.

Lokshin, Michael, Kathleen Mullan Harris, and Barry M. Popkin. "Single Mothers in Russia: Household Strategies for Coping with Poverty." *World Development* 28 (2000): 2183–2198.

Lunyakova, Larissa Grigorevna. "O sovremennom urovne zhizni semei odinokikh materei" [On the contemporary standard of living of single mother families"]. *Sotsiologicheskie issledovaniia* 8 (2001): 86–95.

Macdonald, Cameron. "Life without Father: Single Mothers in the New America." *Qualitative Sociology* 31 (2008): 89–94.

——. *Shadow Mothers: Nannies, Au Pairs, and the Micropolitics of Mothering*. Berkeley: University of California Press, 2010.

MacFadyen, David. "*Moscow Does Not Believe in Tears*: From Oscar to Consolation Prize." *Studies in Russian and Soviet Cinema* 1 (2007): 45–67.

Mackey, Alex. "Tackling 'the Russian God.'" *New York Times*, Nov. 3, 2009.

Malpas, Anna. "Singled Out." *Moscow Times*. June 4, 2004. http://www.themoscowtimes.com/sitemap/paid/2004/06/article/singled-out/365171.html

Manning, Wendy, Susan Stewart, and Pamela Smock. "The Complexity of Fathers' Parenting Responsibilities and Involvement with Nonresident Children." Journal of Family Issues 24 (2003): 645–667.

Marcotte, Amanda. "Romney Blames Single Parents for Gun Violence." *Slate*, Oct. 17, 2012. http://www.slate.com/blogs/xx_factor/2012/10/17/romney_on_gun_control_at_the_presidential_debate_ladies_please_stop_having.html

Mathur, Aparna, Hao Fu, and Peter Hansen. "The Mysterious and Alarming Rise of Single Parenthood in America." *Atlantic*, Sept. 3, 2013. www.theatlantic.com/business/archive/2013/09/the-mysterious-and-alarming-rise-of-single-parenthood-in-america/279203/.

Mazzei, Julie, and Erin E. O'Brien. "You've Got It, So When Do You Flaunt It? Building Rapport, Intersectionality, and the Strategic Deployment of Gender in the Field." *Journal of Contemporary Ethnography* 38 (2009): 358–383.

Mayor, Tracy. "Single Mom Stigma, Alive and Kicking." *Brain, Child Magazine*, Summer 2011. http://www.brainchildmag.com/essays/summer2011_mayor.asp.

McAuley, Alastair. *Economic Welfare in the Soviet Union: Poverty, Living Standards, and Inequality*. Madison: University of Wisconsin Press, 1979.

——. *Women's Work and Wages in the Soviet Union*. London: George Allen & Unwin, 1981.

McKinney, Judith Record. "Lone Mothers in Russia: Soviet and Post-Soviet Policy." *Feminist Economics* 10 (2004): 37–60.

McLanahan, Sara, and Gary Sandefur. *Growing up with a Single Parent: What Hurts, What Helps*. Cambridge, MA: Harvard University Press, 1994.

McMullin, J. A., and E. D. Berger. "Gendered Ageism/Age(ed) Sexism: The Case of Unemployed Older Workers." In *Age Matters: Realigning Feminist Thinking*, edited by T. M. Calasanti and K. F. Slevin, 201–223. New York: Routledge, 2006.

Moskoff, William. "Divorce in the USSR." *Journal of Marriage and the Family* 45 (1983): 419–425.

Motivans, Albert. "Family Formation, Stability and Structure in Russia." In *Single Parents and Child Welfare in the New Russia*, edited by J. Klugman and A. Motivans, 27–52. New York: Palgrave, 2001.

Moynihan, Daniel Patrick. *The Negro Family: A Case for National Action*. Office of Policy Planning and Research. United States Department of Labor. 1965. http://www.dol.gov/dol/aboutdol/history/webid-meynihan.htm

Mudge, Stephanie Lee. "What Is Neo-Liberalism?" *Socio-Economic Review* 4 (2008): 703–731.

Murphy, Tim, and Andy Kroll. "Santorum: Single Moms Are 'Breeding More Criminals.'" *Mother Jones*, March 6, 2012. http://www.motherjones.com/politics/2012/03/santorum-single-mothers-are-breeding-more-criminals.

Nakachi, Mie. "N. S. Khrushchev and the 1944 Soviet Family Law: Politics, Reproduction, and Language." *East European Politics and Societies* 20 (2006): 40–68.

Nelson, Margaret K. "Reciprocity and Romance." *Qualitative Sociology* 27 (2004): 439–459.

——. *The Social Economy of Single Motherhood: Raising Children in Rural America*. New York: Routledge, 2005.

Newman, Katherine S. *Falling from Grace: Downward Mobility in the Age of Affluence*. Berkeley: University of California Press, 1988.

Organisation for Economic Co-operation and Development (OECD). *The Future of Families to 2030: A Synthesis Report*. International Futures Programme, 2011.

Parsons, Michelle. *Dying Unneeded: The Cultural Context of the Russian Mortality Crisis*. Nashville: Vanderbilt University Press, 2014.

Pascall, Gillian, and Nick Manning. "Gender and Social Policy: Comparing Welfare States in Central and Eastern Europe and the Former Soviet Union." *Journal of European Social Policy* 10 (2000): 240–266.

Patico, Jennifer. "Kinship and Crisis: Embedded Economic Pressures and Gender Ideals in Postsocialist International Matchmaking." *Slavic Review* 69 (2010): 16–40.

Perelli-Harris, Brienna, and Theodore P. Gerber. "Nonmarital Childbearing in Russia: Second Demographic Transition or Pattern of Disadvantage?" *Demography* 48 (2011): 317–342.

Pesmen, Dale. *Russia and Soul: An Exploration*. Ithaca, NY: Cornell University Press, 2000.

Peterson, Richard R. "A Re-Evaluation of the Economic Consequences of Divorce." *American Sociological Review* 61 (1996): 528–536.

Pleck, Elizabeth H. "Two Dimensions of Fatherhood: A History of the Good Dad–Bad Dad Complex." In *The Role of the Father in Child Development*, 4th ed., edited by Michael E. Lamb, 32–57. Hoboken, NJ: Wiley, 2004.

Poizner, Susan. "The Sorrows of Mother Russia." *Guardian*, June 30, 1992.

Pollert, Anna. "Gender and Class Revisited; or, the Poverty of 'Patriarchy.'" *Sociology* 30 (1996): 639–659.

Pollitt, Katha. "Ann Romney, Working Woman?" *Nation*, May 7, 2012.

Pridemore, William Alex. "Heavy Drinking and Suicide in Russia." *Social Forces* 85 (2006): 415–430.

Pridemore, William Alex, and Sang-Weon Kim. "Research Note: Patterns of Alcohol-Related Mortality in Russia." *Journal of Drug Issues* 36 (2006): 229–247.

Prokofieva, Lidia M. "Feminization of Poverty in Russia." Moscow: World Bank, 2000.

Rampell, Catherine. "Single Parents, around the World." *New York Times*, March 10, 2012.

Randall, Amy E. "'Abortion Will Deprive You of Happiness!': Soviet Reproductive Politics in the Post-Stalin Era." *Journal of Women's History* 23 (2011): 13–38.

Rands, Tania. "The Division of Market and Household Labor in Post-Soviet Russia." Paper presented at the Annual Meeting of the American Sociological Association, Toronto, Aug. 1997.

Richardson, Paul E., and Mikhail Ivanov. "The Little Water of Life." *Russian Life* 41 (4) (1998): 8

Ries, Nancy. *Russian Talk: Culture and Conversation during Perestroika*. Ithaca, NY: Cornell University Press, 1997.

Risman, Barbara J. "Gender as a Social Structure: Theory Wrestling with Activism." *Gender & Society* 18 (2004): 429–450.

Rivkin-Fish, Michele. "Pronatalism, Gender Politics, and the Renewal of Family Support in Russia: Towards a Feminist Anthropology of 'Maternity Capital.'" Slavic Review 69 (2010): 701–724.

Rotkirch, Anna. "'Coming to Stand on Firm Ground': The Making of a Soviet Working Mother." In *On Living through Soviet Russia*, edited by D. Bertaux, P. Thompson, and A. Rotkirch, 146–175. London: Routledge, 2004.

——. *The Man Question: Loves and Lives in Late 20th Century Russia*. Helsinki: University of Helsinki, 2000.

Rotkirch, Anna, Anna Temkina, and Elena Zdravomyslova. "Who Helps the Degraded Housewife? Comments on Vladimir Putin's Demographic Speech." *European Journal of Women's Studies* 14 (2007): 349–357.

Salmenniemi, Suvi, Paivi Karhunen, and Ritta Kosonen. "Between Business and *Byt*: Experiences of Women Entrepreneurs in Contemporary Russia." *Europe-Asia Studies* 63 (2011): 77–98.

Sarkisian, Natalia, and Naomi Gerstel. *Nuclear Family Values, Extended Family Lives: The Power of Race, Class, and Gender*. New York: Routledge, 2012.

Seltzer, Judith A., and Yvonne Brandreth. "What Fathers Say about Involvement with Children after Separation." *Journal of Family Issues* 15 (1994): 49–77.

Semenova, Victoria, and Paul Thompson. "Family Models and Transgenerational Influences: Grandparents, Parents and Children in Moscow and Leningrad from the Soviet to the Market Era." In *On Living through Soviet Russia*, edited by D. Bertaux, P. Thompson, and A. Rotkirch, 120–145. London: Routledge, 2004.

Sewell, William H. "The Concept(s) of Culture." In *Beyond the Cultural Turn: New Directions in the Study of Society and Culture*, edited by V. E. Bonnell, L. A. Hunt, and R. Biernacki, 35–61. Berkeley: University of California Press, 1999.

Shattuck, Rachel M., and Rose M. Kreider. "Social and Economic Characteristics of Currently Unmarried Women with a Recent Birth: 2011." U.S. Census Bureau, American Community Survey Reports (May), 2013.

Shevchenko, Olga. *Crisis and the Everyday in Postsocialist Moscow*. Bloomington: Indiana University Press, 2009.

Sidel, Ruth. *Unsung Heroines: Single Mothers and the American Dream*. Berkeley: University of California Press, 2006.

Silva, Jennifer M. "Constructing Adulthood in an Age of Uncertainty." *American Sociological Review* 78 (2012): 505–522.

Smith, Raymond T. *The Matrifocal Family: Power, Pluralism, and Politics*. New York: Routledge, 1996.

Smith, S. A. "The Social Meanings of Swearing: Workers and Bad Language in Late Imperial and Early Soviet Russia." *Past and Present* 160 (1998): 167–202.

Sobolevskaya, Olga. "Fragmented Families: A Common but Temporary Phenomenon." *Open Economy,* June 6, 2013. http://opec.ru/en/1538920.html.

Stack, Carol B. *All Our Kin: Strategies for Survival in a Black Community*. New York: Harper and Row, 1974.

Stanley, Alessandra. "Russian Mothers, from All Walks, Walk Alone." *New York Times*, Oct. 21, 1995.

Stephenson, Svetlana. Review of *Single Parents and Child Welfare in the New Russia*, edited by Jeni Klugman and Albert Motivans. *Europe-Asia Studies* 54 (2002): 1174–1176.

Sternheimer, Stephen. "The Vanishing Babushka: A Roleless Role for Older Soviet Women?" *Current Perspectives on Aging and the Life Cycle* 1 (1985): 315–333.

Swidler, Ann. "Culture in Action: Symbols and Strategies." *American Sociological Review* 51 (1986): 273–286.

——. *Talk of Love: How Culture Matters*. Chicago: University of Chicago Press, 2001.

Tartakovskaya, Irina. "The Changing Representation of Gender Roles in the Soviet and Post-Soviet Press." In *Gender, State and Society in Soviet and Post-Soviet Russia*, edited by Sarah Ashwin, 118–136. London: Routledge, 2000.

Taylor, Shelley E., and Marci Lobel. "Social Comparison Activity Under Threat: Downward Evaluation and Upward Contacts." *Psychological Review* 6(4) (1989): 569–575.

Tchernina, Natalia V., and Efim A. Tchernin. "Older People in Russia's Transitional Society: Multiple Deprivation and Coping Responses." *Ageing and Society* 22 (2002): 543–562.

Teachman, Jay D. "Contributions to Children by Divorced Fathers." *Social Problems* 38 (1991): 358–371.

Teplova, Tatyana. "Welfare State Transformation, Childcare, and Women's Work in Russia. *Social Politics* 14 (2007): 284–322.

Townsend, Nicholas W. *The Package Deal: Marriage, Work, and Fatherhood in Men's Lives*. Philadelphia: Temple University Press, 2002.

Turbine, Vikki, and Kathleen Riach. "The Right to Choose or Choosing What's Right? Women's Conceptualizations of Work and Life Choices in Contemporary Russia." *Gender, Work and Organization* 19 (2012): 166–187.

Twohey, Meghan. "1 in 3 Babies Born to Unmarried Moms," *Moscow Times*, November 29, 2001. http://www.themoscowtimes.com/news/article/tmt/249943.html.

Utrata, Jennifer. "Counting on Motherhood, Not Men: Single Mothers and Social Change in the New Russia." PhD diss., University of California, Berkeley, 2008.

——. "Keeping the Bar Low: Why Russia's Nonresident Fathers Accept Narrow Fatherhood Ideals." *Journal of Marriage and Family* 70 (2008): 1297–1310.

——. "Youth Privilege: Doing Age and Gender in Russia's Single-Mother Families." *Gender & Society* 25 (2011): 616–641.

Utrata, Jennifer, Jean Ispa, and Simone Ispa-Landa. "Men on the Margins of Family Life: Fathers in Russia." In *Fathers in Cultural Context*, edited by D. W. Shwalb, B. Shwalb, and M. E. Lamb, 279–302. New York: Routledge, 2013.

Vannoy, Dana, Natalia Rimashevskaya, Lisa Cubbins, Marina Malysheva, Elena Meshterkina, and Marina Pisklakova. *Marriages in Russia: Couples during the Economic Transition*. Westport, CT: Praeger, 1999.

Waller, Maureen R. *My Baby's Father: Unmarried Parents and Paternal Responsibility*. Ithaca, NY: Cornell University Press, 2002.

Wallerstein, Judith S., and Sandra Blakeslee. *Second Chances: Men, Women, and Children a Decade after Divorce*. New York: Ticknor & Fields, 1989.

White, Stephen. *Russia Goes Dry: Alcohol, State and Society*. Cambridge: Cambridge University Press, 1996.

Williams, Joan. *Unbending Gender: Why Work and Family Conflict and What to Do about It*. New York: Oxford University Press, 2000.

Wilson, Ara. "The Empire of Direct Sales and the Making of Thai Entrepreneurs." *Critique of Anthropology* 19 (1999): 401–422.

Wilson, William Julius. *The Truly Disadvantaged: The Inner City, the Underclass, and Public Policy*. Chicago: University of Chicago Press, 1987.

World Bank. "Russian Federation: Country Brief 2004." Washington, DC: World Bank, 2004. Retrieved February 22, 2008.

——. "Russian Federation: Country Brief 2008." Washington, DC: World Bank, 2008. Retrieved April 9, 2008.

World Health Organization. *Global Status Report on Alcohol and Health*. Geneva, Switzerland: WHO, 2011.

Yurchak, Alexei. *Everything Was Forever, Until It Was No More: The Last Soviet Generation.* Princeton: Princeton University Press, 2005.

——. "Russian Neoliberal: The Entrepreneurial Ethic and the Spirit of 'True Careerism.'" *Russian Review* 62 (2003): 72–90.

Zabel, Cordula. "Patterns of Partnership Formation among Lone Mothers in Russia." Rostok, Germany: Max Planck Institute for Demographic Research. MPIDR Working Paper 2008–20.

Zakharov, Sergei. "Russian Federation: From the First to Second Demographic Transition." *Demographic Research* 19 (2008): 907–972.

Zavisca, Jane. *Housing the New Russia.* Ithaca, NY: Cornell University Press, 2012.

Zdravomyslova, Elena. "Working Mothers and Nannies: Commercialization of Childcare and Modifications in the Gender Contract (A Sociological Essay)." *Anthropology of East Europe Review* 28 (2010): 200–225.

Zdravomyslova, Elena, and Elena Chikadze. "Scripts of Men's Heavy Drinking." *Idatutkimus* 2 (2000): 35–52.

Zigon, Jarrett. *"HIV Is God's Blessing": Rehabilitating Morality in Neoliberal Russia.* Berkeley: University of California Press, 2011.

✒ INDEX